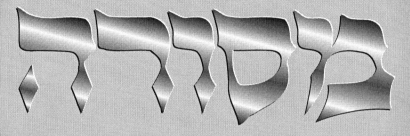

פירוש

ArtScroll Mesorah Series®

Rabbi Nosson Scherman / Rabbi Meir Zlotowitz

General Editors

A PROJECT OF THE

Mesorah
Heritage
Foundation

shemoneh

by
Rabbi Avrohom Chaim Feuer

שמונה עשרה

ESREI

THE AMIDAH / THE EIGHTEEN BLESSINGS
INSPIRATIONAL EXPOSITIONS AND INTERPRE-
TATIONS OF THE WEEKDAY SHEMONEH ESREI

Published by
Mesorah Publications, ltd

FIRST EDITION
Eight Impressions . . . August 1990 — June 2009

Published and Distributed by
MESORAH PUBLICATIONS, Ltd.
4401 Second Avenue
Brooklyn, New York 11232

Distributed in Europe by
LEHMANNS
Unit E, Viking Business Park
Rolling Mill Road
Jarrow, Tyne & Wear NE32 3DP
England

Distributed in Australia & New Zealand by
GOLDS WORLD OF JUDAICA
3-13 William Street
Balaclava, Melbourne 3183
Victoria Australia

Distributed in Israel by
SIFRIATI / A. GITLER — BOOKS
6 Hayarkon Street
Bnei Brak 51127

Distributed in South Africa by
KOLLEL BOOKSHOP
Ivy Common 105 William Road
Norwood 2192, Johannesburg, South Africa

Typography by Compuscribe at ArtScroll Studios, Ltd.

Printed in the United States of America by Noble Book Press
Bound by Sefercraft, Quality Bookbinders, Ltd. Brooklyn, N.Y.

Both our fathers endured the fire
and fury of Churban Europe.

Both prayed to Hashem for salvation and
He mercifully delivered them from the shadow of death.

Both came to these shores and beseeched Hashem
to help them raise "Yiddishe Doros"
and again Hashem answered their pleas.

Both our fathers bequeathed to us a tri-fold treasure
of Torah, Tefillah and Tzedakah,
and they remain our most sacred heirlooms.

The Yiddish word for prayer "Davenen" derives
from the Aramaic term "D'avunan" — from our fathers;
because prayer is the precious legacy
handed down to us from our forefathers, the Avos.
We therefore dedicate this Book of Prayer,
the Shemoneh Esrei, to our fathers.

ר׳ אברהם בן ר׳ מרדכי אפפעל ז״ל

נפטר ב׳ ראש השנה תשנ״ב

Reb Avrohom ben Reb Mordecai Appel z''l

Sitchel, Roumania / Long Beach, New York

ר׳ שמואל ב״ר יצחק מנחם הלוי אפפעל ז״ל

נפטר ד׳ אדר תשמ״ח

Reb Shmuel ben
eb Yitzchok Menachem HaLevi Appel z''l

Beled, Hungary / Montreal, Canada

Dedicated by their children
Barry and Esther Appel and Family

Miami Beach, Florida

ᴥ§ Preface

Prayer stands at the highest level of the universe, yet people treat it without respect (see *Berachos* 6b). The core of our prayers is *Shemoneh Esrei* — we recite it more than one thousand times a year — but the years and decades of daily repetition have hardly improved the quality of our prayer. The words that impact on the highest heavens seem to have little impact on us. We must learn not only to open a *siddur*, but to open our hearts and minds to its words. *Yesod V'shoresh HaAvodah* advises us to reflect on every two or three words of *Shemoneh Esrei* before continuing. He also suggests that one should mentally translate the words into his mother tongue in order to make them more meaningful. *Abudraham* quotes *Raavad* that *tefillah* is called עֲבוֹדָה, *service*, because the supplicant must concentrate on every word like a servant who cannot allow himself to be distracted.

The purpose of this volume is to acquaint the reader with the general message of each blessing of *Shemoneh Esrei*. This will help the supplicant discover his own insights in the *Shemoneh Esrei*. It is my sincere hope that this work will inspire the reader to pray with increased feeling and fervor, and thereby merit all the blessings of the *Shemoneh Esrei*.

ᴥ ᴥ ᴥ

I take this opportunity to express my deep appreciation to Congregation Ohr Chaim, where I have been privileged to serve as *Rav* for the past decade. The primary purpose of a *shul* is to serve as a *beis tefillah*, a house of prayer, where we communicate with our Creator in dignity and decorum. My *kehillah's* exemplary devotion to *tefillah* inspired me to delve into the *Shemoneh Esrei* and to compose this work.

My good friends, Rabbi Meir Zlotowitz and Rabbi Nosson

Scherman, encouraged me to devote an entire volume to *Shemoneh Esrei*. Their unstinting cooperation and wise advice and guidance made this work into a reality.

As always, Rabbi Sheah Brander's artistic skills have made this volume a thing of beauty — a delight for the eye and the mind.

Rabbi Avrohom Biderman served as project coordinator for this volume and his expertise, patience and good nature make it a pleasure to work with him.

Rabbis Yehezkel Danziger, Avie Gold and Shimon Golding made valuable suggestions and comments at many stages of the work.

Yisroel Epstein edited this work, skillfully polishing every sentence and thought.

Mrs. Estie Dicker typed the manuscript skillfully and with dispatch, and Mrs. Esther Feierstein, Mrs. Zissi Landau, Bassie Goldstein, and Mordechai Golding assisted expertly in the final version. Mrs. Faygie Weinbaum proofread meticulously and perceptively.

The entire Mesorah Publications staff helps make it possible for such works to be produced and disseminated; the Jewish public is in their debt.

Seldom do the headquarters of a high-tech firm have the atmosphere of a *beis hamedrash*, but *Origin Technologies* is the exception. The company graciously provided me with a fully equipped private office where I could research and write this *sefer* undisturbed. I am deeply grateful to the entire staff for making me feel at home. My special thanks to Avraham Poznanski, Yitzchok Turetsky and Matti Laserson for their hospitality.

I cannot adequately express my gratitude to my beloved parents who introduced me to the world of prayer. My father's sweet and melodious *tefillos* as a *shliach tzibbur* always echo in my heart. Observing my dear mother, I saw how one converses freely and intimately with Hashem, relying on God with unshakeable faith and devotion. May Hashem bless them with many years of health and *nachas*.

My father-in-law, HaGaon HaRav Mordechai Gifter, שליט"א, the *Rosh Yeshivah* of Telshe, is one of the precious resources of our generation, but as the crown and guide of our family, he is even more to us. As rebbe, guide, father, and inspiration, his presence hovers over every word of this volume. Together with my dear mother-in-law, may he enjoy many more productive years blessed with robust health and vigor.

Last to be mentioned, yet foremost in mind, is my wife Luba Rochel, מנב״ת. Her enthusiasm for this project always inspired me and made every moment of work a pleasure.

This week our son Shmuel Zalman begins his Torah studies at Telshe Yeshivah in Wickliffe, Ohio. We pray that *Hashem Yisbarach* will grant us much Torah *nachas* from him and his older brothers, Tzvi, Eliyahu Meir, Simcha Yeshaya and Eliezer, נ״י. May they all be inspired by the opening verse of *Shemoneh Esrei*, "*My Lord, open my lips that my mouth may declare Your praise.*"

Finally, my inexpressible gratitude to *Hashem Yisborach* for His continuous blessings and for permitting me to help spread His word.

Avrohom Chaim Feuer

Miami Beach, Florida
24 Av 5750 / August 15, 1990

יהי רצון שכל

התפלות בספר זה

יעלו לזכות

יהודה בן פריידא

לרפואה שלמה

An Overview —
Prayer: Sovereignty Through Surrender

I. Key to the World

וְכֹל שִׂיחַ הַשָּׂדֶה טֶרֶם יִהְיֶה בָאָרֶץ וְכָל עֵשֶׂב הַשָּׂדֶה
טֶרֶם יִצְמָח כִּי לֹא הִמְטִיר ה׳ אֱלֹהִים עַל הָאָרֶץ וְאָדָם
אַיִן לַעֲבֹד אֶת הָאֲדָמָה

Now no tree of the field was yet on the earth and no herb of the field had yet sprouted, for Hashem God had not sent rain upon the earth and there was no man to work the soil (Genesis 2:5).

The verse describes the state of the earth on the sixth day before man was created. Although vegetation had been 'brought forth' from the earth on the third day (ibid. 1:12), it remained just beneath the earth's surface and did not emerge until the sixth day. Why? 'For Hashem God had not sent rain upon the earth,' and without rain there can be no vegetation. And the reason He did not send rain was because *there was no man to work the soil*, no one to appreciate the need of rain. But when Adam was created, he recognized that life could not survive without it. He prayed, and rain fell, causing trees and vegetation to spring forth (*Rashi*).

Without rain there can be no vegetation.

Everything remained dormant until there was prayer.

The world began with a prayer. In six days God created and fashioned the marvels of heaven and earth and the fullness thereof, yet everything remained dormant, frozen, undeveloped — until there was prayer.

In six days God set a lavish table for Adam, overflowing with a bounty of delights, and when the preparations were complete God created man and invited him to eat once his prayer made it possible.

When God gifted the world to Adam — not just this planet earth, but the expanse of the entire universe — He presented Adam with the keys. The key to unlocking the cosmos is prayer.

Terms of Transfer

The Creator fashioned spiritual forces to bridge the awesome chasm that separates the infinity of the Master of the universe from this finite world.

In his infinite wisdom, the Creator fashioned spiritual forces to serve as transfer agents, so to speak, to bridge the awesome chasm that separates the infinity of the Master of the universe from this finite world. These "transfer agents," known as מַלְאָכִים, *angels*, are the forces that control every aspect of nature. When God was about to create man on the sixth day of Creation, He informed the angels that man would be their master. The Talmud (*Sanhedrin* 38b) relates that the angels protested: *"What is frail man that You should remember him, and the son of mortal man that you should be mindful of him?"* (*Psalms* 8:5). But the angels did not prevail; Man alone is worthy to represent the Master of the universe. Only to man did God give all the keys, fulfilling the verse: *"You give him dominion over Your handiwork, everything You placed under his feet"* (*Psalms* 8:7).

By Divine license, man controls the world; the keys are in his hand and will remain there as long as man does not break the terms of his contract. It makes but one demand: Man can rule only if he acknowledges that he rules only by the grace of God. Man is master of the world provided he recognizes his Master. Oblivious of God, man becomes a treacherous usurper, a false pretender to the cosmic throne. When he is grateful to God, man is strengthened by his very act of surrender, for it legitimizes his license to control Creation.

Man can rule only if he acknowledges that he rules only by the grace of God.

R' Yehudah said in the name of Shmuel: "One who derives pleasure from this world without offering the appropriate blessing is as if he derived illegal pleasure from a sacred object [which belongs to the

Temple], as it says, *Hashem's is the earth and its fullness* (*Psalms* 24:1). Rav Levi noted an apparent contradiction between two verses. Here it says, *'Hashem's is the earth and its fullness.'* Elsewhere it is written, *'The heavens are Hashem's, but the earth He has given to mankind'* (*Psalms* 115:16). However, there is no difficulty. Before one recites a blessing, all objects belong to God; after the blessing they belong to man (*Berachos* 35a).

Before one recites a blessing, all objects belong to God; after the blessing they belong to man.

Elsewhere, the Talmud (*Berachos* 10b) says that from the verse לֹא תֹאכְלוּ עַל הַדָּם, *you shall not eat on the blood* (*Leviticus* 19:26), we derive the rule: "Do not eat until you pray for your blood." Not only does man have no rights to the earth and its bounty before he acknowledges God, man's body does not belong to him until he addresses God in prayer! Even the respiratory and circulatory systems that we take for granted are Divine gifts, and they are not ours until we acknowledge their Giver.

Defiance and Downfall

Vividly, the Talmud (*Sanhedrin* 59b) describes how Adam enjoyed the Garden of Eden, where the ministering angels responded to his every wish, preparing his food and pouring his wine. But his most trusted and capable servant was the serpent. Rabbi Shimon ben Menasya laments: "Alas that this great servant was lost to the world, for had the serpent not been cursed [by God], every Jew would have two good serpents. . . who would gather precious gems and pearls for him. . ."

But, consumed with envy, the serpent begrudged Adam's power. Perceptively, the serpent recognized that the source of Adam's sovereignty was his surrender to God, so it devised a way to transform Adam's attitude from obedience to defiance. Having broken the terms of his license, Adam was driven from paradise, and the world awaited a new sovereign who would rule through surrender.

Perceptively, the serpent recognized that the source of Adam's sovereignty was his surrender to God.

II. Above the Stars

וַיּוֹצֵא אֹתוֹ הַחוּצָה וַיֹּאמֶר הַבֶּט נָא הַשָּׁמַיְמָה וּסְפֹר הַכּוֹכָבִים אִם תּוּכַל לִסְפֹּר אֹתָם וַיֹּאמֶר לוֹ כֹּה יִהְיֶה זַרְעֶךָ

And He took him outside and said, "Gaze now, towards the Heavens, and count the stars if you are able to count them!" And He said to him, "So shall your offspring be!" (*Genesis 15:5*).

God elevated Abraham and lifted him *outside* of the sphere of this world to a position high above the stars (*Rashi*).

Rav Yehudah said in the name of Rav: "How do we know that no star controls the destiny of Israel? From the verse, *"And He took him outside. . ."* Because Abraham said, "Master of the universe! I have studied my astrological pattern and it is clear that I will not sire a son." God responded, "Go outside the sphere of the stars because אֵין מַזָּל לְיִשְׂרָאֵל, *no star controls the destiny of Israel!"* (*Shabbos 156a*). Rather, prayer and merit can change a Jew's predetermined destiny from bad to good (*Rashi*).

> *Prayer and merit can change a Jew's predetermined destiny from bad to good.*

The angels and the constellations are very similar in their function as Divinely appointed intermediaries that translate the spiritual blessings of heaven into material bounty on earth. The word מַזָּל is cognate with נוֹזֵל, *flow*, because all that emanates from the celestial source flows to earth through the channels of the star formations.

A discussion of angels and stars may appear to be mystical and esoteric, but an appreciation of these concepts is essential to a fundamental teaching of Judaism, which emphasizes that we must perceive this world on not one, but two levels; the natural and the supernatural. The Almighty Who created the world

> *We must perceive this world on not one, but two levels; the natural and the supernatural.*

continues to control its every detail with an omnipotence that defies human comprehension, but He chooses to hide Himself behind a curtain called Nature, which operates by predictable laws and cycles that appear to be independent of a Divine Master.

Lifting the Veil

God issued a challenge, "Lift the veil of nature and discover that I stand behind it!"

The curtain of nature divides between God and man, and God issued a challenge, "Lift the veil of nature and discover that I stand behind it!" Since nature itself is controlled by heavenly intermediaries, we must be aware of the forces controlling nature — the angels and the stars — that stand, so to speak, with one foot in heaven and one foot on earth. Our Sages made this clear when they taught: אָמַר ר' סִימוֹן: אֵין כָּל עֵשֶׂב וְעֵשֶׂב שֶׁאֵין לוֹ מַזָּל בָּרָקִיעַ שֶׁמַּכֶּה אוֹתוֹ וְאוֹמֵר לוֹ גְּדֵל, Rabbi Simon said: There is no blade of grass without a guiding star in heaven, which strikes it and commands, "Grow!" (*Bereishis Rabbah* 10:7).

A Prayer Perspective

When man tarries in the service of his Creator, nature tarries in serving man.

In truth, just as the stars influence man, man influences the stars, because the forces of nature not only challenge man, they serve him as well. However, they serve man only to the extent he serves his true Master, the Almighty. Should man's service of God slacken, nature will turn against him. Thus, the Midrash (*Bereishis Rabbah* 10:4) teaches that prior to the sin of Adam the planets and celestial spheres traveled at an extremely rapid speed, so that they could quickly bring him God's blessings. As a result of Adam's sin, however, the planetary orbits were enlarged and their speed was drastically diminished. When man tarries in the service of his Creator, nature tarries in serving man.

These fundamental concepts and beliefs were revealed to Abraham when God took him הַחוּצָה, *outside*, and elevated him above the stars. Hitherto, Abraham's perspective had been limited by nature's narrow field of vision. Now God raised Abraham's perception of reality by providing him with an elevated vantage point from which to view the world. God encouraged him to soar high above the forces of nature by means of his faith and free-willed service of God. In effect, God said,

"Appeal to Me, the Creator, the Controller, the Source. You will surely arouse My compassion and I will tailor nature to suit your needs."

"No star controls the destiny of Israel"; rather, through prayer and merit a Jew can change his destiny.

Therefore the Talmud perceives in Abraham's encounter with God a quintessential source for the power of prayer: *"No star controls the destiny of Israel"* (*Shabbos* 156a); rather, through prayer and merit a Jew can change his destiny (*Rashi*).

III. Negate Nature; Negotiate with God

M iracles are unpredictable, they are in the hands of God, apparently independent of the laws of cause and effect. But God taught Abraham that prayer is not a miracle. It is a tool, man's paintbrush in the art of life. Prayer is man's weapon to defend himself in the struggle of life. It is a reality, a fact of life.

The miracles performed by the prophets came as a result of their prayers.

Ramban supports this view in his commentary to *Deuteronomy* 34:10, where he observes that all the miracles performed by the prophets came as a result of their prayers. By virtue of sincere prayer, Joshua stopped the sun and Elijah and Elisha resurrected the dead. Thus, even the greatest prophets were not endowed with mysterious supernatural powers; rather, their prophetic spirit brought them closer to God so that they could pray with great intimacy and trust in the Almighty.

The Sages of the Talmud taught: אֵין סוֹמְכִין עַל הַנֵּס, *we may not rely on miracles* (*Pesachim* 64b). *Maharsha* (comm. to *Kiddushin* 29b) observes that when a person is in danger he should not rely on miracles but he may rely on prayer, for prayer is not a miracle.

Does this mean that every prayer is guaranteed a positive response? Absolutely not!

Does this mean that every prayer is guaranteed a positive response? Absolutely not! The story is told of the unsuccessful merchant who, after repeated prayers, approached Rabbi Elimelech and demanded to know why God did not answer him. The rabbi replied, "God *has* answered your prayer. The answer was, "No."

We have only one guarantee. Before prayer, we seem to be gripped by many forces beyond our control — history, heredity, society, competitors, nature — all conspiring to trap us in their tenacious web. After prayer there is hope. When we pray, we elevate ourselves and leave the world behind. Prayer places us in the presence of God, and we deal with Him directly, exclusively. In His kindness, God allows us to negotiate with Him, as it were. The very act of recognizing and acknowledging the Creator has made us His partners in Creation.

Where there is prayer, nothing else exists — only man and God. All that matters is the plea of man and the will of God. Where there is prayer, nothing else exists — only man and God. Facts and figures fall away; precedents and predictions disappear. All that matters is the plea of man and the will of God. Prayer is not a duel, a struggle between two opposing wills, rather it is an attempt to achieve a merger of wills. Indeed, our prayers are an opportunity to yield ourselves to *His* will, but by virtue of our submission to God, we can hope that He will grant our plea. As our Sages taught: "Treat His will as if it were your will, so that He will treat your will as if it were His will. Nullify your will before His will, so that He will nullify the will of others before your will" (*Avos* 2:4).

"There Is Nothing Besides Him"

The Talmud (*Berachos* 33a) tells of the poisonous viper which threatened the neighborhood of the pious Rabbi Chanina ben Dosa. The *tzaddik* placed his foot over the viper's pit, and when the viper bit him, it fell dead. How could he endanger himself and rely on miracles? The Jerusalem Talmud says that while he stood over the viper's pit, Rabbi Chanina was praying fervently to Hashem — and prayer is not a miracle.

Rabbi Yosef Leib Bloch of Telshe (Shiurei Daas, II:44) explains that natural forces that threaten mankind can be compared to a vicious dog on a long leash. When the animal pounces, a victim can save himself by calling upon the dog's master to restrain the beast. If the victim fails to recognize the presence of the master, then he is *When man fails to perceive the "leash" upon the forces of nature, he places himself at their mercy.* truly in grave danger. Similarly when man fails to perceive the "leash" upon the forces of nature, he places himself at their mercy.

Rabbi Chaim of Volozhin (Nefesh HaChaim III:12:13) cites the Talmud (*Chullin* 7b), that if a person internalizes the verse: ה׳ הוּא הָאֱלֹהִים אֵין עוֹד מִלְבַדּוֹ, *HASHEM,*

He is God, there is nothing else beside Him (*Deuteronomy* 4:35), he will be protected from harmful forces. When one accepts God's absolute sovereignty he places himself fully under His protective wing, for the man of faith understands that nature's destructive elements are but marionettes in the hands of the Creator.

When one accepts God's absolute sovereignty he places himself fully under His protective wing.

Rabbi Yosef Albo (*Sefer Halkkarim*, IV: 18) asks: "How does a mortal dare to ask the Almighty to change His decrees?" He answers that one who prays properly changes himself for the better. Thus, אִם תִּשְׁתַּנֶּה הַהֲכָנָה תִּשְׁתַּנֶּה הַגְּזֵרָה, *When one's character changes, then the Divine decree against him changes accordingly.*

What specific personality trait must man change in order to endow his prayers with meaning and effectiveness? Again we examine the character of our ancestor Abraham who introduced the power of prayer to the world.

From Dust to Dominion

Real humility is a feeling of total dependence on God. Even triumph and dazzling success did not dim Abraham's humility.

When God raised Abraham above the stars, He released him from the absolute rule of nature. By what virtue did Abraham merit to be elevated to such heights? He possessed the striking quality of genuine humility. Real humility is a feeling of total dependence on God. Even triumph and dazzling success did not dim Abraham's humility.

The Holy One, Blessed is He, said to Israel: "My children! I yearn for you because even when I shower glory upon you, you make little of yourselves in deference to Me. I gave great glory to Abraham and he said: *I am but dust and ashes* (*Genesis* 18:27). I bestowed greatness upon Moses and Aaron and they said: *What are we?* (*Exodus* 16:7). I elevated David to lofty heights and he said: *And I am a worm and not a man* (*Psalms* 22:7). But when I lifted the gentile rulers to glory — Nimrod, Pharaoh, Sennacherib and Nebuchadnezzar — they waxed proud and reacted with blasphemous arrogance" (*Chullin* 89a).

Arising from the Ashes

It is noteworthy that, "*I am but dust and ashes*" (*Genesis* 18:27), Abraham's hallmark expression of helplessness and humility, was uttered as part of his plea for the survival of Sodom. Indeed, this encounter is the first mention of prayer in the Torah. The Divine decree had been issued, the angels of destruction had been dispatched, yet Abraham did not despair, for prayer can turn aside decrees and overpower angels. But sometimes prayer is not enough. Lacking a minimum quorum of even ten righteous citizens, Sodom was devoid of merit, so Abraham's prayer elicited no positive response to save the city from doom.

Sodom was devoid of merit, so Abraham's prayer elicited no positive response to save the city from doom.

Fire and brimstone consumed Sodom, but from its ashes and from the dust and ashes of Abraham's humility, arose a cosmic force, the power of prayer — which became the legacy which the Patriarchs bequeathed to their descendants.

The Patriarchs introduced prayer:

☐ Abraham introduced *Shacharis*, the morning prayer.
☐ Isaac introduced *Minchah*, the afternoon prayer.
☐ Jacob introduced *Maariv*, the evening prayer (*Berachos* 26b).

IV. Disciples of Abraham

Whoever designates a permanent place for his prayer service, the God of Abraham will surely come to his assistance. And when this person passes away they will mourn for him and say, "Woe, where is the humble one! Woe, where is the pious one, disciple of Abraham!" (*Berachos* 6b).

A permanent place where one prays fervently again and again is an asset to one who wishes to intensify the merit of his tefillos.

A permanent place where one prays fervently again and again is an asset to one who wishes to intensify the merit of his *tefillos*. *Rabbeinu Yonah* (ibid.) observes that when someone goes to such lengths to enhance his prayers, he demonstrates humility, because he considers himself unworthy on his own. Such a person is considered a disciple of Abraham, the first to display his humility and helplessness through prayer. *Rabbeinu*

One who lacks humility will never be able to pray with sincerity. *Yonah* concludes with a penetrating insight: one who lacks humility will never be able to pray with sincerity, and his prayers will never be received favorably by the Omnipresent One, Blessed is He.

Subdue Pride

Proud man! How can you expect God to help you if you do not feel that you need Him? Therefore, the Sages (*Berachos* 26b) also taught that formal prayer was introduced to parallel the sacrificial offerings of the Temple, which inspired the sinner to break his pride and repent.

The essence of prayer and sacrifice are the same. The *Vilna Gaon* (*Proverbs* 21:27) comments: "The essence of prayer and sacrifice are the same; to subdue our insufferable arrogance and our towering pride."

Before one begins to pray, let him meditate upon the loftiness of God and the lowliness of man; let him pluck from his heart his yearning for the mundane pleasures of this world (*Rama; Orach Chaim* 98:1).

Noam Elimelech (*Parshas Vayechi*) observes how the humble are truly identified as disciples of the Patriarchs: "When a person prays with helpless surrender before God, his prayers rise heavenward through the Cave of Machpelah in Hebron, so that the merit of the humble Patriarchs buried therein will accompany this sincere supplication."

The Chant of the Angels

The humble ones, Abraham, Isaac and Jacob, taught their progeny how to pray and how to awaken the entire world to the presence of God with their prayers. The universe was asleep, so to speak, before the Patriarchs aroused it with their prayer. They even stirred the angels to rise to new heights.

Bais Yosef in his commentary to the *Tur Shulchan Aruch* (*Orach Chaim* 112) quotes extensively from the words of the *Shibbolei Halekket* who cites a *Midrash Aggadah* which traces the origins of our prayer. The Talmud (*Megillah* 17b) teaches that the one hundred and twenty sages who were collectively called the Men of the Great Assembly composed the Eighteen Blessings of the *Amidah*.

The Midrash, however, reveals that the Great Assembly did not invent the benedictions, they only expanded upon earlier themes. The first to actually verbalize these Eighteen Blessings were the ministering angels, in response to the heroic actions of the Patriarchs and their progeny:

- When Abraham was saved from the furnace of Ur Kasdim, the ministering angels chanted, *"Blessed are You, Hashem, Shield of Abraham."*

- When Isaac was saved from slaughter at the *Akeidah*, the angels chanted, *"Blessed are You, Hashem, Who resuscitates the dead."*

- When Jacob approached the heavenly gates of mercy and sanctified the Name of the Holy One, Blessed is He, the ministering angels chanted, *"Blessed are You, Hashem, the Holy God."*

The key events in the history of the Patriarchs and their offspring aroused the angels to chant all eighteen benedictions.

The Midrash goes through all the blessings of *Shemoneh Esrei*, demonstrating how the key events in the history of the Patriarchs and their offspring aroused the angels to chant all eighteen benedictions. In our commentary on the blessings we will indicate these events.

V. The Posture of Prayer

To Bow and to Stand

אַבְרָהָם תִּקֵן תְּפִלַּת שַׁחֲרִית, שֶׁנֶּאֱמַר: וַיַּשְׁכֵּם אַבְרָהָם בַּבֹּקֶר אֶל הַמָּקוֹם אֲשֶׁר עָמַד שָׁם אֶת פְּנֵי ה'.
Abraham instituted the morning prayer, as it says (Genesis 19:27): And Abraham arose early in the morning to stand in the place where he had stood in the presence of Hashem (Berachos 26b).

אָמַר ר' יִצְחָק: הַכֹּל בִּזְכוּת הִשְׁתַּחֲוָיָה! אַבְרָהָם לֹא חָזַר מֵהַר הַמּוֹרִיָּה בְּשָׁלוֹם אֶלָּא בִּזְכוּת הִשְׁתַּחֲוָיָה שֶׁנֶּאֱמַר וְנִשְׁתַּחֲוֶה וְנָשׁוּבָה אֲלֵיכֶם

Everything happens only in the merit of bowing.

Rabbi Yitzchok said: Everything happens only in the merit of bowing. Abraham returned from Mt. Moriah in peace only because he bowed to God, as it says: *We will bow down and return to You (Genesis* 22:5). Similarly, the Jews were redeemed from Egypt ... They received the Torah ... Hannah's prayers were answered ... The exiles will be ingathered ... The Temple will be rebuilt ... the dead will be resurrected, in the merit of bowing down before God (*Bereishis Rabbah* 56:3).

When reciting *Shemoneh Esrei*, we emulate the posture of Abraham who *arose ... to stand in the place where he always stood in the presence of Hashem*. So significant is the posture of prayer that its very name, *Amidah*, standing, derives from it.

If prayer is an intimate encounter between man and his Maker, would not a different posture be more conducive to set the proper mood of contemplation?

Many ask, if prayer is an intimate encounter between man and his Maker, a moment of serious meditation and introspection, would not a different posture be more conducive to set the proper mood of contemplation? Perhaps it would be better to sit huddled in a corner, wrapped in deep thought?

Maharal (Derech Hachaim) provides an insight into the significance of man's upright posture. The Mishnah (*Avos* 3:18) teaches: "Beloved is man for he was created in God's image!" God, of course, is incorporeal and has no physical form that we can call an "image." When He fashioned man, however, God sought to endow the human body with one unique characteristic that would demonstrate to the rest of creation that only man represent's God's sovereignty over the world. Therefore, He made the other creatures walk or crawl or swim or fly horizontally, with the spine hunched over or bent, as a symbol of their subservience to man, who alone was created with a perfectly upright spine, a symbol of unbending, uncompromising mastery over all creatures.

Man stands upright as he recites the Amidah to symbolize that he recognizes and accepts his awesome responsibility to represent God's sovereignty on earth.

Man stands upright as he recites the *Amidah* to symbolize that he recognizes and accepts his awesome responsibility to represent God's sovereignty on earth.

Following closely the example of Abraham, man begins prayer with the proclamation that he is sovereign only through surrender. In the very first blessing, dedicated to Abraham, we bow twice, at the beginning and at the end, for only after surrender do we earn the privilege to stand upright as sovereign.

Anatomy of the Amidah — Vertebrae and Ribs   The eighteen blessings of the *Amidah* — what do they signify? The Talmud teaches that the number eighteen corresponds with the eighteen times God's Name is found in Psalm 29; the eighteen times it is found in the recitation of the *Shema*; and the eighteen vertebrae in the spinal column. The Talmud adds that these vertebrae must bulge noticeably when one bows during the *Amidah*. But now there are nineteen blessings — to what does the extra blessing correspond? The Talmud explains that there is a further reference to God in Psalm 29; in the *Shema* the word אֶחָד, [He is the only] *One*, is a reference to God; and there is one more tiny vertebra — a nineteenth — at the lower end of the spine (*Berachos* 28b).

Everything in creation was designed for but one purpose: to proclaim the glory of the Creator. It was by Divine choice, not chance that man's spine contains nineteen vertebrae. He was endowed with an upright spine for one reason only — so that he could surrender and bow before the nineteen utterances of God's Name in *Psalms* and *Shema*.

The greater a person is, the more he must surrender his sovereignty to God,   Indeed, the greater a person is, the more he must surrender his sovereignty to God, as the Talmud teaches (*Berachos* 34b), a common Jew bows only four times in the *Amidah*; the high priest bows at the beginning and end of every blessing; but the king remains bent over in bowed submission from the beginning of the *Amidah* to the very end.

Maharal (*Nesivos Olam*, *Avodah* 9) observes that of the eighteen main vertebrae, twelve spread out into ribs, while six do not. This symbolizes that originally the central core of the *Amidah* consisted of twelve requests, like ribs that protect the body. The six vertebrae without ribs correspond with the first three blessings of שֶׁבַח, *praise*, and the last three blessings of הוֹדָאָה, *thanksgiving*, which are not personal requests for our needs.

Depen-
dence and
Surrender

We communicate
our needs to You to
impress upon
ourselves how
utterly dependent
we are on Your
gracious help.

Chovos Halevavos emphasizes that even our personal requests are intended to enhance God's glory. We say to Hashem: "We communicate our needs to You not in order to make You aware of them, because You surely know what is in our heart; rather we verbalize our needs in Your presence to impress upon ourselves how utterly dependent we are on Your gracious help, and to demonstrate how much we place our trust in Your kindness" (*Cheshbon Hanefesh, cheshbon* 18).

Total surrender to God, spontaneous outpouring of feeling — this was the nature of prayers from the days of our Patriarchs to the foot of Sinai and beyond. A standard text was not instituted because it was not yet needed. Our forefathers brought this legacy into the Holy Land and incorporated it into the Holy Temple, which was a House of Prayer for all the nations. So it

Dramatic historic
events changed
both the fortunes
of Israel and the
form of her
prayers.

continued for centuries upon centuries, until dramatic historic events changed both the fortunes of Israel and the form of her prayers. Those events brought into being the standard liturgy of *Shemoneh Esrei* as we know it today.

An Overview — The Prayer Code

I. A Standard Siddur

וַעֲבַדְתֶּם אֵת ה׳ אֱלֹהֵיכֶם
*And you shall serve Hashem your God
(Exodus 23:25) ... true service of God is
through prayer. From this we learn that it is
a Biblical commandment to pray to God
every day (Rambam, Sefer Hamitzvos;
mitzvah 5).*

In the first chapter of *Hilchos Tefillah, Rambam*
sketches the history and development of Jewish
prayer. For many centuries, from the time Moses gave
the Torah to Israel, Jews prayed to God daily,
expressing their heartfelt praises, making their requests,
offering their thanksgiving. Everyone could communicate with God in his own very personal fashion. The
Patriarchs of Israel had opened the lines of communication between heaven and earth, and their descendants
followed their example.

*For many
centuries,
everyone could
communicate with
God in his own
very personal
fashion.*

All this came to an end with the destruction of the
First Temple and the ensuing Babylonian Exile. Wan-
dering among alien cultures in foreign lands, Jews
became estranged from the God of their fathers and
ultimately they became strangers to themselves. No
longer were Jews capable of reaching down into the
depths of their souls to extract the proper words with
which to express their innermost yearnings to serve God
with all their heart and all their resources. Exile ravaged
the Jews and rendered them spiritually speechless. Mute
and dumb they stood before God, having lost the gift of
prayer.

*Exile ravaged the
Jews and rendered
them spiritually
speechless.*

A formidable task faced the spiritual leaders of that
silent generation of Jews who returned tongue-tied and
confused from the exile of Babylon. The Holy Land was

in their hands, but the holy language had been plucked from their hearts. These leaders — teachers, scribes, sages and prophets — convened, and gathered in every holy phrase, every sacred thought, every inspired idea, every essential value of Judaism. Then they skillfully wove them into a magnificent tapestry of uniform prayers.

These leaders convened and gathered in every holy phrase, every sacred thought, every inspired idea, every essential value of Judaism.

They regrouped the spiritual treasures of Judaism and restored the gift of prayer to the Patriarchs' descendants. In appreciation of their formidable accomplishments, these one hundred and twenty men earned the title The Men of the Great Assembly.

Words Which Shake the Heavens

Rabbi Chaim of Volozhin writes of the importance of every word of the *Amidah* prayer:

Anshei Knesses HaGedolah, the Men of the Great Assembly who composed the text of the *Amidah*, numbered one hundred and twenty scholars. Some of these were prophets as well as Sages. What they achieved can never be duplicated. They invested each word of the liturgy with a power to affect all of creation, from the smallest atomic particle to the most enormous galactic mass. Moreover, the effect of every word leaves a different impression on the cosmos. The impact of the evening prayer is not the same as the impact of the prayer offered on the previous morning. All this is possible because a spirit of Divine holiness guided the authors: Through them the Almighty Himself implanted within each word infinite power and unlimited effect.

The effect of every word leaves a different impression on the cosmos.

Since no human being can possibly fathom the awesome depth of each word of prayer, one should rather pray with pure and simple intent. As he pronounces each word, he should picture in his mind's eye a mental image of the actual word as it is written. He should concentrate on raising the words heavenward to their celestial source ... One

Since no human being can possibly fathom the awesome depth of each word of prayer, one should rather pray with pure and simple intent.

who prays in this fashion will make an impact with every word.

Therefore the Talmud (*Berachos* 6a) describes the words of prayer as "matters which stand in the height of heaven," because every phrase of prayer actually rises up to heaven in its shape of letters and words, and impacts on the entire cosmos (*Nefesh HaChaim* II:13).

Prayer: A Cosmic Force

Chassidei Ashkenaz meticulously studied the significance of each word in the Shemoneh Esrei.

Tur Shulchan Aruch (*Orach Chaim* 113) writes of *Chassidei Ashkenaz*, the pious mystics of medieval Germany, who meticulously studied the significance of each word in the *Shemoneh Esrei*, that they demonstrated how no word is superfluous, and derived insights from even the number of letters in each benediction. His brother, *Rabbeinu Yechiel* (son of the *Rosh*), counted the words in each benediction and found that they correspond to the number of words in the Scriptural verses that address the same themes. The blessing for healing, for instance, is composed of twenty-seven words, corresponding to the verse in *Exodus* (15:26) that conveys God's promise to be the Healer of the Jewish people.

Analyzing the text of *tefillah*, *Tur* (*Orach Chaim* 118) notes that the numerical value of the initial letters of each blessing of *Shemoneh Esrei* [ב, א, א, ה, ס, ר, ר, ב, ת, ה, ה, ו, ע, ו, א, ש, ר, מ, ש] equals eighteen hundred, corresponding to the eighteen hundred celestial angels who receive our prayers as they soar heavenward.

Many of our greatest sages made similar computations. *Rokeach* calculated that there are a total of one hundred and thirteen words in all the endings of the blessings of *Shemoneh Esrei* [בָּרוּךְ אַתָּה ה' מָגֵן אַבְרָהָם; בָּרוּךְ אַתָּה ה' מְחַיֵּה הַמֵּתִים and so on], corresponding to the one hundred and thirteen words in the Song of Chana (*I Samuel* 2:1-10) and the one hundred and thirteen times that the word לֵב, *heart*, is mentioned in the Five Books of Moses. This teaches that the more one focuses his heart and mind on the words of prayer, the more blessing he will merit (cited in *Tur, Orach Chaim* 101).

This teaches that the more one focuses his heart and mind on the words of prayer, the more blessing he will merit.

Abudraham notes that the numerical value of the word תְּפִלָּה, *prayer*, 515, equals the value of בְּכַוָּנַת הַלֵּב, *with intent of the heart*, and עֲבוֹדַת הַלֵּב, *service of the heart*. If one desires that God hear his prayers he must plead sincerely, as Moses did when he said, וָאֶתְחַנַּן אֶל ה', *And I pleaded with Hashem (Deuteronomy 3:23)*. The numerical value of וָאֶתְחַנַּן is 515, equal to תְּפִלָּה, *prayer*.

If one desires that God hear his prayers he must plead sincerely.

What is the real significance of these computations?

II. Aleph-Beis: Brick and Mortar of the Universe*

יוֹדֵעַ הָיָה בְּצַלְאֵל לְצָרֵף אוֹתִיּוֹת שֶׁנִּבְרְאוּ בָהֶם שָׁמַיִם וָאָרֶץ. כְּתִיב הָכָא וָאֲמַלֵּא אֹתוֹ רוּחַ אֱלֹהִים בְּחָכְמָה וּבִתְבוּנָה וּבְדַעַת וּכְתִיב הָתָם ה' בְּחָכְמָה יָסַד אָרֶץ כּוֹנֵן שָׁמַיִם בִּתְבוּנָה.

Bezalel [the builder of the Tabernacle in the Wilderness] knew how to combine the letters with which heaven and earth were created. For it is written (Exodus 31:3) [with regard to Bezalel]: I have filled him with a Godly spirit, with wisdom, understanding, and knowledge; and it is written (Proverbs 3:19): [with regard to Creation]: Hashem founded the world with wisdom, He established heaven with understanding ... (Berachos 55a).

אִילּוּ הָיוּ הָאוֹתִיּוֹת מִסְתַּלְּקוֹת כְּרֶגַע ח"ו וְחוֹזְרוֹת לִמְקוֹרָן, הָיוּ כָּל הַשָּׁמַיִם אַיִן וָאֶפֶס מַמָּשׁ.

If the letters [with which heaven was created] were to remove themselves for an instant, God forbid, and return to their source, the entire heaven would become an absolute vacuum (Tanya, Shaar HaYichud V'haEmunah I).

---

* This treatment of the letters of the *Aleph-Beis* is based on Rabbi Nosson Scherman's Overview to *The Wisdom in the Hebrew Alphabet*.

The twenty-two sacred letters are profound, primal spiritual forces. They are, in effect, the raw material of Creation. When God combined them into words, phrases, and commands, they brought about Creation, translating His will into reality, as it were. There is a Divine science in the Hebrew alphabet. *Sefer Yetzirah*, The Book of Creation, the early Kabbalistic work ascribed to the Patriarch Abraham, describes how the sacred letters were used as the agency of creation.

The letters can be ordered in countless combinations.

The letters can be ordered in countless combinations, by changing their order within words and interchanging letters in line with the rules of various Kabbalistic letter-systems. Each rearrangement of the same letters results in a new blend of the cosmic spiritual forces represented by the letters. An analogy can be found in the physical sciences. One combination of hydrogen and oxygen produces water, while another produces hydrogen peroxide. So it is with all the elements and the infinite number of possible combinations.

Each rearrangement results in a new blend of the cosmic spiritual forces represented by the letters.

Rabbi Dov Ber, the *Maggid of Mezritch*, writes:

It is known in Kabbalistic literature that the letters of the *Aleph-Beis* were created first of all. Thereafter, by use of the letters, the Holy One, Blessed is He, created all the worlds. This is the hidden meaning of the first phrase in the Torah, *"In the beginning God created אֵת"* — that is, God's first act was to create the letters from א to ת (*Or Torah*).

The Words and Letters Are Eternal

לְעוֹלָם ה' דְּבָרְךָ נִצָּב בַּשָּׁמָיִם

Forever, Hashem, Your word stands firm in heaven (Psalms 119:89).

The *Baal Shem Tov* explained that the "word" of God to which the verse refers is His utterance יְהִי רָקִיעַ, *let there be a firmament (Genesis 1:6).* With these words, the heaven came into existence at that primeval instant — but what prevents the heaven from aging, decaying, crumbling?

What prevents the heaven from aging, decaying, crumbling?

The Psalmist answered these questions when he said: *Forever, Hashem, Your word stands firm in heaven.* The word of God that brought the heaven into being remains with them. The heaven continues to exist because not an instant goes by without God continuing to say, in effect, *'Let there be a firmament'* — otherwise it would return to the status that prevailed before God's will was uttered. So it is with every aspect of Creation. God's original Ten Utterances are repeated constantly in the sense that the Divine will of the original six days remains in force. Otherwise, everything would revert to the nothingness of before Creation.

God's original Ten Utterances are repeated constantly in the sense that the Divine will of the original six days remains in force.

The letters of the *Aleph-Beis* are the array of individual spiritual forces through which God articulates His will in creation.

Degel Machneh Ephraim teaches that man has the power to affect the sacred letters with which God created heaven and earth. When he sins, he cheapens and sullies the Divine powers allotted him. But when he acts properly, he enables the powers within the *Aleph-Beis* to achieve their purpose and reflect their full holiness. He can elevate not only his personal universe, but that of everyone around him.

The Sages expounded that Bezalel, the builder of the *Mishkan* [i.e., the Tabernacle in the Wilderness], knew the art of combining the sacred letters:

יוֹדֵעַ הָיָה בְּצַלְאֵל לְצָרֵף אוֹתִיּוֹת שֶׁנִּבְרְאוּ בָהֶם שָׁמַיִם וָאָרֶץ

Bezalel knew how to combine the letters with which heaven and earth were created (Berachos 55a).

Since the purpose of human existence is to make earthly life worthy of God's Presence and to lead all mankind to acknowledge Him, it stands to reason that the wisdom exercised by God in creating the universe should — to the extent humanly possible — be had by those who build His Tabernacle on earth. Bezalel, who did so, was qualified by virtue of his ability to utilize the spiritual forces inherent in the sacred letters.

The wisdom exercised by God in creating the universe should be had by those who build His Tabernacle on earth.

A Combination of Letters

By referring to the primal sanctity of the *Aleph-Beis*, *Chidah* answers a question that perplexes many people. Why is it necessary to articulate the prescribed text of the prayers — doesn't God know what is in our hearts?

Wouldn't it be a greater sanctification of His Name if He were to fulfill *unspoken* human desires? *Chidah* explains that the combinations of letters — as formulated by the spiritual masters who composed the prayers — have the power to arouse spiritual forces beyond our imagination. Thereby new spiritual lights can be created through the agency of human beings. To accomplish this, we must *articulate* the prayers. This causes the sacred letters to arouse their spiritual roots. It brings about a totally unprecedented combination: The interacting of the *Aleph-Beis* is combined in the respective prayer and the particular set of circumstances prevailing on earth at the instant the prayer is uttered (*Shem HaGedolim*, entry on *R' Yitzchak of Acco*).

New spiritual lights can be created through the agency of human beings. To accomplish this, we must articulate the prayers.

Ezra the Sofer

Why were the Sages of early times called סוֹפְרִים, *Soferim*? Because they counted [סוֹפֵר] all the letters of the Torah (*Kiddushin* 30a).

The predominant figure in the Great Assembly was Ezra HaSofer. The title "*HaSofer*" is commonly translates as "The Scribe", and it is correct, because Ezra did, in fact, write Torah scrolls and toiled to insure the authenticity and accuracy of our written tradition. The term *Sofer*, however, literally means "one who counts" (see comm. to the thirteenth blessing וְעַל פְּלֵיטַת סוֹפְרֵיהֶם), because Ezra and his colleagues counted the number of letters in the Scriptures and derived important lessons from the numbers, shapes, and positions of the sacred letters.

The Great Assembly knew that the Torah was the blueprint which dictated the design of the universal structure built upon the sacred words and letters.

The *Soferim* of the Great Assembly knew well that the *Aleph-Beis* was the brick and mortar of the universe, and that the Torah was the blueprint which dictated the design of the universal structure built upon the sacred words and letters.

When the *Soferim* composed the eighteen benedictions of *Shemoneh Esrei*, they carefully counted the words and letters of each benediction to match corresponding verses in Scripture. Verbalizing the prayer had an impact on the Scriptural passage and activated its letters to exercise their influence in all the worlds!

Similarly, *Pnei Yehoshua* (*Berachos* 28b) says that when Shmuel HaKattan composed the nineteenth benediction, he arranged it so that its number of words and letters would have a cosmic effect.

Early commentaries went to such lengths to show the relationship between tefillah and Torah, because prayer activates the letters of the Torah.

This is why *Tur, Abudraham* and other early commentaries went to such lengths to show the relationship between *tefillah* and Torah, because prayer activates the letters of the Torah. Indeed *Pnei Yehoshua* (ibid.) explains that even when a person prays in a language other than the original Hebrew, as long as the translation adheres to the original version of *Shemoneh Esrei*, it will activate the corresponding Hebrew words and letters to impact on the entire world in their customary fashion.

Control by Code

Even when the supplicant fails to pray with proper intent, feeling, and understanding, his words still have a great impact on the world.

Nefesh HaChaim (II:13) emphasizes that the standard prayer text composed by the Men of the Great Assembly is so powerful that even when the supplicant fails to pray with proper intent, feeling, and understanding, his words still have a great impact on the world.

This can be illustrated with a contemporary parable: Imagine, if you will, a spaceship hurtling at an incredible speed millions of miles away from this mother planet. At mission-control headquarters down on earth the spaceship is guided by a computer technician operating a control console. The computer operator knows nothing about spacecraft — he has never seen and will never see the vehicle he is now guiding. The operator doesn't even understand the top-secret, classified commands he is issuing, because every message is carefully encoded and only the spacecraft's computer can unscramble and decipher the secret orders. The computer operator knows only one

Tefillah is a thrice-daily transmission of cosmic proportions, broadcast by simple operators who are unaware of the far-reaching power at their fingertips.

thing — if he presses a few buttons and keys down below he makes important things happen in space! A few small numbers and letters on earth can change the space vehicle's course and destination by millions of miles.

Tefillah works in similar fashion. It is a thrice-daily transmission of cosmic proportions, broadcast by simple operators who are unaware of the far-reaching power at their fingertips.

Chassidic masters were fond of relating the touching story of the ignorant illiterate shepherd boy who came to *shul* on *Yom Kippur* but was unable to read the siddur. He sat all day and fervently repeated the only thing he knew — the letters of the *Aleph-Beis* — adding this one plea, "Hashem, I don't know how to pray! Please accept these letter of the *Aleph-Beis* and You organize them into words and sentences of prayer!"

The Chassidic masters assure us that these sincere words had the most profound effect on the highest heavens, and opened up many a celestial gate hitherto sealed shut.

Even those who are fortunate enough to be able to read the lines of the *Siddur* should realize that we are ignorant of the inner code and its mystical combinations of which *Tur* gives us a tiny glimpse. Humbly, we offer our prayers to God and beg Him to arrange the words and letters to arouse the blessings of the universe.

A Confluence of Prayer Forces

Jacob was a powerful warrior, yet he knew that God, not man, wages war. Man's most potent weapon is prayer. On his death bed Jacob related that he conquered Shechem בְּחַרְבִּי וּבְקַשְׁתִּי, *with my sword and with my bow* (Genesis 48:22), which *Targum Onkelos* renders as בִּצְלוֹתִי וּבְבָעוּתִי, *with my prayer and with my supplication.* [For an explanation of *Targum's* simile, see the Sixteenth Blessing.]

The *Shemoneh Esrei* integrates two essential elements of *tefillah.* From our Patriarchs we received a legacy of personal supplication and surrender. But personal prayer can be only as powerful as the devotion, concentration, and merit of the supplicant — like a bow that can dispatch an arrow tellingly only to the extent it is properly strong, supple, and stretched by the archer.

When the ravages of exile rendered the mass of Jewish people incapable of such skill and devotion, the Men of the Great Assembly composed an effective, universal text. Thus even if his own concentration and comprehension is lacking, the prayer can still be efficacious —

like a sword, which, by virtue of the sharpness of its blade, can be effective even when it is not wielded well.

Today we start with the standard text, the "sword," which, in addition to its inherent and efficacy, elevates the supplicant to new heights of devotion and feeling. This, in turn, arouses him to compose personal supplications which resemble well-aimed arrows (see *Sefer Chassidim* 158).

❀ ❀ ❀

פָּנָה אֶל תְּפִלַּת הָעַרְעָר וְלֹא בָזָה אֶת תְּפִלָּתָם. תִּכָּתֶב
זֹאת לְדוֹר אַחֲרוֹן וְעַם נִבְרָא יְהַלֶּל יָהּ

He turned to the prayer of the lonely one and has not despised their prayer. Let this be recorded for the last generation, so the newborn nation will praise God (Psalms 102:18,19).

Rabbi Yitzchok said: This refers to these lonely generations, isolated and abandoned in exile without the leadership of a prophet or a High Priest. The only sacred power left to the exiled Jew is the power of his prayers. David begged, "Master of the universe, do not despise their prayer [in whatever fashion they pray], and in the merit of their prayers may we be the last generation to pine in exile, and may we behold the newborn, redeemed nation, which will dedicate itself to the full praise of God!" (*Midrash Shocher Tov*).

The only sacred power left to the exiled Jew is the power of his prayers.

The Blessings of Shemoneh Esrei

Introductory Verse
אֲדֹנָי שְׂפָתַי תִּפְתָּח – *My Lord, open my lips*
Asking Permission to Pray

שָׁלֹשׁ בְּרָכוֹת רִאשׁוֹנוֹת שֶׁל שֶׁבַח
The First Three Blessings – God's Praise

1
Patriarchs – אָבוֹת
Divine service began when the Patriarchs recognized the Creator.

2
God's Might – גְּבוּרוֹת
Divine service reaches its historical conclusion with the Resurrection of the Dead and Final Judgment.

3
Holiness of God's Name – קְדֻשַּׁת הַשֵּׁם
The purpose of Divine service is to emulate God's holiness and to sanctify His Name.

שְׁלֹשׁ עֶשְׂרֵה בַּקָּשׁוֹת
The central core of thirteen requests for necessities of life in order to serve God.

Six Personal Requests
4. דַּעַת – Intellect
5. תְּשׁוּבָה – Repentance
6. סְלִיחָה – Forgiveness
7. גְּאֻלָּה – Personal Salvation
8. רְפֻאָה – Health and Healing
9. בִּרְכַּת הַשָּׁנִים – Year of Prosperity

Six Communal Requests
10. קִבּוּץ גָּלֻיּוֹת – Ingathering of Exiles
11. דִּין – Restoration of Justice
12. בִּרְכַּת הַמִּינִים – Against Heretics
13. צַדִּיקִים – The Righteous
14. בִּנְיַן יְרוּשָׁלַיִם – Rebuilding Jerusalem
15. מַלְכוּת בֵּית דָּוִד – Davidic Reign

16

Acceptance of Prayer — קַבָּלַת תְּפִלָּה

הוֹדָאוֹת שֶׁל שָׁלוֹשׁ אַחֲרוֹנוֹת
The Last Three Blessings — Thanksgiving to God
for the opportunity to serve Him . . .

17

Temple Service — עֲבוֹדָה

We yearn to resume the sacrificial service in the Temple.

18

Thanksgiving — הוֹדָאָה

We are grateful for all blessings in our lives.

19

Peace — שָׁלוֹם

And we give thanks for tranquility and peace of mind.

Conclusion — Personal Supplication

יִהְיוּ לְרָצוֹן אִמְרֵי פִי — *May the expressions of my mouth find favor*

אֱלֹהַי נְצֹר — *My God, guard my tongue from evil*

יְהִי רָצוֹן — *May it be Your will*

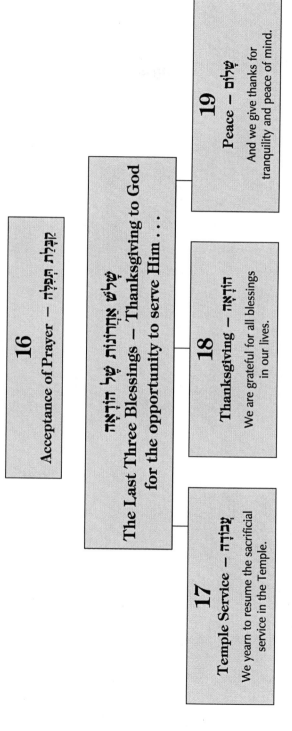

See pages 91-93 for an explanation of this pyramid of prayer.

The Juxtaposition of Prayer and Redemption

יְהִיוּ לְרָצוֹן אִמְרֵי פִי וְהֶגְיוֹן לִבִּי לְפָנֶיךָ ה׳ צוּרִי וְגֹאֲלִי.

May the expressions of my mouth and the thoughts of my heart find favor before You, HASHEM, my Rock and my Redeemer.
(Psalms 19:15)

לַמְנַצֵּחַ מִזְמוֹר לְדָוִד. יַעַנְךָ ה׳ בְּיוֹם צָרָה יְשַׂגֶּבְךָ שֵׁם אֱלֹהֵי יַעֲקֹב.

For the Conductor, a psalm by David. May HASHEM answer you on the day of distress; may the name of Jacob's God make you impregnable.
(Psalms 20:1-2)

The *Talmud* and *Rashi* (*Berachos* 4b) take note of the fact that the psalmist was careful to juxtapose the last verse of Psalm 19, which speaks of redemption (*HASHEM, my Rock, and my Redeemer*), with the first verse of *Psalm* 20, which speaks of beseeching God in prayer (*May HASHEM answer you on the day of distress*). This teaches that immediately before beginning the recitation of the *Shemoneh Esrei* [*Amidah*] prayer, one should recite the benediction which praises God as the Redeemer: צוּר יִשְׂרָאֵל . . . גֹּאֲלֵנוּ ה׳ צְבָאוֹת שְׁמוֹ קְדוֹשׁ יִשְׂרָאֵל. בָּרוּךְ אַתָּה ה׳, גָּאַל יִשְׂרָאֵל, *Rock of Israel . . . Our Redeemer, — HASHEM, Master of Legions, is His — Name is the Holy One of Israel. Blessed are You, HASHEM, Who redeemed Israel.*

> Rabbi Yochanan said: "Who is assured of a portion in the World to Come? He who juxtaposes the benediction of גְאוּלָה, *redemption*, with תְּפִילָה, *prayer*.

Rabbeinu Yonah (commentary to *Berachos* 4b) offers two beautiful explanations for the importance of the juxtaposition of redemption and prayer.

1) The Jewish people are servants of God, and their main עֲבוֹדָה, *service*, is prayer, which is also called עֲבוֹדָה שֶׁבַּלֵּב, *service of the heart*. The Jewish people officially became God's servants on the night of Passover, when He redeemed us from the bondage of Egypt. Until then we were עַבְדֵי פַרְעֹה, *servants of Pharaoh*, but from the moment God redeemed us from human bondage, we became exclusively עַבְדֵי ה', *servants of HASHEM*. Therefore, it is most appropriate that we bless God, our Redeemer, and proclaim that we are His servants, before we perform our primary act of service.

2) When we pour out our hearts to God in sincere prayer, we demonstrate that we have complete faith in His unlimited power to fulfill every one of our requests. This is actually the main purpose of prayer: It is not so much an opportunity for man to declare his desires to God as it is an opportunity for him to proclaim his absolute faith that God can fulfill those desires.

Therefore, before one begins to pray he should fortify his faith by remembering the awesome wonders God performed when He redeemed us from Egypt. Nowhere else in history did God manifest so clearly and dramatically His control over the entire cosmos. After blessing God for His incredible demonstration of power as our collective national Redeemer, we go on to pray to Him to be our personal Redeemer as well, by granting our personal requests. Surely the person who lives with such intense trust in God will merit a portion in the World to Come.

The Gerrer Rebbe offers an additional insight into the juxtaposition of redemption and prayer:

The primary power of the Jewish people is not in their hands but in their mouths; the Jews are God's chosen people because they have mastered the act of communicating with Him through their verbal prayers and pleas. Moreover, the Jewish mouth has the unique ability to express the yearning of our souls. Although the flesh, in its pursuit of baser desires, seeks to stifle the soul's aspirations, the Jewish mouth gives voice to the soul and empowers it in its battle over the allures of the sensual world.

The Egyptians were a stark contrast to the Jews. In their obsession with the pleasures of the flesh they made themselves like speechless animals: בְּשַׂר חֲמוֹרִים בְּשָׂרָם, *the flesh of donkeys is their flesh* (Ezekiel 23:20). Therefore, their leader was called פַּרְעֹה, because the letters of his name can be transposed to read פֶּה רַע, *the wicked mouth,* for his mouth gave expression only to the desires of his flesh and not those of his spirit.

The primary tragedy of the Jews in Egypt was not so much the physical hardship they endured, but rather the shackling of their souls. The insidious influence of the Egyptian overlords was so powerful that for a period of time the Jews themselves became mute. Their spirits were silenced, and they lost the ability to pray and communicate with God.

The redemption of Israel really began long before Passover night. It started when the Jews struggled to regain their "voice," their ability to speak words of prayer. When they began to cry out to God in pain, when they screamed of the torment of their souls, then the redemption process was set in motion. It was Moses who taught the Jews how to pray on an ever-higher level, and they ultimately celebrated their verbal freedom with a holiday called פֶּסַח, which can also be read as פֶּה סָח, *the mouth which speaks.*

Therefore, we juxtapose these two themes to demonstrate that the גְּאוּלָה, the *redemption* from Egypt, as well as future redemptions, is a result of only one power — the power of sincere תְּפִילָה, *prayer.*

(*Likutei Yehudah; Parshas Vaeira* pg. 45)

Introductory Verse

אֲדֹנָי שְׂפָתַי תִּפְתָּח, וּפִי יַגִּיד תְּהִלָּתֶךָ.

My Lord, open my lips,
that my mouth may declare Your praise.

◄§ To Be Able to Pray

אֲדֹנָי שְׂפָתַי תִּפְתָּח וּפִי יַגִּיד תְּהִלָּתֶךָ — *My Lord, open my lips, that my mouth may declare Your praise* (Psalms 51:17).

This introductory verse is the key to effective, successful prayer. It did not appear in the original version of the *Amidah*, because in earlier generations even simple Jews were capable of concentrating intensely on their prayers. However, with the passage of time men paid less and less attention to God throughout the workday, and so they had to struggle to focus their minds on Him at prayer time. Therefore, the Sages of later times inserted this verse from *Psalms* as a *special prayer to be able to pray* (*Kedushas Levi, Parshas Va'eschanan*).

Although we may not interrupt between גְּאוּלָה, *the Blessing of Redemption*, and תְּפִלָּה, *the Amidah* (especially in the morning prayers), this verse is *not* considered an interruption. Rather, since it is a crucial plea for concentration in prayer it is called a תְּפִילָה אֲרֻכְתָּא, *an extension of the prayer* (*Berachos* 9b).

◄§ A Perfect Prayer Offering

This verse sets the time of prayer and reminds us that today prayer replaces the Temple's sacrificial offerings. It is taken from *Psalm 51*, in which David expresses his deep remorse over his sin with Bath-sheba. He laments and pleads: *My Lord, open my lips that my mouth may declare Your praise. For You desire no offering, else I would give it; a burnt offering You do not favor. The offerings of God are a broken spirit; a heart broken and crushed, O God, You will not despise* (*Psalms* 51:17-19). [Based on *Beis Yosef, Tur Orach Chaim* 111, in the name of *Rabbeinu Yonah*.]

The purpose of prayer is for man to stand in the Presence of the Master of the universe and to recognize God's greatness and man's insignificance. Alone, man is worthless, only in God do we discover self-worth. This awareness, this humility, is called a *broken spirit* and a *crushed heart* — and as the *Kotzker Rebbe* said so pithily: "I have found nothing so perfect and complete as a humble, broken heart!"

◄§ Be a 'No-limits' Person

Ramban (*Emunah U'Vitachon*, Chapter 5) maintains that in the context of this verse the term שְׂפָתַי, *my lips*, is related to שְׂפַת הַנָּהָר, the river bank, the barrier which confines the river to its narrow channel.

HaRav Mordechai Gifter שליט"א elaborates on this theme: Man's soul is restricted and stifled within the very narrow confines of his finite body. But when man stands in prayer before the infinity of his Maker, his eternal soul is aroused and it surges until it 'overflows' the restrictive 'banks' of the body.

Man's worst crimes are the crimes he commits against himself. How wantonly he wastes every one of God's gifts, and how irresponsibly he creates obstacles in the paths that God has cleared for him!

The ultimate purpose of prayer is to remove these impediments and energize oneself. In the presence of my Creator I am inspired to make the following commitment to myself:

"Today is a fresh start. I will surpass all past performances! I cast aside those mental blocks and emotional locks which I placed in my own path."

"Today I am a free man, exercising my Divine gift of completely free choice. I have an open mind, and I unlock the chains of prejudice and preconceived notions. Today I embark wholeheartedly upon the path of excellence, and I put the world on notice: אֵין דָּבָר עוֹמֵד בִּפְנֵי הָרָצוֹן, Nothing can withstand the force of the human will."

⇜§ The Divine Dialogue

Rav Tzadok Hacohen (Tzidkas Hatzaddik #209) explains why we must pray for our lips to be opened before we can commence prayer.

God, the Omnipresent, is everywhere; and yet, so to speak, He took a fragment of His spirit and embedded it within a human body. This is the human נְשָׁמָה, *soul*. The sliver of God constantly yearns to reattach itself to its Divine source, but the human body is a physical obstruction which interferes.

However, at the times ordained for prayer the supplicant "strips his body away from his soul" (*Rabbeinu Yonah*) so that the soul may embrace its source. Thus, prayer is not *man speaking to God* — it is *the God inside man speaking to the God outside of man!*

Therefore, the introduction to prayer is a plea for God to open our lips and remove all physical impediments to the dialogue between the Divine within us and the Divine all around us.

Furthermore, the Talmud (*Berachos* 34b) relates that the pious Rabbi Chanina ben Dosa had a clear indication whether his prayers were effective:

"If my words flow smoothly and my mind is concentrated and clear, I am sure that my prayer was accepted. But if I stumble over my words and my mind is distracted, I know that my prayer was unacceptable."

When prayer flows smoothly it emanates from the soul; if one prays with difficulty, he is merely moving his lips but his soul remains silent.

⊷§ God's Gift to Mankind

The Talmud (*Berachos* 7a) says: From where do we know that God Himself prays? From the verse: *And I will bring them to My Holy Mountain and cause them to rejoice in the House of My Prayer* (*Isaiah* 56:7). The prophet doesn't call the Temple 'the House of *their* Prayer'; he calls it 'the House of *My* Prayer,' meaning that God Himself prays.

Rav Chaim Stein of Telshe explains that God's prayer is that man should be inspired to pray to Him. When we say that God prays, it means that He arouses in us a desire to pray to Him. Without this Divine Inspiration, how would frail, mortal man dare to approach the Master of the universe? This is God's most precious gift to man, His most precious creation, and it causes man to rejoice in God's House of Prayer.

⊷§ He Gives Speech to the Dumb

אֲדֹנָי שְׂפָתַי תִּפְתָּח — *My Lord, open my lips.*

When man, so frail and insignificant stands before his Maker and contemplates His praises, he should be struck silent with awe. Therefore, man must appeal for Divine assistance to open his mouth and endow it with the ability to declare God's praises.

God's greatest gift to humanity is the power of intelligent speech. When God blew the breath of life into Adam, He made him into a רוּחַ מְמַלְלָא, "a creature of speech" (see *Targum* to *Genesis* 2:7). God may bestow this gift on dumb animals as well, for regarding Bilaam's donkey it says: *"And HASHEM opened up the mouth of the ass"* (*Numbers* 22:28). *Sforno* (ibid.) observes: The gift of intelligent speech to an ass reminds us of the words of the Psalmist: *"My Lord, open my lips, so that my mouth may declare Your praise."*

HaRav Yaakov Yitzchak Ruderman zt"l, of Yeshivas Ner Israel, explained that *Sforno* is teaching us to appreciate human speech as no less a miracle than the speech of an ass. Man should never take this gift for granted, and should regard his every utterance as a renewal of the Almighty's blessing of verbal communication.

❧ A License to Speak

Tradition has it that every human being is allotted only a specific number of words to be utilized over his lifetime; once the allotment is depleted, life must come to an end! (*Derech Pikudecha, Lo Sa'aseh* 34). Awareness of this would certainly encourage a person to use his words most carefully and sparingly.

Moreover, even those words allotted to man are not his personal property; they belong to the Almighty, Who grants a temporary concession. The license to use this concession must be renewed three times a day at the commencement of prayer, but may be revoked by God in the case of a thoughtless, callous speaker. Indeed, a careless speaker is far more dangerous than a reckless driver. King David, who was the victim of much false and malicious slander, cried out: "*HASHEM, rescue my soul from lying lips, from a deceitful tongue*" (*Psalms* 120:2).

When God created the tongue, He recognized its potential to cause harm, so He concealed it inside the mouth and secured it with a double lock (*Midrash Shocher Tov* ibid.). Despite these precautions the tongue causes an immeasurable amount of trouble, causing the Holy One, Blessed is He, to moan: "O tongue! I have imprisoned you within two formidable walls: one hard (the clenched teeth), one soft (the pursed lips). Still, you break loose and wreak havoc. What more can I do to keep you in check?" (*Arachin* 15b).

When we stand in prayer and renew our license to speak we take note of the potential hazards of careless speech. We remember that our license only allows positive speech, our lips are sealed against gossip, slander, insults, anger, lies and curses. *My Lord, open my lips that my mouth may declare Your praise* — and nothing else! (based on *Yaaros Dvash*).

❧ Pray as if Your Life Depended on It

It is noteworthy that at the very outset of our prayers our first word is אֲדֹנָי, *my Lord*! We are reminded that the Patriarch Abraham, who was the first to pray, was also the first to refer to God in this way. The Talmud (*Berachos* 7b) teaches: Rabbi Yochanan said in the name of Rabbi Shimon ben Yochai, "From the day that the Holy One, Blessed is He, created the world no human being ever referred to Him as אָדוֹן, *Lord*, until Abraham appeared and called God אֲדֹנָי, *my Lord*."

Before Abraham began disseminating his teachings there were many theological misconceptions. Some proclaimed that there was no specific act of creation, but believed that the world evolved on its own. Others acknowledged that the Almighty created the world in six days, but claimed that He never established His providential conduct of world affairs, turning them over rather to the forces of "nature." Yet a third school of belief maintained that God continued to be interested in His creation and would occasionally intervene in its workings, but by and large He let nature work on "automatic pilot."

Abraham introduced a new and dynamic doctrine which revealed that the work of the Creator never ended, but that creation is an enduring, perpetual process. On the first six days God created the world יֵשׁ מֵאַיִן, something from nothing; afterward God constantly *recreates* the world, renewing יֵשׁ מְיֵשׁ, *something from something*.

So we say in our prayers: הַמְחַדֵּשׁ בְּטוּבוֹ בְּכָל יוֹם תָּמִיד מַעֲשֵׂה בְרֵאשִׁית, "In His goodness He renews daily, perpetually, the work of creation" (see *Beis HaLevi, Parshas Bereishis*).

God renews our worlds and our lives daily, and we must express our appreciation in our daily prayers. Never take the gift of life for granted.

Before commencing *Shemoneh Esrei* it is customary to take three steps backwards in order to come three steps forward. The *Baal Shem Tov* explained this with a parable. When a parent teaches his child to walk, he beckons the toddler to take two or three steps towards him. As the child slowly comes closer, the parent backs away in order to encourage the youngster to walk a bit more. Similarly, God often appears to withdraw from our lives and conceal Himself, as the prophet says, *You are God Who hides Himself (Isaiah 45:15)*. This is not a sign of Divine displeasure and rejection. To the contrary, God often withdraws to arouse us to intensify our search for Him. He steps back, as it were, so that we will take the steps to follow Him (*Kedushas Levi, Parshas Shemos*). As we prepare to renew our relationship with God through the *Amidah* encounter, we symbolically reenact this concept, as if to say, "We are not discouraged when God takes three steps backward because we realize that His purpose is to encourage us to take three steps forward — towards Him."

The First Three Blessings

✺§ The Three Prefatory Blessings of Praise

Rabbi Simlai taught: "One should never deviate from this procedure — first recount God's praises and afterwards make your requests" (*Berachos* 32a).

Rabbi Yehudah ruled: "A person should never make personal requests during the first three blessings because, as Rabbi Chanina taught, during the first three blessings the supplicant resembles a servant who expresses only his master's praises" (*Berachos* 34a).

✺§ Stepping Closer to God

Prayer marks man's transformation from a self-centered to a God-centered existence. Thus, to negate personal wants by concentrating on God's attributes is the essence of prayer, because prayer's primary goal is to shift man's focus away from himself and toward God.

Maharal (*Nesivos Olam; Avodah* 5) observes that this is the meaning of the Talmudic teaching (*Sotah* 22a) that it is preferable to pray in a synagogue that is far from a person's home, because God rewards a person for every step he takes as he walks to *shul*. This concept of שְׂכַר פְּסִיעוֹת, *reward for steps*, is unique to prayer, as the Talmud never encourages a person to walk a great distance for the fulfillment of any other *mitzvah* such as *succah* or shofar. *Maharal* explains that distancing oneself from the home, the center of personal needs, in order to come close to God is an integral part of prayer itself, which requires the shift of man's focus from himself toward God.

❧ Springboard to Heaven

Before one begins to pray, he should meditate upon the loftiness of God and the lowliness of man. He should pluck from his heart any desire for the mundane pleasures of the world. One is prohibited to kiss his children in the synagogue, so as to establish in his heart that there is no love comparable to the love for the Almighty God (*Rama, Orach Chaim* 98:1).

Similarly, *Ramban* writes in his ethical will to his son, "Cast all worldly matters from your mind when you stand to pray; carefully prepare your heart in the presence of the Holy One." How can the *Ramban* encourage his son to "cast all worldly matters from your mind when you stand to pray" when *Shemoneh Esrei* includes requests that God grant us the blessings of this world — health, prosperity, freedom, and success?

We find an answer in the carefully chosen words of *Rama* quoted above: "In prayer . . . he should pluck from his heart any desire for *the mundane pleasures* of this world." Certainly we pray for the bounty of this world, but we strive to elevate our requests above the mundane. We ask God to make the resources of this world available to us so we can utilize them to serve Him properly and with peace of mind.

Rabbi Chaim of Volozhin (*Nefesh HaChaim, Shaar* II) explains that the true purpose of prayer is to increase God's influence over the world. We ask for blessings from His hand so that His kindness will permeate the world with greater intensity. The supplicant uses genuine prayer as a springboard, propelling himself heavenward to new spiritual heights, even while remaining physically on this world.

❧ We Are Your Creations

In his commentary to the Torah (*Exodus* 13:12), *Ramban* offers a stirring description of the purpose of prayer.

> The intent of every commandment is to help one acquire a firm belief in God, and to proclaim Him as the One Who has created us. This is, in fact, the very purpose of creation; there is no other motive known to us . . . The synagogues we build, the services we hold, the prayers we recite are all designed to provide outward expression for our inner conviction that He is our Creator. We assemble in the houses of prayer and cry out, בְּרִיּוֹתֶךָ אֲנַחְנוּ, *We are Your creations!*

Through the ages, the prophets of Israel demanded that the people never forget the Jewish nation's essential purpose: עַם זוּ יָצַרְתִּי לִי תְּהִלָּתִי

יְסַפֵּרוּ, *This nation I fashioned for Myself, that they shall recount My praises (Isaiah 43:21).*

~§ The Shell and the Kernel

One should never forget that recounting God's praises is meaningful only when the words are heartfelt and sincere. *Chovos Halevavos (Shaar Cheshbon Hanefesh*, Ch. III, section 9) gives detailed instructions on how to prepare for prayer:

> One must disengage himself from this world and free his mind of any thought which will distract his attention from prayer. One should take to heart seriously that he stands before his Maker, and carefully choose both the words and the themes he intends to contemplate.
>
> Understand full well that the words of prayer enunciated by the mouth are merely the shell. The heart's meditation upon these words is the inner kernel. Words of prayer are like a body, while meditation is its soul. One who prays only with his tongue while his mind wanders resembles an empty body, a husk devoid of a kernel. Such a person is compared to the servant whose master had just returned home from a journey. The servant sent his children to greet the master, while he himself ignored the master's presence. The master was infuriated by this wanton disrespect. Similarly, if the heart sends the body and the mouth to greet the Almighty in prayer, but the heart turns its attention elsewhere, God will surely be displeased.

He concludes:

> My dear brother, it is only proper that you realize what prayer really is! It is nothing less than the passionate yearning of the soul for God, and its utter surrender to His service.

~§ Kavanah — Direction in Prayer

The Talmud (*Berachos* 31a) teaches, "He who prays must direct his heart to heaven." Prayer is the pathway to God, and when following any path, direction — *kavanah* — is everything. תְּפִלָּה בְּלִי כַוָּנָה כְּגוּף בְּלִי נְשָׁמָה, *Prayer without proper intention is like a body without a soul.* The essence of direction is to know one's destination:

When Rabbi Eliezer was on his sickbed his disciples came to visit him and asked, "Our master, teach us the proper pathways of life so that we may reach the World to Come." Rabbi Eliezer responded, "When you stand in prayer, know before Whom you are praying, and through that you will merit the World to Come" (*Berachos* 28b).

We must exert ourselves when we pray, lest we merely daydream and allow vague thoughts to float lazily through our stream of consciousness. In prayer we must discipline our minds to focus on specific objectives which become our daily goals.

⋅§ Concentrate on Every Word

The Talmud (*Berachos* 30b) relates that *Chassidim HaRishonim* — the pious men of earlier generations — would spend a full hour reciting *Shemoneh Esrei*. Since there are approximately 500 words in *Shemoneh Esrei*, they would spend an average of seven seconds on each word. This demonstrates how slowly and deliberately one must concentrate on every word.

⋅§ A Crown of Prayers

Arvei Nachal (Vayakhel) writes that God wears a wreath woven from the prayers of Israel. He uses each word of prayer, uttered with pure intent, as a precious gem to adorn this crown. God also scattered holy sparks all over the world. Whenever a person prays with intent, his words attract one of these sparks and propels it heavenward to add brilliance and sparkle to God's glorious crown.

Arvei Nachal (Va'eschanan) states that prayer also serves as the key to a heavenly vault of blessing. With proper concentration and pure intent, words of prayer unlock treasures from above that descend to earth, not just for the benefit of the supplicant but for the good of the entire world.

1

אָבוֹת / Patriarchs

בָּרוּךְ אַתָּה יהוה אֱלֹהֵינוּ וֵאלֹהֵי אֲבוֹתֵינוּ, אֱלֹהֵי אַבְרָהָם, אֱלֹהֵי יִצְחָק, וֵאלֹהֵי יַעֲקֹב, הָאֵל הַגָּדוֹל הַגִּבּוֹר וְהַנּוֹרָא, אֵל עֶלְיוֹן, גּוֹמֵל חֲסָדִים טוֹבִים וְקוֹנֵה הַכֹּל, וְזוֹכֵר חַסְדֵי אָבוֹת, וּמֵבִיא גוֹאֵל לִבְנֵי בְנֵיהֶם, לְמַעַן שְׁמוֹ בְּאַהֲבָה. מֶלֶךְ עוֹזֵר וּמוֹשִׁיעַ וּמָגֵן. בָּרוּךְ אַתָּה יהוה, מָגֵן אַבְרָהָם.

Blessed are You, HASHEM, our God and the God of our forefathers, God of Abraham, God of Isaac, and God of Jacob; the great, mighty, and awesome God, the supreme God, Who bestows beneficial kindnesses and creates everything, Who recalls the kindnesses of the Patriarchs and brings a Redeemer to their children's children, for His Name's sake, with love. O King, Helper, Savior, and Shield. Blessed are You, HASHEM, Shield of Abraham.

✺ The Patriarchs

Prayer, the opportunity to communicate intimately with the Master of the universe, is a precious legacy bequeathed by our forefathers, Abraham, Isaac, and Jacob. Prayer is so closely identified with our forefathers that it is popularly called *davenen*, a corruption of the Aramaic term *d'avuhon*, of our fathers. What made our forefathers so beloved to God?

The Talmud states: "Only three men are worthy of the title Patriarch [even the twelve sons of Jacob, the Tribes, did not merit this title]. Why? Because only these three were of the highest caliber; no others achieved that level" (*Berachos* 16b).

The Midrash (*Bereishis Rabbah* 47) describes the unique level of the *Avos:* הָאָבוֹת הֵן הֵן הַמֶּרְכָּבָה, *the Patriarchs — they are the Divine chariot.* Abraham, Isaac and Jacob are called God's "chariot" because through them His Presence descended to earth. Their greatness was achieved by their ability to put aside their personal desires and dedicate every feeling and fiber of their being to His service. Because they negated their individual rights and desires, they could absorb Godliness and become the bearers — the chariot — of His *Shechinah*.

✺ Trailblazers

The Talmud (*Berachos* 26b) describes how each Patriarch introduced Godliness to the world in his own way: "Prayer was introduced by the Patriarchs ... Abraham introduced *Shacharis* ... Isaac introduced *Minchah* ... Jacob introduced *Maariv*" (*Berachos* 26b).

Rav Elya Lopian likened the role of the *Avos* to that of the pioneers of the telegraph and telephone industry. The early inventors and engineers toiled to build the delicate equipment and lay down the wires for a vast communications system that was later available to everyone. Similarly, before the Patriarchs, mankind was spiritually deaf and dumb, and no one knew how to recognize or communicate with his Creator. The Patriarchs demonstrated how one can detect the imprint of the Creator on every wonder of nature, and express his admiration and gratitude through prayer. Abraham, for example, was overwhelmed by God's majesty when he beheld the dazzling morning sunrise. In response, he composed the morning prayer. Similarly, Isaac set up the lines of communication for the afternoon prayers, and Jacob for the evening prayers. The *Avos'* enthusiasm and love continue to reverberate to this very day in the passionate prayer of their children. Over thirty-seven centuries ago God stood daily at the gateway of Heaven to hear the *Avos* pray; today, He listens every morning to the voices of their descendants.

When we stand to pray, therefore, we should not feel alone because our prayers echo the outpourings of the hearts of the Patriarchs and all of their descendants. Our personal prayers are amplified by over three thousand seven hundred years of prayer. If one considers the tens of millions of Jews who have repeated this *Amidah* for over two thousand years, the figures are astronomical. The sounds, sighs, and tears of every Jewish prayer are interwoven in today's prayer — is it any wonder that God listens eagerly to this supplication?

◄§ Lovingkindness Above All

God promised the Patriarchs that their descendants would remember them at the commencement of every prayer service. According to the Talmud (*Pesachim* 117b), this is the meaning of God's pledge to Abraham: וְאֶעֶשְׂךָ לְגוֹי גָּדוֹל וַאֲבָרֶכְךָ וַאֲגַדְּלָה שְׁמֶךָ וֶהְיֵה בְּרָכָה, *And I shall make of you a great nation; I shall bless you and make your name great, and you shall be a blessing (Genesis 12:2). I shall make of you a great nation* refers to the opening of the *Amidah* prayer with the phrase, "God of Abraham"; *and I shall bless you* refers to the phrase, "God of Isaac"; *and I will make your name great* refers to the phrase, "God of Jacob." However, God promised Abraham, *you shall become a blessing*, meaning that only his name will appear at the end of the blessing of *Avos*: Blessed are You, HASHEM, Shield of Abraham.

Rav Elya Lopian (*Lev Eliyahu* I, p. 245) explains that the mission of the *Avos* was to attract mankind to God's service, and each Patriarch had a unique approach. Abraham showered people with hospitality to give them a taste of God's boundless lovingkindness. Isaac trembled in incessant prayer and penitence and gave mankind a glimpse of God's awesomeness. Jacob was profoundly scrupulous in revealing God's attribute of truth. All three approaches were necessary and effective, but which is most relevant to us? The obvious choice is kindness, the attribute of Abraham. The reverence of Isaac and the truth of Jacob are lofty intellectual ideals, but they are effective only with people who are already attuned and receptive to spiritual values. Ordinary people respond to more immediate, physical stimuli, like the hot meal and cool shade which Abraham offered his pagan guests. Since Abraham demonstrated genuine concern for the needs of their bodies, they willingly entrusted him with the welfare of their souls. Therefore, the blessing of the *Avos* concludes exclusively with Abraham, because his influence surpasses all others.

◄§ *The Final Merit*

Rav Shimon Shkop offered another insight: In every generation one outstanding method of Divine service seems to be more effective than others. Some generations witnessed a renaissance of intense Torah study, stressing the truth of Jacob. Other generations saw a resurgence of intense piety and penitence, reflecting the reverent service of Isaac. But which motif will predominate in the generation that heralds the advent of the Messiah? God Himself answers, בְּךָ אֲנִי חוֹתֵם, *With you, Abraham, I will conclude* the final chapter of Jewish history. When the gentile world is engulfed in senseless hatred and brutality, the Jewish world will respond by practicing kindness on an unprecedented scale, inspired by the example of Abraham. This may well be the sign that the Messiah's arrival is imminent.

◄§ *Abraham Was One*

The first blessing is dedicated to Abraham, the first person to clearly recognize God on his own. The first letter of His name begins with an *aleph*, the first letter of the Hebrew alphabet, which has a numerical value of one. This signifies that Abraham stood alone, one man opposite the entire world. The prophet says of him, אֶחָד הָיָה אַבְרָהָם, *Abraham was one [alone]* (*Ezekiel* 33:24).

Abraham introduced the world to monotheism, the belief in one God. With him began a new era in history. Though all mankind was worshiping a multiplicity of gods, Abraham began his quest for the true God when he was only three years old. He saw the sun rise and bathe the earth in light and activity, and thought the sun must be God. But when the sun was banished by the moon, it seemed that the moon must be God because it had overpowered the sun. When the moon, too, disappeared, Abraham deduced that there had to be a supreme God Who made them both; Hashem is the One God, who rules over all! (*Rambam*).

Abraham was the first mortal to call Him אָדוֹן, *Master* of the universe (*Berachos* 7b). Although Adam, too, referred to God as the Master of all, Abraham added a new dimension to this title. He was the first to recognize that God *retains* mastery over all His creations, despite the laws of nature that appear to be unchangeable and resistant to change. He can perform miracles and reverse any natural process at will (*Maharsha, Berachos* 7b).

It is reported that the *Vilna Gaon* was once studying a newly published commentary on the prayers, which stated that the *Shacharis* (morning) service begins with the hymn עוֹלָם אֲדוֹן [*Adon Olam*], *Master of the universe*, because *Shacharis* was instituted by Abraham (*Berachos* 26b), the first person to address the Creator as Master. Upon reading this explanation, the Gaon exclaimed that for this insight alone the publication was worthwhile.

◄§ *Increasing God's Presence*

בָּרוּךְ אַתָּה ה' — *Blessed are You,* HASHEM.

Rabbi Chaim of Volozhin (*Nefesh HaChaim* II:2) negates the widespread misconception that the term בָּרוּךְ is an accolade meaning *praised* or *blessed*. The Almighty Master of the universe hardly needs our compliments. Rather the most precise connotation of בָּרוּךְ is *increase, expand, intensify,* from the word בְּרֵכָה, *spring*.

God desires to increase His Presence in this world, but He Himself has ordained that His involvement depends on mankind. When people recognize God as Sovereign of the World and invite Him to enter their lives, He will responds with His abundant goodness. If, however, people ignore God, He retreats and His blessed influence recedes into the background. When one recites the word בָּרוּךְ, therefore, he is in fact proclaiming that God is the source of all blessing, and He is welcome to increase and intensify the flow of His bounty.

◄§ *Personal Discovery*

אֱלֹהֵינוּ וֵאלֹהֵי אֲבוֹתֵינוּ — *Our God and the God of our forefathers.*

First we call Him *our God* because we are obligated to serve and know Him to *our* fullest capacity. But there is much about His ways that we cannot understand. In response to this lack of clarity we proclaim that He is *the God of our forefathers*, and we have complete faith in the tradition they have transmitted (*Dover Shalom*). Similarly, the Israelites sang God's praise after witnessing the wondrous splitting of the Sea of Reeds: זֶה אֵלִי וְאַנְוֵהוּ אֱלֹהֵי אָבִי וַאֲרֹמְמֶנְהוּ, *This is my God and I shall praise Him, the God of my father and I shall exalt Him* (*Exodus* 15:2).

~§ Every Jew Is Special

The introspective mood of prayer helps us discover our unique talents and qualities of character. The Talmud (*Berachos* 58a) observes that just as no two faces look alike, no two minds think alike. We are not meant to be clones of our forebears or carbon copies of our social peers.

Rav Naftali Amsterdam once lamented to his teacher, Rav Yisrael Salanter, "If only I had the mind of the author of *Sha'agas Aryeh;* the heart of the author of the *Yesod V'Shoresh Ha'avodah;* and the sterling character of the Rebbe [Rav Yisrael Salanter himself]!"

Rav Yisrael retorted, "No, Naftali! Serve Hashem with your *own* mind; your *own* heart; your *own* character!"

Four centuries ago, the *Maharal* of Prague (*Netzach Yisrael*) foretold that, according to the Divine plan of history, most Jews in the pre-Messianic era will be irreligious and estranged from the Torah legacy of their forefathers. Ultimately, these lost Jews will make independent decisions to repent and return to their heritage. This chain of events is necessary, explains the *Maharal*, because if all Jews would serve God only because they accepted the word of their parents, the service would be mechanical, routine, and lifeless. God wants Israel to greet the Messiah with a level of enthusiasm that be attained only through personal inquiry, struggle, and hard-earned discovery of the truth.

~§ Father of All Nations

Some say that a convert to Judaism cannot include the phrase, אֱלֹהֵינוּ וֵאלֹהֵי אֲבוֹתֵינוּ, *Our God and the God of our fathers,* in his prayers because his ancestors were not Jewish and did not recognize our God. However, the accepted ruling is otherwise, because God said to Abraham, וְלֹא יִקָּרֵא עוֹד אֶת שִׁמְךָ אַבְרָם וְהָיָה שִׁמְךָ אַבְרָהָם כִּי אַב הֲמוֹן גּוֹיִם נְתַתִּיךָ, *You shall no longer be called by your name Abram, but your name shall be Abraham, for I have made you the father of a multitude of nations (Genesis 17:5).* Since Abraham is referred to as the father of many nations, even a convert is considered his descendant and may call the God of Israel, "the God of my fathers," (see *Orach Chaim* 53:19 and *Mishnah Berurah* 49,50; *Tosafos Bava Basra* 81a in the name of *Ri*).

~§ Protectors of the World

אֱלֹהֵי אַבְרָהָם אֱלֹהֵי יִצְחָק וֵאלֹהֵי יַעֲקֹב — *God of Abraham, God of Isaac, and God of Jacob.*

God's Name is associated with each Patriarch individually to empha-size that each one stands on his own special merits, as intimated in God's promise: וְזָכַרְתִּי אֶת בְּרִיתִי יַעֲקוֹב וְאַף אֶת בְּרִיתִי יִצְחָק וְאַף אֶת בְּרִיתִי אַבְרָהָם אֶזְכֹּר, *I shall remember My covenant with Jacob, as well as My covenant with Isaac, as well as My covenant with Abraham will I remember* (*Leviticus* 26:42). Why are the Patriarchs mentioned separately, and in reverse order? To teach that the merit of Jacob [the last Patriarch] is sufficient to stand on its own, as is the merit of Isaac, as is the merit of Abraham. Each of the Patriarchs was great enough to protect the entire world (*Vayikra Rabbah* 36:4). Another reason why God's Name is joined separately with each Patriarch is to remind us that even to this day the *Avos* continue to pray on behalf of their children, but that each Patriarch prays to God separately, invoking his own unique merits (see *Bava Metzia* 85b).

◆§ *A Personal Approach*

The Patriarchs are listed in this blessing separately to emphasize that each one represents a unique approach to Divine service. Abraham represents חֶסֶד, *kindness*, the desire to seek out the welfare of others. Such a person takes God Himself as his role-model and, like the Creator, desires to give and share everything he possesses. This trait is similar to רַחֲמָנוּת, generally translated as *mercy*, but there is a difference between the two terms. The merciful person is aroused to help only after he learns of another's suffering. The *chesed*-oriented person, on the other hand, is self-motivated, constantly searching for new opportunities to benefit others. The *merciful* person seeks merely to solve problems and alleviate suffering. The *kind* person wants to help every man achieve success and good fortune, even if he has not been suffering.

Isaac represents the attribute of גְּבוּרָה, *strength*, or as it is often called, פַּחַד or יִרְאָה, *fear* of God. Whereas Abraham's service was outwardly directed, Isaac's mission was internal. Such a person is driven by a fear of transgression and a powerful drive for self-perfection. Isaac constantly subjected his every deed and desire to an exacting standard of purity and excellence.

Jacob dedicated himself to the characteristic of אֱמֶת, *truth*, which seeks to combine *chesed* and *gevurah*, kindness and strength, in the proper balance. Indulgent kindness and love can lead to undesirable excess, while self-critical *strength* can lead to stifling despair. The man of *truth* finds the middle course between these two extremes, creating a harmonious mixture.

When we recite the names of the Patriarchs in our prayers, we commit ourselves to adopting each of their characteristics and values.

◆§ Renaissance of Greatness

הָאֵל הַגָּדוֹל הַגִּבּוֹר וְהַנּוֹרָא — *The great, mighty and awesome God.*

In these four words we detect the signature of the authors of the *Amidah*, אַנְשֵׁי כְּנֶסֶת הַגְּדוֹלָה, the *Men of the Great Assembly*. The Talmud (*Yoma* 69b) explains that they merited the title "The Men of the Great Assembly" because they restored God's crown to its original greatness. In the Wilderness, Moses proclaimed that God was הָאֵל הַגָּדוֹל הַגִּבּוֹר וְהַנּוֹרָא — *the great, mighty and awesome God* (*Deuteronomy* 10:17). Centuries later, after Nebuchadnezzar and his hordes sacked the Holy Temple, the prophet Jeremiah cried out, "The gentiles desecrate His Sanctuary without restraint — where is God's awesomeness?" So Jeremiah deleted the term הַנּוֹרָא, *the awesome*, from his prayers. Then the prophet Daniel witnessed the gentiles oppressing the Jewish exiles and exclaimed, "Where is God's might?" And he deleted the term הַגִּבּוֹר, *the mighty*, from his prayers. But later the Men of Great Assembly determined that matters must be viewed from a different perspective. God displays His might, they declared, when the Jews are persecuted, yet He controls His wrath and fury for many years, waiting for the right moment to punish the gentile oppressors. God displays His awesomeness when Israel is in exile. How else can one explain the survival of a helpless band of Jews surrounded by hostile nations? [They resemble a tiny lamb surrounded by seventy savage, hungry wolves (*Tosafos Yeshanim*).] Beyond doubt, consciously or subconsciously, the gentiles are awestruck by God, and do not dare annihilate His people! Thus the Men of the Great Assembly earned the accolade "great," for they reinstituted all of God's praises: *The great, mighty and awesome God.* Similarly, all who recognize God's true greatness and teach it to others deserve for themselves the accolade *great.*

◆§ Imitate His Ways

The highest form of praise is imitation. When we recount these praises of God we must resolve to follow His example. As the Talmud (*Shabbos* 133b) teaches, הֱוֵי דוֹמֶה לוֹ, *Emulate Him!*

God is גִּבּוֹר, *mighty*. But His might is neither brutal nor vindictive. It is the strength of patience and perseverance. God is long suffering. The

Men of the Great Assembly earned their title not merely for their insight into God's attributes. They were called 'great' because they emulated God's attributes and patterned their own behavior after Him.

As we recite this blessing we resolve to strengthen ourselves by practicing self-control. We will not act or speak upon impulse, nor will we allow ourselves to be overwhelmed by anger. We thus fulfill one of the essential purposes of prayer — to recognize God and וְהָלַכְתָּ בִּדְרָכָיו, *to follow in His ways* (*Deuteronomy* 28:9).

⋑ *A Word of Caution*

As we recite this list of God's Attributes, we must always bear in mind that it is impossible to adequately describe God's virtues, for He is beyond our comprehension. We are privileged to utter these few praises of God in an attempt to understand him a little better. The Talmud (*Berachos* 33b) relates the following story:

Once, R' Chanina overheard someone praying, "the Great, the Mighty, the Awesome," as we are accustomed to saying in the *Shemoneh Esrei*. But then he added further praises, "the Brave, the Bold, the True, the Fearsome, the Strong, the Sure, the Esteemed." After the man finished his prayer, R' Chanina asked him, "Are you attempting to enumerate all of the praises of your Creator? Are these all the adjectives that you can think of to glorify the Name of Hashem? If Moshe Rabbeinu had not used the praises, 'the Great, the Mighty, the Awesome,' then the Men of the Great Assembly would never have dreamed of using those words in referring to Hashem. But you come along on your own and dare to add praises of your own invention. Let me tell you a parable:

"A wealthy king possessed millions of gold and silver pieces. If one were to say that he has only hundreds of silver pieces, the king would not feel complimented by the gesture. On the contrary, he would be insulted, for it is a disgrace to say that he owns less than he does, for we would be measuring his enormous wealth in trivial terms.

"When you praise Hashem by attempting to mention all of His praises, you are doomed to fall short. Wherever you step, you will have left out an infinite number of praises that should have been included, and that is not praise at all."

⋑ *Hashem Comes First*

אֵל עֶלְיוֹן — *The supreme God* [lit. *God most high*].

The word עֶלְיוֹן, *supreme*, means that God is so exalted that He is far beyond the comprehension of even the holiest angels. We can understand Him only superficially, by studying how He treats His creations, such as the fact that He *bestows beneficent kindnesses (Siach Yitzchok)*.

✍ High Command

The Midrash (*Koheles Rabbah* 4:18) observes: "When a weaker force occupies a strategic, high position, it can vanquish a much mightier army that is below it. Certainly, when the upper force is the mightiest of all, the Omnipotent God, and frail man is below, the Almighty will prevail."

Rav Dessler (*Michtav MiEliyahu* vol. III p. 82) illustrates this: Hundreds of thousands of mighty soldiers, heavily armed with spears and swords and war chariots, poised for invasion. Suddenly they are attacked from above by a lone pilot dropping bombs. There is no contests, because the jet is in a class of superiority that the primitive ground forces cannot begin to approach. Similarly, the might of God is in a class of its own, beyond comparison with mortal forces.

This title first appears in conjunction with Malchizedek, King of Shalem, whom the Torah describes as כֹּהֵן לְאֵל עֶלְיוֹן, *priest of the supreme God (Genesis* 14:18). Malchizedek expressed his admiration and gratitude to Abraham for defeating the four kings who threatened his country. As the verse states: *He blessed him saying, 'Blessed is Abram of God the Most High, Master of heaven and earth; and blessed be the Supreme God Who has delivered your foes into your hand'* (ibid. 14:19-20). The Sages take special note of the fact that Malchizedek first blessed Abram (as if to credit him for the victory), and only later (in the next verse) thanked and blessed God. Rav Zechariah said on behalf of Rav Yishmael: The Holy One, Blessed is He, intended to bring forth the priesthood from Shem [identified as Malchizedek], but because Malchizedek blessed Abraham before blessing God, God brought it forth from Abraham. Indeed, Abraham himself reprimanded Malchizedek, "Does a servant's blessing precede his Master's?" God then gave the priesthood to Abraham. Therefore, the verse reads: *And he was a priest of God, the Most High — only he* [Malchizedek] was a priest, but not his descendants (*Nedarim* 32b).

The above offers an insight into the next segment of the blessing: . . . *the supreme God . . . Who recalls the kindnesses of the Patriarchs and brings a Redeemer to their children's children, for His Name's sake.* God created the universe *'for His Name's sake,'* so that mankind should know that He is supreme and so that His Name should be *foremost* in their minds and on their lips. Malchizedek, who failed to make the *Name* of the *supreme God* foremost, did not transmit his legacy to his descendants. The Patriarchs, who made אֵל עֶלְיוֹן, *supreme God*, first and foremost, merited that their legacy and blessing continue in an unbroken chain for all time.

◄§ The World Is Built on Kindness

גוֹמֵל חֲסָדִים טוֹבִים וְקוֹנֵה הַכֹּל — *Who bestows beneficial kindnesses and creates everything.*

God created *everything* so that He might bestow beneficial kindnesses upon it — using *everything* created.

Abraham personified kindness as the prophet *Micah* (7:20) said: תִּתֵּן . . . חֶסֶד לְאַבְרָהָם, *You shall grant . . . kindness to Abraham.* Abraham taught the world that all the kindness he was doing was merely a reflection of God's boundless kindness. Thus, the Midrash states that Malchizedek praises Abraham as קֹנֵה שָׁמַיִם וָאָרֶץ, *He who has "acquired" heaven and earth* (Genesis 14:19), as if he had become an owner of the universe; by disseminating the knowledge of God among men, Abraham became a partner in the realization of creation's purpose.

Rav Yitzchak said: Abraham used to entertain wayfarers, and after they had eaten he would say to them, "Recite a blessing."

"What shall we say?" they asked.

"Blessed be the God of the universe Whose bounty we have eaten," he replied.

God said to Abraham: "My Name was unknown among My creatures, and you have made it known. I will therefore regard you as My partner in the creation of the world" (*Midrash*).

King David devoted an entire psalm to this theme: מַשְׂכִּיל לְאֵיתָן הָאֶזְרָחִי: חַסְדֵי ה׳ עוֹלָם אָשִׁירָה לְדֹר וָדֹר אוֹדִיעַ אֱמוּנָתְךָ בְּפִי. כִּי אָמַרְתִּי עוֹלָם חֶסֶד יִבָּנֶה שָׁמַיִם תָּכִן אֱמוּנָתְךָ בָהֶם — *Maskil by Eisan the Ezrachite. Of* HASHEM's *kindnesses I will sing forever; to every generation with my mouth I shall make Your faithfulness known. For I said, "The world is built on kindness; the heavens — You establish Your faithfulness in them"* (Psalms 89:1-3)

Targum, based on the Talmud (*Bava Basra* 14b), identifies Eisan, the author of the psalm, as the Patriarch Abraham, for he was אֵיתָן [lit. *strong*] in his faith (*Aggadah Bereishis* 55). Since Abraham traveled from Chaldea in the מִזְרָח, *east,* in order to spread belief in God, he was called הָאֶזְרָחִי, *the Ezrachite* [lit. *the easterner*].

◆§ Identifying with the Patriarchs

וְזוֹכֵר חַסְדֵי אָבוֹת — *Who recalls the kindnesses of the Patriarchs.*

Of course, God forgets nothing, says *Rav Dessler (Michtav MiEliyahu* vol. III p. 83). Rather this praise means that God made the Patriarchs the focus of His attention for the last thirty-seven centuries. Nothing in the world interests God more than the destiny of the *Avos* and their descendants, and all events revolve around the fate of the Jewish people. The kindness and selflessness of the *Avos* bonded them so intimately with God that nothing they or their offspring do can weaken God's fond remembrance of their deeds.

The Jewish standard of behavior is ordained by God, and its models are the Patriarchs. As the Sages teach, a Jew must always demand of himself, מָתַי יַגִּיעוּ מַעֲשַׂי לְמַעֲשֵׂי אֲבוֹתַי, *When will my deeds approach the deeds of my forefathers, Abraham, Isaac and Jacob (Tanna d'Bei Eliyahu Rabbah* 28).

The prophet records the Almighty's pledge to the Jewish people: כִּי הֶהָרִים יָמוּשׁוּ וְהַגְּבָעוֹת תְּמוּטֶינָה וְחַסְדִּי מֵאִתֵּךְ לֹא יָמוּשׁ וּבְרִית שְׁלוֹמִי לֹא תָמוּט אָמַר מְרַחֲמֵךְ ה', *For the mountains may slip away and the hills may falter, but My lovingkindness will not slip away from you, nor will My covenant of peace falter, says* HASHEM, *Who shows you mercy (Isaiah* 54:10).

The Midrash *(Vayikra Rabbah* 36) comments: If you see the merit of the fathers slipping away, and the merit of the mothers faltering, go and occupy yourself with kind deeds.

As the above verse teaches:

"For the mountains may slip away ..."

This refers to the merits of the Patriarchs.

"And the hills may falter ..."

This refers to the merits of the Matriarchs.

"But My lovingkindness will not slip away from you ..."

[If you practice kindness, I will always identify you with your pious ancestors.]

There were black periods in Jewish history when the Jews had sinned so greatly that certain Sages *(Shabbos* 55a) held that the merits of the Patriarchs have lost their ability to protect their descendants. Nevertheless, Isaiah proclaimed that if we emulate their kindness, God will always remember us favorably. *Maharal (Chiddushei Aggados, Shabbos* 55a) explains that this is precisely the purpose of prayer: Even if our sinful ways have obliterated the merits of our Patriarchs, sincere prayer will bring those very merits back to life!

◄§ Selflessness

Abraham excelled in kindness, Isaac in fear, and Jacob in truth, yet here we mention חַסְדֵי אָבוֹת, *the lovingkindness of [all] the Patriarchs,* because this trait is the root of all Divine service.

The most accurate definition of חֶסֶד is "selflessness" — to live for others, to live for a cause outside and greater than oneself. An egocentric person always serves himself, even when he appears to serve others. The *Avos* taught the world how to breach the constraints of selfishness.

Because the *Avos* were selfless in their service of God, they earned the title חָסִיד, *selfless one. Mesillas Yesharim* (chapter 18) describes this level: Unlike the servant who fulfills his obligation by rote, the *chassid* has a vibrant love for God, like that of a son for his beloved father. The *chassid* studies the ways of God constantly in order to discover new opportunities to please his Creator.

◄§ People-pleaser or God-pleaser?

We devote much effort to please important people. We strive in myriad ways to ingratiate ourselves to our clients, customers, congregants, patients, employers, and teachers. But no one is more important to our success than God. How much time do we spend trying to please Him?

First and foremost the *Avos* were "God-pleasers." They shared good fortune with others because they knew it pleased God. Therefore, God never forgot them and graciously remembers us, their descendants, to this very day.

◄§ Ongoing Redemption

וּמֵבִיא גוֹאֵל לִבְנֵי בְנֵיהֶם לְמַעַן שְׁמוֹ — *And brings a Redeemer to their children's children, for His Name's sake.*

This phrase is written in the present tense to emphasize that redemption is not an event that will occur abruptly in the future; rather, it is a steady, ongoing process that is happening right now. Every event, no matter how terrible it appears, is actually a step toward the ultimate redemption by the Messiah (*Siach Yitzchok*).

The First Blessing / 61

◄§ Redemption and Sanctification

The redemption of Israel occurs not only for our sake, but also for the glory of God's Name. Speaking through Ezekiel, God describes how there is no greater חִלּוּל ה', *desecration of the Name*, than the conditions of Jews in exile: *When the House of Israel dwelt in their own land, they defiled it by their ways and by their deeds . . . So I scattered them among the nations and they were dispersed through the countries. And when they came among the nations they profaned My Holy Name, because people said of them, "These are* HASHEM's *people and they left His land." So I am concerned for My Holy Name that Israel has profaned among the nations. Therefore say to the House of Israel, "Thus says the Lord, Hashem, 'I do not do this for your sake, O House of Israel, but for the sake of My Holy Name which has been profaned among the nations, because you profaned It in their midst. And the nations shall know that I am the Lord,' says the Lord Hashem, 'when I shall be sanctified in your midst before their eyes. For I will take you from among the nations, and gather you out of all countries and I shall bring you into your own land'* " (Ezekiel 36:17-24).

◄§ Double Reward

The Talmud (*Berachos* 63a) teaches: "Whoever incorporates the Name of God into his own personal pain will receive double reward." *Rabbi Chaim of Volozhin (Nefesh HaChaim* II:12) explains that we cannot realize how much pain our sins cause God. We are like the wayward son who becomes a drunkard, and, in his stupor, falls and lapses into a coma. His father is overwrought with anguish and pain, while the unconscious son is completely oblivious to the danger he is in. Doctors attempt to arouse him. He screams as they inject painful medicines into his veins. Though the compassionate father winces at his son's suffering during his treatment, his pain is nothing like what he felt when his son was injured, for now he knows that recovery is on the way. Similarly, when a Jew (who is God's son) sins, he causes God double pain. First, by sinning he inflicts injury upon himself, which causes pain to God. Secondly, he must now be punished so that suffering will atone for his sin. This, too, causes God sorrow. When a Jew prays, his primary concern should not be to alleviate his personal woes, but to remove the pain he has caused God. If that is his prayer's prime purpose, he will certainly receive God's help, measure for measure.

⇜ Wholehearted Loyalty

בְּאַהֲבָה — *With love.*

God's boundless love for the Patriarchs overflowed to all their descendants, as it is written: רַק בַּאֲבֹתֶיךָ חָשַׁק ה׳ לְאַהֲבָה אוֹתָם וַיִּבְחַר בְּזַרְעָם אַחֲרֵיהֶם בָּכֶם מִכָּל הָעַמִּים כַּיּוֹם הַזֶּה — *God yearned only for your forefathers — to love them, and He chose their offspring after them, that is you; from all the nations, to this very day* (Deuteronomy 10:15). The verse differentiates between God's feelings for the Patriarchs, for whom He *yearned,* and that toward their offspring, whom He merely *chose.*

Haamek Davar (ibid.) explains that the difference reflects the difference between our own devotion to God and that of our ancestors. As human beings, we have freedom of choice, which implies that we have many options from which we eventually make a final selection. The descendants of the Patriarchs do not love God wholeheartedly, without deviation. Many ungodly desires stir up their hearts, where a battle rages between their spiritual and physical sides. Finally, we choose to serve God, but somewhat reluctantly. Measure for measure, God's feeling for us is equally cool. He *chooses* us from among the nations — but only because we are the lesser of evils.

Not so the Patriarchs. They had an intense yearning for the Almighty. For them nothing else mattered. And God responded in kind to their wholehearted love and loyalty, and yearned for them — to love them.

We, their descendants, should strive for that quality of love, for by virtue of it God will ultimately redeem us.

⇜ Love Your Neighbor

"And He brings a Redeemer to their children's children . . . with love" also suggests the brotherly love that Jews should have for one another. The second Temple was destroyed and the Jews were dispersed as a result of שִׂנְאַת חִנָּם, *hatred without cause.* Conversely, we shall be redeemed only by virtue of genuine brotherly love. As we begin to pray we must generate love not only for God, but for our fellow man. *Arizal* teaches that at the outset of prayer one should fully accept upon himself the *mitzvah* of וְאָהַבְתָּ לְרֵעֲךָ כָּמוֹךָ, *Love your fellow as yourself* (*Leviticus* 19:18). Our prayers are in the plural to demonstrate that we think not only about ourselves, but that we are concerned for our fellow Jews.

Rav Chaim Vital (*Shaarei Kedushah* II:4) teaches that hating another Jew is equivalent to hating God, for every Jewish soul is but a fragment of the Creator's "super-soul." [Moreover, since all Jews descend from the Patriarchs, one who hates a fellow Jew is casting aspersions on his enemy's forebears, the Patriarchs, and thereby diminishes his own זְכוּת אָבוֹת, *merit of the Patriarchs*.]

❧ Helper of the Helpless

מֶלֶךְ עוֹזֵר וּמוֹשִׁיעַ וּמָגֵן — *O King, Helper, Savior, and Shield*.

God *'helps'* [עוֹזֵר] those who try to help themselves. But often a person is absolutely helpless; nevertheless, even then God *'saves'* [מוֹשִׁיעַ] without the victim's participation [*Iyun Tefillah*]. However, the highest level of Divine assistance is reserved for the believer who voluntarily endangers himself in the service of God, as Abraham did when he destroyed His father's idols and was thrown into the inferno. In such instances God is the *'shield'* [מָגֵן] that protects His believers from every form of danger (*Vilna Gaon*).

Moreover, although God uses conventional, natural methods when He acts as *Helper* and *Savior*, when He acts as our Shield He employs supernatural means to protect us (*Lev Eliyahu*, Vol. I p. 301).

❧ Undiminished Reward

בָּרוּךְ אַתָּה ה' מָגֵן אַבְרָהָם — *Blessed are You, HASHEM, Shield of Abraham*.

This phrase derives from God's assurance to Abraham after he vanquished the four kings who invaded the Land of Canaan: אַל תִּירָא אַבְרָם אָנֹכִי מָגֵן לָךְ שְׂכָרְךָ הַרְבֵּה מְאֹד, *Fear not, Abram, I am your shield; your reward is very great* (Genesis 15:1).

Yalkut Shimoni (ibid.) notes that in Aramaic מָגֵן means *'free, at no cost'*. Abraham was apprehensive that since he had benefited from a miraculous victory, his merits had been consumed in This World, leaving nothing for the Hereafter. God assured him, therefore, that because he fought exclusively for the glory of God and with no desire for personal gain, his great reward would not be diminished at all.

By reciting this blessing at the outset of our personal prayers, we proclaim to God: "Master of the universe, I am about to make many requests of You, but I fear that if You grant my wishes my future reward will be diminished. I declare, therefore, that I desire to follow in the footsteps of my forefather, Abraham, who acted only for Your glory and thus did not deplete his reward at all!"

⊸§ The "Pinteleh Yid"

One of the primary teachings of the Chassidic masters is that although evil influences may corrupt a Jew and alienate him from his roots, a Jew is never completely lost. In the deepest recesses of the soul there survives a tiny spark of Jewishness, pure and untainted. From such a spark a brilliant flame of faith can be rekindled. This indestructible *pinteleh* Yid [tiny dot of Jewishness] was implanted into the genetic design of our people by Abraham, and Hashem promised to protect and preserve it forever when He assured Abraham: *"I am your shield."*

Similarly, King Solomon referred to this indestructible spark when he sang of Israel's love for God: אֲנִי יְשֵׁנָה וְלִבִּי עֵר, [Although] *I am* [outwardly] *asleep, my heart is still awake* (Song of Songs 5:1). We should bear this assurance in mind when reciting the blessing, *Shield of Abraham* (*Chiddushei HaRim; Sefer Hazechus, Parshas Tazria*).

⊸§ In God's Footsteps

Rambam (*Guide* III:51) reveals that God shielded Abraham and the other Patriarchs from all harm because they focused their every thought on Him and never interrupted their concentration as they attempted to follow in His footsteps.

One who walks with God, writes *Rambam*, rivets his attention to the Almighty and allows nothing to distract him. This walking in the way of God, the highest level of human existence, can be attained only through intense discipline. One who aspires to such closeness to his Maker should begin by training himself to concentrate on his prayers. After successfully doing so, he will be able to sense God's Presence more easily throughout the day, even when he is involved in mundane pursuits.

Rambam continues:

When a man frees his thoughts from all worldly matters — when he obtains a correct understanding of the true nature of God and rejoices in that knowledge — it is impossible for any kind of evil to befall him. He is always with God and God is always with him.

⊸§ There Is Nothing Besides Him

Rabbi Chaim of Volozhin (*Nefesh HaChaim* III:12-13) cites the Talmud (*Chullin* 7b) that if a person internalizes the verse: ה' הוּא הָאֱלֹהִים

אֵין עוֹד מִלְּבַדּוֹ, HASHEM, He is God, there is nothing else beside Him (Deuteronomy 4:35), he will be protected from harmful forces. By accepting God's absolute sovereignty, one places oneself fully under His protective wing. Although nature contains many destructive elements, the man of faith understands that they are but marionettes in the hands of the Creator.

∞§ Nature's Leash

The *Brisker Rav, Rav Yitzchok Zev Soloveitchik*, a descendant of Rav Chaim of Volozhin, testified how the above statement of faith recorded in *Nefesh HaChaim* served as his guide throughout his life. When he was a young man, "Reb Velvel" — as the Brisker Rav was known — was commanded to appear before the Russian draft board to be inducted into the Czar's army. This fate was tantamount to both a spiritual and physical death sentence. As the date of his appearance neared, his father, Rav Chaim Brisker, instructed him to concentrate on the above passage from *Nefesh HaChaim*. To Reb Velvel's great relief, his meeting with the draft board came, and he was exempted from the draft.

Later, when the Germans occupied Poland at the beginning of World War II, Reb Velvel fled to Vilna. The roads were filled with German troops. The danger was awesome. Yet, Reb Velvel traveled undaunted, for he never stopped reviewing the guarantee of the *Nefesh HaChaim*: "If you always think of God, He will always think of you, and protect you from all harm."

Just once, Reb Velvel was distracted and his mind wandered. Immediately, as if from nowhere, an armed Nazi approached him threateningly. In a flash, Reb Velvel collected his thoughts and focused on the *Nefesh HaChaim*, and the Nazi moved on (*Rabboseinu* p. 170).

This level of concentrated, uninterrupted faith in God is the real *Shield of Abraham*, which he handed down as a protective legacy to his descendants.

2

גְּבוּרוֹת / God's Might

אַתָּה גִּבּוֹר לְעוֹלָם אֲדֹנָי, מְחַיֵּה מֵתִים אַתָּה, רַב
לְהוֹשִׁיעַ. (מַשִּׁיב הָרוּחַ וּמוֹרִיד הַגֶּשֶׁם,) מְכַלְכֵּל
חַיִּים בְּחֶסֶד, מְחַיֵּה מֵתִים בְּרַחֲמִים רַבִּים, סוֹמֵךְ נוֹפְלִים,
וְרוֹפֵא חוֹלִים, וּמַתִּיר אֲסוּרִים, וּמְקַיֵּם אֱמוּנָתוֹ לִישֵׁנֵי עָפָר.
מִי כָמוֹךְ בַּעַל גְּבוּרוֹת, וּמִי דוֹמֶה לָּךְ, מֶלֶךְ מֵמִית וּמְחַיֵּה
וּמַצְמִיחַ יְשׁוּעָה. וְנֶאֱמָן אַתָּה לְהַחֲיוֹת מֵתִים. בָּרוּךְ אַתָּה
יהוה, מְחַיֵּה הַמֵּתִים.

You are eternally mighty, my Lord, the Resuscitator of the
dead are You; abundantly able to save. (He makes the wind
blow and He makes the rain descend,) He sustains the living
with kindness, resuscitates the dead with abundant mercy,
supports the fallen, heals the sick, releases the confined, and
maintains His faith to those asleep in the dust. Who is like
You, O Master of mighty deeds, and who is comparable to You,
O King Who causes death and restores life and makes
salvation sprout! And You are faithful to resuscitate the dead.
Blessed are You, HASHEM, Who resuscitates the dead.

◆§ Isaac's Blessing

The *Amidah* begins with the blessing of the Patriarchs who initiated Israel's mission of Divine service. This next blessing takes us to the end of history and the culmination of Divine service: the Day of Final Judgment. At that time, the Resurrection of the Dead will occur, demonstrating the enormity of *God's might* and His total mastery over every detail of existence. That event will be coupled with the final accounting of mankind's activities throughout history.

The first blessing is dedicated to Abraham, the progenitor of Israel. The second blessing is dedicated to his son Isaac who provided a glimpse of the final resurrection at the *Akeidah*. Although he was never actually sacrificed, tradition teaches that Isaac's soul left his body for a brief instant and ascended to celestial heights, and then God returned it to revive his momentarily lifeless flesh.

Pesikta D'Rav Kahana (32) states that in the future God will restore the dead in the merit of Isaac. In this vein, *Shibbolei Halekket* quotes the Midrash that when Isaac was bound to be sacrificed, the ministering angels chanted, "Blessed are You, HASHEM, Who resuscitates the dead."

◆§ Death Is not Forever

Contemplation of God's mighty power to resurrect the dead can infuse one with a faith and conviction so strong that he will gladly offer his life to sanctify God's Name. Abraham's progression of faith began when he fearlessly faced the menacing flames of Nimrod's furnace rather than recant his belief in the One, true God. The specter of death is terrifying only to those who believe that death is final and forever. Death cannot intimidate men of God who know that their demise only brings them one step closer to a blissful afterlife that comes to its climax at the Resurrection of the Dead.

When the *Rebbe of Lubavitch* was arrested in Russia for violating the ban against promulgating Torah, an interrogating officer pointed a gun at his head, but the *Rebbe* was not intimidated. He remarked, "Fear of death occurs only when a person has only one world, but many gods. However, when the reverse is true, when one has only one God and two worlds, death is not frightening."

As we recite this blessing we commit ourselves to following in the footsteps of our Patriarchs no matter how hazardous that mission might be. No danger, not even death, can deter us, because we know that even death is not forever.

ᴥᴥ Life in Two Worlds

Blessing number two teaches us that we live in two worlds — this one and the Hereafter. Even in this world, we exist on two planes, the lower physical level of the body and the higher spiritual level of the soul. *Malbim* (comm. to *Chayei Sarah*) describes how Abraham introduced these concepts to the world when he purchased the Cave of Machpelah for Sarah's burial place. It was called *Machpelah*, meaning *double*, because, the Talmud (*Eruvin* 53a) teaches, it was a two-level structure, symbolizing the relationship of body and soul. The Canaanites were reluctant to sell prime real estate to be wasted on a burial site. Because they denied the existence of the soul, a cemetery was no more than a dump for the disposal of decaying human flesh. Abraham, however, revealed to them that the body, too, could be eternal. Body and soul separate at death temporarily, but they will yet reunite.

ᴥᴥ Burial: Planting a Seed

In this world, the first stage of existence, the relationship between the body and the soul is not harmonious: Each struggles to gain control over the other, and the incessant friction and attrition caused by this bitter struggle is actually the cause of death (comm. of *Sforno* to *Numbers* 25:12). When the body finally releases its grip on the soul each combatant retires to its corner for "rehabilitation." This Divinely designed process prepares them for a second union which *will* be perfectly harmonious. At death, the liberated soul soars to the celestial bliss of the World of Souls where it is purged of any taint left from its earthly sojourn. It is then exposed to intense Divine light which fortifies it against any mundane influence, forever.

On earth meanwhile, the body is reverently purified and prepared for interment in the soil where it is planted, as it were, like a seed. The old, scarred flesh falls away and dust returns to dust. As the Resurrection of the Dead nears, the seed germinates. A dramatic transformation takes place and a new body is sculpted to conform perfectly to every desire of the soul.

In the future, the refurbished body and soul will rejoin to exist in absolute harmony. They will form a perfectly integrated unit without any trace of feud. Together, they will be judged for their past actions in this world and then go on to enjoy eternal bliss, as one (based on *Ramban*, שַׁעַר הַגְּמוּל, *The Gate of Reward*).

~§ The Foundation of Our Faith

The Talmud (*Shabbos* 88b) teaches that when the Jews received the Torah at Sinai they were so overwhelmed by the voice of God that their souls departed from their bodies. God gently resuscitated them with a refreshing dew only to have them pass away again with the pronouncement of the next commandment. Once more He revived them. This process repeated itself over and over again for every Divine utterance at Sinai, to underscore that belief in the future resurrection is the foundation of our faith. When the time comes, that same dew will be used to resurrect the lifeless.

Rambam's Thirteen Principles of Jewish Faith lists the final principle as: "I believe with perfect faith that the dead will be brought back to life when God wills it to happen." In his commentary to Mishnah (*Sanhedrin* 10:1), *Rambam* adds: "The Resurrection of the Dead is one of the fundamentals handed down by Moses. One who does not believe in it cannot be associated with Judaism." Finally, *Rambam* rules in *Mishneh Torah* (*Hilchos Teshuvah* 3:6): "These have no portion in the World to Come... Those who deny the Resurrection of the Dead."

~§ The Four Keys to Life

In addition to the restoration of life in the future, this blessing speaks of God's "might" in sustaining life in this world. Our Sages taught (*Taanis* 2a) that although God controls many aspects of the world through His intermediaries, the angels, three primary functions remain under God's direct control. "Three keys are in the hands of the Holy One, Blessed is He: the key to open the mother's womb at birth, the key to open the skies for rainfall, and the key of life to resurrect the dead." *Tur* (*Shulchan Aruch*, *Orach Chaim* 114) adds to the list the key of sustenance and livelihood, which God entrusts to no one. *Tur* notes that the word מַפְתֵּחַ, *key*, is an acronym for these four blessings — מָטָר, *rainfall*; פַּרְנָסָה, *livelihood*; תְּחִיָּה, *resurrection*; and חַיָּה, *mother at birth*. Furthermore, this blessing contains fifty-one words, the exact sum of all the words in the four Scriptural verses that refers to God's keys.

The keys of resurrection, rain, and sustenance are clearly mentioned in this blessing; childbirth is not. *Prishah (Tur Orach Chaim* 114), however, explains that the phrase וּמַתִּיר אֲסוּרִים, *releases the confined*, alludes to the mother who was confined by חֶבְלֵי לֵידָה, *the bonds of birth*, and to the infant who had been imprisoned in the womb. At the *Bris Milah* ceremony, just after the baby is named, everyone cries out, *Give thanks to* HASHEM *for He is good; His kindness endures forever* (Psalms 107:1), because Psalm 107 teaches that a person released from prison must recite this verse of thanksgiving. Likewise, we publicly thank God for releasing both mother and child.

⊷§ Prayer Restores Life

"Resurrection of the Dead" is not a remote event relegated to the distant future. Anyone who prays with sincerity feels renewed, because prayer restores vitality to both body and soul. Before praying, we may feel exhausted, disheartened, drained of strength and enthusiasm. But as we turn our hearts heavenward in prayer, we attach ourselves to the Source of life's energy. The more we concentrate on the words the more vitality we absorb from the Almighty, and find within ourselves. Prayer releases hidden reserves of dormant potential.

King David sang: לֹא הַמֵּתִים יְהַלְלוּ יָהּ וְלֹא כָּל יֹרְדֵי דוּמָה, *Neither the dead can praise* YAH, *nor any who descend into silence* (Psalms 115:17). The Sages (*Yalkut Shimoni* #573) cite this verse in their ruling that a dried-out, bleached or brittle *lulav* is invalid, because the *lulav* symbolizes the human spine and body which must be supple and fresh in the service of God. When a person is cold and apathetic, he resembles the silent dead who cannot praise God. In this blessing, therefore, we implore God to revive us with fresh enthusiasm for life and Divine service.

⊷§ Concealed but in Control

אַתָּה גִבּוֹר לְעוֹלָם אֲדֹנָי — *You are eternally mighty, my Lord.*
Human might is short lived. The boastful youth shows off his muscle early in his life, only to become weak and infirm in his old age. God's might, however, endures for eternity and is never diminished (*Etz Yosef*).

As explained above, Moses bestowed upon God the title הַגִּבּוֹר, *the Mighty One*. Later, when the Jews languished in the oppression of the Babylonian exile, the prophet Daniel deleted this title, arguing, "The Jews are slaves to heathens; where is God's might?" But the Men of the

Great Assembly reinstated the title *Mighty One* in the *Amidah*, explaining, "To the contrary, the greatest evidence of God's might is the fact that He is patient and doesn't punish His enemies instantly" (*Yoma* 69b).

In this blessing we therefore emphasize that God is גִּבּוֹר לְעוֹלָם, *eternally Mighty*. Even when he chooses to hide His Presence and allow the heathens to triumph, He always remains in full control of the universe (*Rav Yitzchok Zev Soloveitchik, Brisker Rav zt"l*).

◆§ The Source of All Life

מְחַיֶּה מֵתִים אַתָּה רַב לְהוֹשִׁיעַ — *The Resuscitator of the dead are You; abundantly able to save.*

Scripture records several instances where human beings resuscitated the dead, such as the prophet Elijah, who did it once, Elisha who did it twice, and Ezekiel who did it for an entire valley full of dry bones. The Talmud also relates numerous instances where the Sages revived the dead. Nevertheless, we declare here that no human being can ever accomplish such a feat independent of God Who is the sole source of all life. *The Resuscitator of the dead are You* — none other.

At the same time we acknowledge that God's life-restoring powers are so vast and inexhaustible that He generously shares them with select mortals. So He is *abundantly able to save* through human beings, even while retaining the key to life in His own hands (*Iyun Tefillah*).

◆§ Life-restoring Rains

מַשִּׁיב הָרוּחַ וּמוֹרִיד הַגָּשֶׁם — *He makes the wind blow and He makes the rain descend.*

The Talmud (*Taanis* 7a) states: "The day of rainfall is greater than the day of the Resuscitation of the Dead, because the future revival is only for the righteous, whereas rainfall comes for both the righteous and wicked alike. Since rainfall is compared to revival, the Sages included it in the blessing for the Resuscitation of the Dead."

Rain causes the buried seed to rot and disintegrate, after which it germinates and produces a beautiful plant. This parallels the Resurrection when the "planted" body will emerge in a superior form. Both are evidence of God's גְּבוּרָה, *might*.

In addition, rain supplies food and water from which human bodies are formed (65% of the body is moisture). Thus, rain is tantamount to a downpour of human life (*Rav Avigdor Miller*).

⊷§ A Question of Pronunciation

There is a serious debate among halachic scholars as to the correct vowelization of the Hebrew word *rain* used in this phrase. The word is usually pronounced גֶּשֶׁם, unless it appears at the end of a statement, as it does here, in which case it is pronounced גָּשֶׁם. For this reason *Rabbi Moshe Feinstein* (*Igros Moshe, Orach Chaim* Vol. IV, 40:15) endorses גָּשֶׁם. There is evidence for this position in the ruling of *Shulchan Aruch* and *Mishnah Berurah* (*Orach Chaim* 114:6) that one who forgot to say מַשִּׁיב הָרוּחַ וּמוֹרִיד הַגֶּשֶׁם in its customary place may insert it anywhere in this blessing because it is an independent statement.

Others, however, argue that since the Talmud puts great emphasis on merging the themes of life-giving rain and resurrection, it is incorrect to use גָּשֶׁם which implies a conclusion and appears to sever the phrase from the rest of this blessing. Additionally, גָּשֶׁם uses the vowel *komatz* which literally means *a clenched fist*, whereas גֶּשֶׁם uses the vowel *segol*, cognate with *segulah, treasure*. When praying for something as vital as rain, the symbolism of a *treasure* is far more appropriate than that of *a clenched fist*.

⊷§ The Almighty's Benevolence

מְכַלְכֵּל חַיִּים בְּחֶסֶד — *He sustains the living with kindness.*

Men of power often use their strength to oppress and dominate others. This is not true of God, Who uses His might to *sustain the living with kindness*. Human tyrants exercise their might to kill people, but God resuscitates the dead. Human strongmen topple their rivals, torture and imprison them, but God *supports the fallen, heals the sick, releases the confined*. Human bullies lie, steal, and cheat anyone too helpless or weak to retaliate, but God *maintains His faith [even] to those [helplessly] asleep in the dust* (*Iyun Tefillah*; based on *Sefer HaIkkarim*).

⊷§ The Blind Man and the Cripple

מְחַיֶּה מֵתִים בְּרַחֲמִים רַבִּים — *He resuscitates the dead with abundant mercy.*

The Talmud (*Sanhedrin* 91a,b) compares a human body without a

The Second Blessing / 73

soul to a robust person who is blind, while the soul without a body is likened to a sharp-sighted cripple. Individually, each is immobilized by his handicap, but when the sharp-eyed cripple is placed on the back of the strong blind man, together they can go anyplace. Similarly, the body can accomplish nothing until the soul enters and guides it to achieve its ultimate purpose. When body and soul are separated at death, they suffer because each one cannot be fully effective without the other. At the Resurrection, God exercises *abundant mercy* and reunites them harmoniously so that they can resume their symbiotic relationship.

◆§ Garments for the Future

The Talmud (*Sanhedrin* 90b) relates that Queen Cleopatra said to Rabbi Meir, "I fully believe that the dead are destined to be resurrected, but I would like to know if they will emerge from the earth naked or clothed." Rabbi Meir replied, "The dead will arise fully clad and this can be logically proved by observing nature. A naked kernel of wheat is planted in the ground, yet it emerges fully clothed as a stalk of wheat, covered with husks and wrappings. Certainly man who is clothed in shrouds at his burial will emerge from the earth covered with garments."

This is God's mercy to the dead. He preserves their dignity, and they return to life properly attired (*Etz Yosef*).

◆§ Better than Ever

סוֹמֵךְ נוֹפְלִים, וְרוֹפֵא חוֹלִים, וּמַתִּיר אֲסוּרִים — *Supports the fallen, heals the sick, releases the confined.*

The Talmud (*Sanhedrin* 91b) teaches that people with physical handicaps at the time of their death will be resurrected with the same flaw. Immediately after they emerge from their graves, however, God will cure them. Indeed, *Raavad* (gloss to *Hilchos Teshuvah* 8:2) says that when the dead come to life, their bodies will be stronger and healthier than ever, impervious to fatigue, illness, or harm, like the bodies of the celestial beings. Thus, in the future, God will continue to *support the fallen, heal the sick and release the confined* by physical infirmity, just as He does in this world.

◆§ Asleep in the Dust

וּמְקַיֵּם אֱמוּנָתוֹ לִישֵׁנֵי עָפָר — *And maintains His faith to those asleep in the dust.*

The Talmud (*Sanhedrin* 92a) quotes Ravina, who said that the tenet of the Resurrection is derived from the words of Daniel: *Many of those who sleep in the dusty earth shall awaken, some of these for everlasting life, and some of these for shame, for everlasting abhorrence (Daniel 12:2)*. Rav Saadiah Gaon (*Emunos V'De'os*, chapter 7) notes that the prophet does not say that *all who sleep* will return because that promise would include all of mankind and this pledge is only to Israel. Therefore he carefully says *many*.

Taking it one step further, *Rav Saadiah* explains that the verse does not mean that all Jews will be resurrected, *some for everlasting life, some for everlasting abhorrence*. Rather, those who are deserving will be revived, while those who are undeserving — apostates and unrepentant sinners — will remain in the grave eternally.

Rambam (*Commentary* to Mishnah, *Sanhedrin* 10:1) agrees with R' Saadiah Gaon that the Resurrection is destined only for the righteous. *Abarbanel* (*Mayenei Hayeshuah* 11a), however, disagrees and states that the Resurrection will include all of mankind. [This short summary in no way exhausts this topic, which deserves a volume to itself. The reader inclined to pursue this topic should study *Maamar Hatchiyah* (*Rambam*); *Shaar Hagemul* (*Ramban*); *Chiddushei HaRamah* to Sanhedrin Perek Chelek; *Igros Ramah*, etc.]

⧉ Avoid Envy, Avoid Decay

The Talmud (*Shabbos* 152b) states that exceptionally righteous people do not decompose in the grave, but are merely *asleep in the dust*. When Rav Nachman's workers were digging in his land, they inadvertently hit upon the lost grave of Rabbi Achai bar Yoshia whose body remained physically perfect. Rav Nachman was told of this and communicated with Rabbi Achai, who explained that the preservation of his body was quite natural, for King Solomon taught: *A tranquil heart gives vitality to the flesh, but envy is the rot of the bones (Proverbs 14:30)*. When the heart is consumed with envy, the flesh will rot; if the heart is free of envy, the flesh will be preserved. But, Rav Nachman asked, what about the curse God issued to all descendants of Adam, *For you are dust and dust you shall return (Genesis 3:19)*? Rav Achai explained that for the righteous that curse will take effect just before the final resurrection when they will momentarily revert to dust. Then, an instant later, God Himself will open their graves and restore them to everlasting life.

Rav Eliyahu Lopian (Lev Eliyahu, Bereishis, p. 197) explains that there are two kinds of resurrection. Ordinary people whose bodies decay into dust require abundant Divine mercy to be revived, as, indeed, the blessing states earlier that He will resuscitate them *with abundant mercy*. But in referring to the truly righteous who do not actually rot, the blessing does not mention mercy — God *maintains His faith to those asleep in the dust* (i.e. very easily) — because they maintained pure faith in Him.

⇜§ Not a Molecule Will Be Lost

Rav Avigdor Miller observes that God will *maintain His faith* to resurrect even those whose graves are lost and whose bodies have disintegrated. Some bodies have drowned in the ocean, some were eaten by beasts, some were entirely burnt and their ashes scattered without identification. Nevertheless, Hashem is faithful; He keeps account of every molecule of dust and ashes, and will collect them all, despite the passage of thousands of years.

⇜§ Our Lord Is Unsurpassed

מִי כָמְוֹךָ בַּעַל גְּבוּרוֹת וּמִי דּוֹמֶה לָּךְ — *Who is like You, O Master of mighty deeds, and who is comparable to You.*

Throughout history, many prophets and sages have resurrected the dead and performed wonders. Nevertheless, their accomplishments are inferior to those of the Almighty, for God is *Master of mighty deeds* while the prophets and sages are merely God's agents, deriving their powers from Him. Moreover, none are comparable to God, because the people whom God is destined to resurrect will live on forever, whereas every person revived by holy men eventually died once again (*Etz Yosef*).

⇜§ The Cycle of Life

מֶלֶךְ מֵמִית וּמְחַיֶּה — *O King Who causes death and restores life.*

God does both simultaneously: He causes death in this world but restores life in the Hereafter. Even in this world both life and death may occur simultaneously, for at the same time God brings one life to an end, He gives life to a newborn child.

This also alludes to God's kindness in introducing new life into the world to replace what is lost by death. King Solomon observed וְזָרַח הַשֶּׁמֶשׁ וּבָא הַשָּׁמֶשׁ, *The sun rises and the sun sets* (*Ecclesiastes* 1:5), to which the Midrash comments that the rising and setting sun alludes to the life-death cycle, and teaches that before the "sun" of one righteous man sets, God causes the "sun" of another righteous man to rise, so that death should not leave a spiritual void in the world. On the day Rabbi Akiva died, Rabbi Yehudah HaNassi was born ... Before the sun of Sarah set, God caused the sun of Rebeccah to rise. Before the sun of Moses set, God caused the sun of Joshua to rise ... and so on, generation after generation (see *Kiddushin* 72b).

⋅§ Never Despair

וּמַצְמִיחַ יְשׁוּעָה — *And makes salvation sprout.*

Even when every avenue of salvation seems to be shut, one should never give up hope. God has the ability to turn around the most hopeless desperate situation just as He can restore life to a pile of dead bones. Similarly, when we witness the ongoing wonder of lifeless seeds sprouting forth from cold, hard earth, we reinforce our faith in God's power of resurrection and salvation.

⋅§ The Indestructible Bone

Sefer HaBris (Part I, Essay 11, Chapter 10) states that the entire body disintegrates after death with the exception of one indestructible bone at the top of the spinal column. This bone, called *luz* or *nasqui*, can neither be shattered by hammers nor consumed by fires. When God resurrects the dead, this surviving bone will be used as the starting point for the restoration of the rest of the body (*Bereishis Rabbah* 28:3).

When Adam ate from the Tree of Knowledge, all his organs derived pleasure from this sin, and were condemned. Only the *luz* refused to absorb any part of this forbidden fruit and remained immortal.

After the three generous Sabbath meals, the body is surfeited and derives no physical pleasure from the *Melaveh Malkah* eaten after the Sabbath ends. Only the *luz* is nourished by this meal exclusively, for it is eaten only for the sake of enriching the immortal spirit. The *Melaveh Malkah* is called *the feast of King David*, for *David, King of Israel, lives on and endures!* It is he who will restore the immortality of Adam for he will bring the Messianic era which will be followed by the Resurrection of the Dead (whose formation is based on the *luz* bone) for all eternity. Thus, the future Resurrection will sprout from a small, hard bone which resembles the sprouting of a small seed.

⊷§ Many Forms of Revival

וְנֶאֱמָן אַתָּה לְהַחֲיוֹת מֵתִים — *And You are faithful to resuscitate the dead.*

Abudraham observes that we mention God's power to restore life three times in this blessing. This alludes to the three kinds of revival: man's daily awakening, life-restoring rains, and the Resurrection of the Dead in the future.

Chiddushei Ritva (Bava Metzia 85b) explains these three references differently. The first two allude to incidents of the past — the resuscitation of Isaac at the *Akeidah* and the wondrous acts of resuscitation performed by the prophets. The third reference alludes to the future Resurrection of the Dead [see *Chiddushei Ritva, Rosh Hashanah* 16b and *Taanis* 30b].

Kovetz Shiurim (Vol. II:29) quotes *Radvaz* (II:644), who explains that there will be *two* resurrections in the future. The general resurrection for all people will take place after the Messianic era ends. However, at the beginning of the Messianic era a limited revival of the dead will occur, bringing back to life the outstanding individuals, the great scholars and men of piety, of each generation. This is also the opinion of *Ritva*, who explains that these dedicated individuals are entitled to enjoy the bliss and rewards of the Messianic times. [See *Ikrei Hadat, Yoreh Deah Hilchos Aveilus* appendix 66.] Indeed, the Talmud (*Yoma* 5b) indicates that in the Messianic era Moses and Aaron will be alive once again and available to make halachic decisions. [See *Pesachim* 114b, *Tosafos* s.v. אֶחָד זֶכֶר לְפֶסַח and *Sanhedrin* 51b, *Rashi* s.v. הַלְכָה לָמָה לִי.] *Rav Saadiah Gaon* comments that Moses will be revived together with all other prophets of Jewish history, who will assist him in leading the Jewish people.

⊷§ Five Stages of the Soul

בָּרוּךְ אַתָּה ה' מְחַיֵּה הַמֵּתִים — *Blessed are You, HASHEM, Who resuscitates the dead.*

Iyun Tefillah notes that if we carefully count every separate reference to resurrection in this blessing we will see that it is really mentioned five times. This alludes to the Midrashic teaching (*Devarim Rabbah* 2:26) that the soul includes five distinct spiritual levels: נֶפֶשׁ, *spirit*; רוּחַ, *wind*; נְשָׁמָה, *soul*; חַיָּה, *the live one*; and the loftiest level called יְחִידָה, *the one and only*. In this world few people actually relate to all five levels, but at the time of the future Resurrection, people will be in total harmony with all five components.

In *Psalms* (103:1,2,22 and 104:1,35), David repeats the refrain, *Bless* HASHEM, *O my soul*, five times. R' Shimon bar Yochai (*Berachos* 10a) explains that David detected five stages in the soul's development and praised God at each stage.

Pnei Yehoshua (comm. to *Berachos* 10a) observes that the *Zohar* and other Kabbalistic works identify the five phases of the soul's development as נֶפֶשׁ, רוּחַ, נְשָׁמָה, חַיָּה, יְחִידָה.

In the womb, the Divine spark is called נֶפֶשׁ, *spirit*, cognate with נָפַשׁ, *resting*, because before birth the soul has not yet been activated.

At birth, it is called רוּחַ, literally *wind* or *direction*, because the soul is now free to soar in any direction.

When the infant starts to nurse, the soul is called נְשָׁמָה, cognate with נְשִׁימָה, *the breath of survival*, because nourishment is essential for human survival.

Until the age of religious majority, *bar* or *bas mitzvah*, the soul is still relatively dormant. When a man or woman becomes obligated to perform *mitzvos*, God introduces a powerful יֵצֶר טוֹב, *good inclination*, into the soul, which activates it to serve God with dedication. Then the soul is called חַיָּה, *the live one*, because it receives new vigor and vitality.

When the soul finally comprehends that God is the only true power in the universe, the soul is referred to as יְחִידָה, *the one and only*. Most ordinary people never achieve this level of perception, for it is reserved for the righteous, who struggle all their lives to comprehend God. When they die and their souls are released from the distractions of the flesh, they can finally conceive of God as One and Only and their souls enter the sphere of יְחִידָה. All who are resurrected will achieve this fifth level of the soul, יְחִידָה, *the one and only*.

3

קְדוּשַׁת הַשֵּׁם /
Holiness of God's Name

אַתָּה קָדוֹשׁ וְשִׁמְךָ קָדוֹשׁ, וּקְדוֹשִׁים בְּכָל יוֹם יְהַלְלוּךָ
סֶלָה. בָּרוּךְ אַתָּה יהוה, הָאֵל הַקָּדוֹשׁ.

You are holy and Your Name is holy, and holy ones praise
You every day, forever. Blessed are You, HASHEM, the holy
God.

~§ Jacob's Blessing

This third blessing of the *Amidah* corresponds to the third Patriarch, Jacob. *Shibbolei Halekket* cites the Midrash which says: "When Jacob approached the heavenly gates of Mercy (*Genesis* 28:17) and sanctified the Name of the Holy One, Blessed is He, the ministering angels chanted, 'Blessed are You, Hashem, the Holy God.' "

Jacob epitomized holiness. This is evidenced by the fact that, unlike Abraham and Isaac, all of Jacob's sons were holy and righteous (*Abudraham*). As the third Patriarch, Jacob forged the Jewish people into one indivisible unit, fulfilling King Solomon's statement: *"A three-ply cord is not easily severed"* (*Ecclesiastes* 4:12).

~§ The Blessing of Balance

Jacob succeeded in merging the conflicting attributes of the first two Patriarchs.

Abraham personified חֶסֶד, *kindness*, and Isaac epitomized דִּין, *uncompromising justice*. Individually, these principles cannot sustain the world. A world built on both kindness and justice cannot long endure, since these two opposites would clash constantly. Jacob succeeded in merging the conflicting attributes of the first two Patriarchs. With the concept of אֱמֶת, *truth*, as embodied by Jacob, the world finds its necessary balance. "Truth" decides when to utilize kindness, when to utilize justice, and when to temper one with the other. When kindness and justice are blended in the proper measure, the result is truth. This combination gives beauty, meaning, and permanence to each of its components. Because Jacob succeeded in creating the balance between the teachings of his forebears, the Sages call him the greatest of the Patriarchs.

~§ The Art of Originality

Man is like a sponge. As he goes through life, countless influences impact his mind and personality, each leaving a definite trace. He constantly absorbs new words, ideas, impressions, attitudes, preferences and prejudices. What should he retain and what should he repel?

Kedushah, holiness, is the art of designing a Godly personality by determining to absorb the influences which make us more Divine and rejecting the influences which diminish our divinity. This unique art form was perfected by the *Avos*, Patriarchs, who were, by definition, progenitors and originators. Each Patriarch detached himself from the gentile world in a special way and blazed an original path to God.

⋑ Remaining Apart

The Midrash (*Bereishis Rabbah* 77:1) expounds on the verse in *Deut.* 33:26 and states: *There is none like God!* But who is similar to God? *Yeshurun* (i.e. Jacob), our grandfather! In what way does he resemble God? Of God it says: "*HASHEM is exalted — all alone*" (*Isaiah* 2:11), and concerning Jacob it says: "*And Jacob remained all alone*" (*Genesis* 32:25).

God alone is exalted, and He is elevated above and separate from everything He created. This is His holiness — He influences everything, while nothing influences or controls Him.

Jacob emulated the holiness of God. He too was a breed apart, separate from the rest of the world. Jacob was true to himself. He refused to betray his integrity by allowing alien influences to corrupt his moral underpinnings. He resisted temptation because failing to do so would have sullied his character and adulterated his purity. Because Jacob was *true* and *genuine*, he had to be *alone* and *separate* and *holy*.

Therefore, in this third and final blessing of the section of the *Amidah* called שֶׁבַח, *praise*, we allude to Jacob-Israel, in whom the heights of God's praise are to be found. As the Psalmist said: וְאַתָּה קָדוֹשׁ יוֹשֵׁב תְּהִלּוֹת יִשְׂרָאֵל, *You are the Holy One, enthroned upon the praises of Israel* (Jacob) (*Psalms* 22:4).

⋑ Holiness Is Freedom

Without holiness and its characteristic of remaining alone and apart from corruptive influences, man cannot be free. He remains a prisoner of the outside world, which imposes its will on society. Without holiness, man is a conformist, living an alien life style adopted from others. He may assume false pretensions to impress those around him, while inside he is void and empty. Without sanctity, or at least the aspiration to attain it, man is a coward who surrenders to his surroundings.

But when one fills himself with holiness, his strong spirit cries out: "Be true! Initiate — don't imitate!"

This helps to explain why the blessing for holiness adjoins the one dedicated to דַּעַת, *intellect*. As our Sages taught, "If there is no intellect there can be no discernment and separation" (*Jerusalem Talmud, Berachos* 5:2). One must be blessed with the wisdom to appreciate and therefore to maintain his own sanctity, originality, and independence.

⊷§ *Sanctity Restores Life*

Mesillas Yesharim bases his entire treatise on a quote from the holy sage, Rabbi Pinchas ben Yair, which ends: קְדוּשָׁה מְבִיאָה לִידֵי רוּחַ הַקֹּדֶשׁ וְרוּחַ הַקֹּדֶשׁ מְבִיאָה לִידֵי תְּחִיַּית הַמֵּתִים, *Holiness leads to acquisition of the Divine spirit and acquisition of the Divine spirit leads to the revival of the dead* (*Avodah Zarah* 20b).

The holy man comes so close to the holy God that he is actually invested with the Divine power of life itself. With this in mind, one can truly appreciate the juxtaposition of this third *Amidah* blessing about holiness with the second blessing that extols God's might as מְחַיֵּה הַמֵּתִים, *He Who revives the dead*.

Mesillas Yesharim adds that the three Patriarchs reached the pinnacle of holiness. God's holy spirit rested upon them with such intensity that these mortals were considered as holy as the Tabernacle, the Temple, and the Altar. Our Sages further observed that הָאָבוֹת הֵן הֵן הַמֶּרְכָּבָה, *the Patriarchs are the Divine chariot*, upon which God is enthroned (*Bereishis Rabbah* 47:8).

Thus, we can appreciate how the praises of our Patriarchs, which began in the very first blessing of the *Amidah*, culminate with the blessing of "Holiness."

⊷§ *Separate but Related*

אַתָּה קָדוֹשׁ וְשִׁמְךָ קָדוֹשׁ — *You are holy and Your Name is holy.*

The *kedushah*, holiness, of God is that He is exalted above all else, and therefore separated from the limitations of material existence. Every day the celestial angels proclaim that God's level of holiness is unsurpassed, saying: "*Holy, holy, holy is* HASHEM, *Master of Legions, the whole world is filled with His glory*" (*Isaiah* 6:3).

At first glance, this proclamation appears to be self-contradictory. If indeed God is utterly holy and *separate* from this world, how can His glory and His presence *fill* the entire world?

This difficulty can be explained by understanding the phrase וְשִׁמְךָ קָדוֹשׁ, *and Your Name is holy*. The term "Name" suggests *our* perception of God, the way in which He manifests Himself to us. Therefore, we now say that God wants us to recognize His holiness. He desires to reveal His attribute of holiness to Mankind so that we may attempt to identify with Him by striving to emulate His sanctity.

In other words, even though God is holy, i.e. *separated* from this material world and untarnished by it, He nevertheless has not *abandoned* this world. To the contrary, in His infinite kindness, God is totally involved and concerned with every detail of this world so that His proximity and intimacy will elevate and inspire people to live sacred, Godly lives. This is the ultimate separateness — to be completely involved in something and yet remain independent and unsullied by it. Moreover, just as God's holiness inspires us, we should always be cognizant of our responsibility to make others more holy.

This blessing of the *Amidah* is a commitment to practice genuine sanctity. Men who are truly holy do not fear or despise this world. They do not retreat to a cloistered ivory tower, shunning the company of others for fear of contamination. Rather, truly holy people strive to elevate everything and everyone around them. The heaven-ward thrust of their lives is so powerful that nothing can hold them back.

⊷§ Clean Involvement

"When King Solomon ordained the laws of *eruv* and the washing of the hands, a heavenly voice issued forth and proclaimed, 'My son, if your heart be wise, My heart, too, will be glad'" (*Eruvin* 21b). *Rabbi Bunam of P'schis'cha* analyzed the selection of these two particular procedures for such praise. King Solomon instituted many other wise practices, as well. What makes these two special?

The answer lies in their connection, the Rebbe reasoned. The Hebrew *eruv* is from the etymological root meaning "to include," "to be involved." The Sabbath *eruv* laws were introduced in order to increase social interaction and camaraderie among Jews. Conversely, washing the hands indicates not only cleanliness but also holiness: separation from the mundane.

This, he pointed out, is the great wisdom underlying this concept: to be involved with everyone and yet to maintain clean hands — that is indeed laudable!

וּקְדוֹשִׁים בְּכָל יוֹם יְהַלְלוּךָ סֶּלָה — *And holy ones praise You every day.*

The term 'holy ones' may refer to the celestial angels who praise God daily (*Iyun Tefillah*). Most commentaries, however, agree that it refers primarily to the Jewish people to whom God applied this title, as it is stated, קְדֹשִׁים תִּהְיוּ כִּי קָדוֹשׁ אֲנִי ה׳ אֱלֹהֵיכֶם, *You shall be holy for I, HASHEM your God, am holy* (*Leviticus* 19:2).

In the last chapter of *Mesillas Yesharim*, *Rabbi Moshe Chaim Luzatto* describes how the attribute of holiness applies to human behavior. He explains that man cannot make himself heavenly through his efforts alone, nor does God expect him to, because man is mortal and material and cannot divorce himself completely from his base environment and nature. Man must strive, however, to elevate himself as much as he can and to retract from his animalistic lusts and urges. When man sincerely struggles to do this, God reaches out and raises him heavenward. As the Sages teach: אָדָם מְקַדֵּשׁ עַצְמוֹ מְעַט, מְקַדְּשִׁין אוֹתוֹ הַרְבֵּה; מִלְּמַטָּה מְקַדְּשִׁין אוֹתוֹ מִלְמַעְלָה, *If a man sanctifies himself a little, they will sanctify him a great deal; [if he does so] below, they will sanctify him from above* (*Yoma* 39a).

Mesillas Yesharim continues, describing human holiness of the highest degree, that is achieved only after a long, arduous course of self-perfection:

> The essence of holiness is captured when one becomes so attached to God that no matter what he does, he will not be separated from Him, Blessed is He. Even the physical objects that he uses for material purposes are elevated by virtue of his using them, eclipsing the descent he suffers from his attachment to and use of them.

One who strives for holiness must concentrate on certain key areas of self-discipline.

Just before his marriage, the holy *Sh'lah* was told by his teacher Rabbi Shlomo, "Sanctify yourself in these two matters — the holiness of food and the holiness of the marital relationship — and be exceedingly heedful of their holy nature" (*Shaar HaOsios, Kuf*).

This does not mean that one should avoid food; rather, it means that one should elevate it by using it to preserve life and health, not as a means of satisfying lust and overindulging.

◄§ A Martyr's Life

A great rabbi once said: "It is much easier to *die* for the sanctification of God's Name than to *live* for the sanctification of His Name." The highest degree of devotion to God, *mesiras nefesh*, is most often translated as "martyrdom." In fact, however, the words literally mean *transferring one's life over to God* — one can do this best while still living. Those who dedicated every moment of their lives to sanctifying the Name become God's partners in creation.

Rabbi Yerucham Levovitz notes that on various occasions the Talmud refers to the person who lives according to the dictates of God as "one who is a partner in the creation of the world" (see, for example, *Shabbos* 10a). A partner, he explains, is not an employee, but an owner. A partner has a right to express an opinion on the operation of a business. His opinion may be overruled, but unlike a hired worker, he can insist that his opinion be heard.

Reb Yerucham states that the reason the great *tzaddikim* were able to make things happen with their prayers was because they had achieved a status of being "partners with God" in the operation of the world. As partners, they had an authoritative position.

If we think our prayers are not effective enough, perhaps we should think of conducting our lives in such a way that God accords us the status of "partnership." This is not an easy achievement, but we are then in a position not only to pray, but actually demand of God that He reveal His glory in the world, and openly sanctify His name so that all living things can see His majesty.

◄§ A Martyr's Death

His *chassidim* told the *Chiddushei HaRim* about a Jew who had just given up his life to sanctify God's Name publicly. The Rebbe sighed deeply and said: "In just one brief moment of martyrdom a person can acquire his entire portion in the World to Come" (*Avodah Zarah* 18a). However, the frightening thing is that in that very same instant he can forfeit the entire portion he just acquired if he allows his heart to be filled with pride over his exalted status as a *kadosh*, a holy martyr!

Chasam Sofer (*Toras Moshe, Parshas Kedoshim*) notes that many gentile philosophers divorce themselves from worldly pleasures far more than the Sages of Israel. The former's ascetic life style, however, is condemned for its extremism and severity, whereas the more moderate behavior of our pious men is praised as being holy. The gentile ascetics despise this world and deem all human endeavors as exercises in futility. Pious Jews, however, love this world because it is beloved by God, its Creator. With Divine genius, God designed everything on earth to be a tool for discovering and serving Him. The essence of sanctity is to use everything in the world according to God's plan.

בָּרוּךְ אַתָּה ה׳ הָאֵל הַקָּדוֹשׁ — *Blessed are You, HASHEM, the holy God.*

This blessing is the last of the three introductory blessings of Divine praise. Since the ensuing central section of the *Amidah* is a list of personal requests to God for success in all endeavors, it is essential that we preface these worldly requests by affirming our value system in this world. In a word — *sanctity* above all else!

To the secular mind, success is measured by *how much you take from this world*. To the Torah mind, success is measured by *how little you take from this world*.

The most important priority of our value system is that we choose to take from this world only that which will help us to fulfill God's vision for the Jewish people, *"And you shall be for Me a kingdom of priests and a holy nation"* (*Exodus* 19:6).

The Thirteen
Middle Blessings

❧ The Central Core of Thirteen Requests

The Talmud (*Berachos* 34a) compares a supplicant to a servant approaching his master. Only after enumerating the master's praises does the servant go on to his list of personal requests.

❧ The Heart of the Matter

Rabbi Yaakov Lorberbaum of Lisa (Emes L'Yaakov; Aggados, Maseches Rosh Hashanah) ponders this: Our Sages refer to *Shemoneh Esrei* as עֲבוֹדָה שֶׁבְּלֵב, *service of the heart*. It is difficult to see how prayer is viewed as Divine service when its inner core is thirteen personal requests; how, therefore, can it be called service of God? Secondly, since the *halachah* requires us to verbalize and enunciate our prayers, it would be more appropriate to describe it as "service of the lips" rather than "service of the heart."

We must therefore view the purpose of prayer in a new light. The Sages listed thirteen essential needs of the Jew and issued this challenge: "We have created a universal liturgy so that all Jews will *daven* from essentially the same *siddur*. The only thing that will differentiate between them is the intent of their heart. The egocentric person who lives to serve his own needs will read these thirteen requests and think only of his personal welfare. However, the Jew who views Divine service as his *raison d'etre* will arouse his heart to inject deeper meaning into the words of his prayer. He will, for example, ask God to heal his ailments, so that he may serve his Master vigorously, in robust health. He will plead with God for livelihood, so that he will have the financial abilities to fully observe the Master's commandments. Prayer is called 'service of the heart' because in his heart the supplicant's attitude should be to serve God, not himself."

⋗ We Depend on You

Chovos Halevavos makes it clear that even when we make personal requests, our main purpose is to enhance God's glory. We say to Him: "We communicate our needs to You not in order to make *You* aware of them, because You surely know what is in our hearts; rather we verbalize our needs in Your Presence to impress upon ourselves that we are completely dependent on Your gracious help and to demonstrate how much we place our trust in Your kindness" (*Cheshbon Hanefesh* §18).

⋗ For the Sake of God

Rabbi Chaim of Volozhin (*Nefesh HaChaim* sec. II) explains how the Almighty designed the world in such a way that He truly desires our prayers. God's will is to enter this world and to spread His blessings everywhere, but according to His scheme, He can enter this world only if man invites Him and makes Him feel welcome. Man extends this invitation to God through prayer!

The more helpless a person feels, the more helpful he allows God to be. To the extent that he feels dependent on God, God blesses and enriches his existence. On the other hand, when man sins, he is declaring himself to be independent of God's influence. The sinner "paralyzes" God, so to speak, removing His ability to be helpful. This causes God great pain, because He must interrupt the flow of His blessings, and human suffering ensues. Suffering causes the arrogant, independent person to recognize his mistakes. He will then turn to God in sincere prayer. His primary concern, however, should not be for his personal needs, but rather for ending God's "pain" by giving the Almighty an opportunity to intensify His blessings in the world!

This is the proper attitude to assume before commencing with this list of thirteen requests.

⊷ The Pyramid of Prayer

Avudraham records a dissertation of the *Riva* describing the intricate structure of the thirteen blessings that comprise the core of *Shemoneh Esrei. Riva* explains that the first six blessings are requests for personal needs, while the next six are requests for the public needs of the entire nation. Each public need corresponds to one of the private needs. Upon completion of these twelve requests we recite the thirteenth petition, שְׁמַע קוֹלֵנוּ, *Hear our voice,* an all-encompassing plea for *Hashem* to hear our intense, heartfelt prayers. This general plea is the base upon which the other twelve rest.

⊷ Parallel Prayers

Riva pairs up the blessings as follows:

Personal	Public
1) Intellect	7) Ingathering of Exiles
2) Repentance	8) Restoration of Justice
3) Forgiveness	9) Against Heretics and Traitors
4) Redemption	10) The Righteous
5) Health and Healing	11) Rebuilding Jerusalem
6) Prosperity	12) David's Dynasty

Riva explains the parallels:

I) Request One — Request Seven

The personal request for intelligence corresponds with the public request to gather the exiles, because intellect is the first step toward the reconstruction of the Holy Temple. The Talmud (*Berachos* 33a) states that Rabbi Elazar taught: 'The man who uses his intellect properly is considered to have had the Holy Temple rebuilt in his time because in Scripture (I *Samuel* 2:3) we find the word *thoughts* [i.e. intellect] bracketed by Names of God, אֵל דֵּעוֹת ה', *a God of thoughts is Hashem,* and we also find (*Exodus* 15:17) the Holy Temple bracketed by Names of God, ה' ... מִקְדָשׁ אֲדֹנָי *Hashem, the Sanctuary, my Lord.'* Thus, personal intelligence, which brings man to recognize God's Name, pertains to the reconstruction of the Temple by the ingathered Jews where everyone will recognize God's Presence.

II) Request Two — Request Eight

The personal request הֲשִׁיבֵנוּ אָבִינוּ, *Bring us back, our Father,* (in sincere repentance) can be fulfilled only under the guidance of great Torah scholars and holy prophets. Therefore, we make the corresponding public request, הָשִׁיבָה שׁוֹפְטֵינוּ, *Bring back our judges* (and restore our counselors).

III) Request Three — Request Nine

First we request סְלִיחָה, *forgiveness,* for our individual sins, but we realize that as long as the insidious influence of the מַלְשִׁינִים, *informers,* and heretics continues, we will be susceptible to sin. So we ask God to punish the wicked and obliterate evil, thereby inspiring all of Israel to eschew sins forever.

IV) Request Four — Request Ten

We beseech God to take notice of our personal problems and *behold our affliction,* yet realizing that our personal merits are few and insignificant, we pray as well עַל הַצַּדִּיקִים, *for the righteous,* who care deeply about their suffering brethren, and implore God to have mercy on each individual Jew.

V) Request Five — Request Eleven

We cry out, רְפָאֵנוּ ה', *Heal us HASHEM,* from our personal sicknesses, but at the same time we are fully aware that our individual illnesses are an outgrowth of the general malady that afflicts the Jewish nation as a whole. As long as the Temple is destroyed, Jerusalem is considered to be in ruins. The Temple and the Holy City are the heart of our nation; when they were destroyed we suffered a national cardiac arrest. If we are crippled as a nation, how can any one individual be fully healthy? Only when Jerusalem is rebuilt, will Israel be healed: As King David said, *The Builder of Jerusalem is HASHEM, He will gather in the outcasts of Israel. He is the Healer of the broken hearted and the One Who binds up their sorrows (Psalms 147:2,3).*

VI) Request Six — Request Twelve

We ask God for a year of growth and prosperity, and hope He will *Bless on our behalf . . . the year and all its kinds of crops . . .* But we understand that any growth in prosperity will be short lived until all Jews together see צֶמַח דָּוִד, *the flourishing growth of David's dynasty.* The Talmud (*Sanhedrin* 98a) teaches that the clearest sign of the advent of the Messiah is the revitalization of agriculture in *Eretz Yisrael* with blooming trees and flourishing crops.

Riva makes one final observation: These requests are listed in descending order of significance — what comes first is most important, what comes later, less important. The request for wisdom and Torah knowledge is listed first while the plea for material prosperity is mentioned last, demonstrating how much more important knowledge is than wealth. Thus, a merchant who is willing to travel one mile to earn a dollar should be eager to travel six miles to acquire a word of Torah! Similarly, the requests for *repentance* and *forgiveness* come before *prosperity* to demonstrate how we must arrange our priorities. Most people go to great lengths to avoid a financial loss which will only affect their level of prosperity. They should be much more careful to avoid transgression, a spiritual loss, which will adversely affect their character.

Now that we have established our priorities, we can begin our thirteen requests.

4

דַּעַת / Intellect

אַתָּה חוֹנֵן לְאָדָם דַּעַת, וּמְלַמֵּד לֶאֱנוֹשׁ בִּינָה. חָנֵּנוּ מֵאִתְּךָ
דֵּעָה בִּינָה וְהַשְׂכֵּל. בָּרוּךְ אַתָּה יהוה, חוֹנֵן הַדָּעַת.

You graciously endow man with intellect and teach insight to a frail mortal. Endow us graciously from Yourself with intellect, insight, and wisdom. Blessed are You, HASHEM, gracious Giver of intellect.

ও The First Priority

Man's superiority over the animal kingdom is only by virtue of his intellect. The Sages therefore determined that the plea for wisdom should be the first direct request of the *Amidah*, for without intellect and understanding prayer is meaningless (*Shulchan Aruch, Orach Chaim* 115).

ও The Greatest Gift of All

The Talmud (*Nedarim* 41a) quotes Abaye who emphasized that intellect is man's most fundamental possession: "No man is considered truly poor unless he is poor in intellect! He who has intellect possesses everything. He who lacks intellect, of what value are his possessions? He who acquires intellect, what is he lacking? He who lacks intellect, what has he acquired?"

The number of words in this blessing is seventeen, which is the numerical value of טוב, *good*, as nothing is better than wisdom. *Tur* (*Orach Chaim* 115) notes that these seventeen correspond with the seventeen words of the verse which begins, "*And you shall speak to all those who are wise hearted, whom I have filled with a spirit of wisdom*" (*Exodus* 28:3). Furthermore, this blessing contains sixty letters [up to the concluding words חוֹנֵן הַדָּעַת], alluding to the sixty tractates of the Mishnah which cannot be mastered without God's gracious gift of intellect (*Otzar HaTefillos*). With the words חוֹנֵן הַדָּעַת, there are sixty-eight letters, alluding to the numerical value of חַיִּים, *life*.

Additionally, this blessing starts with the letter *aleph* and ends with the letter *tav*, the first and last letters of the alphabet, suggesting that anyone with intellect and wisdom has everything, for wisdom is an all-encompassing blessing.

ও Knocking on Heaven's Door

The request section of *Shemoneh Esrei* begins with the fourth blessing which alludes to the fourth letter of the Hebrew alphabet. This letter, דָּלֶת, *dalet*, has the shape of an open doorway and is cognate with the word דֶּלֶת, door. The letter is also related to דַּל, *a pauper*, who pitifully knocks on doors begging for alms (see *Shabbos* 104a). When we bring our many requests before God we stand like beggars at His door, pleading for God's mercy. Unworthy and undeserving, we make no demands, we merely invoke God's compassion. Above all else, we petition God for the gift of intellect for without it we are truly paupers, possessing nothing.

✌ Divine versus Human Intellect

Torah tradition describes two distinct types of intellect — Divine and human — and it is crucial to distinguish between them. When exercising "human intellect," one relies on his five empirical senses (sight, sound, smell, touch, and taste) and his logical abilities to make decisions that guide him through life. Human intellect tends to reject anything that cannot be physically sensed or logically proven. It sees man and his mind as the measure of all things, drawing every experience down to its own limited level and reducing all phenomena to its own terms. A person who limits himself to human intellect is truly arrogant, for he idolizes his own mental prowess and never looks beyond his own perception.

In contrast, Divine intellect is humbling. One who possesses it employs spiritual guidance, recognizing a source of knowledge and perception high above the frail human mind. He accepts God and His will as the measure of all things. He begins his search for truth with the first commandment, אָנֹכִי ה' אֱלֹקֶיךָ, which, *Rambam* (*Yesodei HaTorah* 1:1) explains, is the first *mitzvah* and the foundation for everything that follows — to know that God exists. One who uses Divine intellect deeply mistrusts the human mind, which can be easily corrupted and misled, for people are more short sighted and narrow minded than they may imagine, blinded by pride, passion, and prejudice.

✌ I Am Senseless and Know Nothing

King David expressed his mistrust of human intellect in a pithy verse that is so meaningful the Midrash (*Koheles Rabbah* 1:12) exclaims it is worthy of being the introduction to the entire Book of *Psalms:* וַאֲנִי בַעַר וְלֹא אֵדָע בְּהֵמוֹת הָיִיתִי עִמָּךְ, *I am senseless and know nothing, like a beast was I with You* (*Psalms* 73:22). The word בַּעַר, *senseless*, is related to בֹּעֵר, *burning*, describing the animal as ablaze with instinctive desires, burning unbridled and unchecked. Similarly, man can imitate the animal when he allows his superb mind to become devoid of sensibility and surrenders to the desires of his flesh.

Alone, the human mind is unreliable because it falls prey to outside influences which distort it, as the Talmud teaches: "Man sins only after a spirit of madness takes hold of his mind" (*Sotah* 2a). Man easily becomes the victim of imagination and fantasy which literally render him temporarily insane.

Furthermore, King David admitted that his awareness of God made him feel "senseless" because he realized that it is impossible for mortal man to comprehend the mystery of God and His ways. *Rambam* summed it up well when he said, תַּכְלִית הַיְדִיעָה שֶׁלֹּא נֵדַע, "The ultimate goal of knowledge is to admit that we know nothing!"

◄§ *Divine Intellect — Holy Spirit*

In this blessing, we request knowledge, intellect, perception, wisdom, but we want these mental capacities to operate from a Divine perspective; we want to view the world from God's vantage point. We are deeply grateful for God's gift of five senses and a rational mind, but we view these endowments as means to a loftier end. We do not shun the techniques and tools of science. We will use the same microscope as the biologist, the same telescope as the astronomer, but we are looking for different things. While the scientist searches for stars, we look beyond the stars and search for God.

Rashi (comm. to *Exodus* 31:3) therefore observes that the most precise definition of דַּעַת, *intellect*, is רוּחַ הַקֹּדֶשׁ, *the holy Divine spirit*, that permeates the human mind. *Etz Yosef* notes the blessing of *intellect* was placed after the blessing of קְדוּשָׁה, *holiness*, to underscore this idea that we request holy, Divine intellect. The Talmud (*Megillah* 17b) observes that Isaiah noted the connection between these two themes saying, וְהִקְדִּישׁוּ אֶת קְדוֹשׁ יַעֲקֹב וְאֶת אֱלֹהֵי יִשְׂרָאֵל יַעֲרִיצוּ, וְיָדְעוּ תֹעֵי רוּחַ בִּינָה, *For they shall sanctify the Holy One of Jacob and revere the God of Israel. And those of confused spirit shall gain understanding (Isaiah 29:23,24).*

◄§ *From the Mouth of God*

King Solomon wrote in *Proverbs:* כִּי ה' יִתֵּן חָכְמָה מִפִּיו דַּעַת וּתְבוּנָה, *For HASHEM gives wisdom; from His mouth come intellect and insight (Proverbs 2:6).*

The Talmud (*Niddah* 70b) relates that the citizens of Alexandria once asked Rabbi Yehoshua ben Chananya, "What must a person do to become wise?" He replied, "He should decrease his business affairs and increase the time he spends studying." But the Alexandrians were unsatisfied with his answer claiming, "Many have attempted to follow this method, yet wisdom has eluded them!" "If so," concluded Rabbi Yehoshua, "let the sincere seeker of wisdom pray to the Almighty Who is the Source of all wisdom, as it says: *For HASHEM gives wisdom; from His mouth come intellect and insight.*"

The Midrash (*Yalkut Shimoni; Mishlei* 2) states: Wisdom is great, for it is written, *HASHEM gives wisdom.* But far greater than wisdom are intellect and understanding for they are granted only to those whom He loves very much, as it is written, *From His mouth come intellect and insight.* This interpretation of the verse can be illustrated with the parable of a king and his beloved son. One day the prince came home from school while his father, the king, was eating. The king took a piece of food from the pot and gave it to his son, but the child refused it. "Father, all I want is a piece of the slice you are about to eat," he said. Because the king loved his son so much, he shared his piece with him.

This parable teaches a deep lesson about a loving relationship. The devoted son is not as hungry for food as he is to share with his father to whom he is so deeply attached. He yearns for a token of his father's love, he pines for a piece of his father's being. Similarly the Jew, as scholarly as he may seem, is not hungry for knowledge *per se;* his real desire is to cleave to God Who is the Source of intellect. *From His mouth come intellect and insight* to those who have a strong bond to Him. It is for this sort of intellectual enlightenment that we ask in this blessing.

✍ Tapping Our Mental Reservoir

Shibbolei Halekket quotes the Midrash, which says: When the angel Gabriel visited Joseph in his Egyptian prison cell and taught him seventy languages in one night, the ministering angels chanted, "Blessed are You, HASHEM, gracious Giver of intellect." Thus, this blessing fosters an awareness of man's vast intellectual potential which usually lies dormant and untapped.

A minuscule amount of mental capacity may be sufficient for man to meet his everyday needs, but in order to achieve mastery of the Torah's limitless knowledge, man must utilize all of the mental powers at his command. An auspicious time to request success in Torah studies both for oneself and one's children is during the recitation of this blessing for intellect. Moreover, even after mastering a Torah topic, we need Divine assistance to retain it in our memories. *Rashi* (comm. to *Avodah Zarah* 8a) advises anyone who frequently forgets his Torah learning to prolong his recital of this blessing and fervently ask for Divine assistance to strengthen his memory.

◆§ Only from God

אַתָּה חוֹנֵן לְאָדָם דַּעַת — *You graciously endow man with intellect.*

It is noteworthy that this is the only one of the thirteen personal requests of the *Amidah* that begins with a direct pronouncement of God's praise and *not* an immediate plea for assistance. In the other requests it is clear what we want — forgiveness, health, redemption, etc., but in asking for wisdom one may easily be confused as to what he wants. He must differentiate between human intellect and Divine intellect and declare that it is Divine intellect that he truly seeks. This can be acquired only through Divine grace. Only אַתָּה, *You,* [O God, can] *graciously endow man with* [the gift of Divine] *intellect.*

It is also interesting to note that this is the third and last time we address Hashem with the word אַתָּה to open a blessing. The second blessing of the *Amidah* begins, אַתָּה גִבּוֹר לְעוֹלָם ה', *You are eternally mighty, HASHEM,* and the third blessing begins, אַתָּה קָדוֹשׁ , *You are holy.* The first two blessings explain and highlight this one, as if to say, "אַתָּה, *You* alone, Hashem, can bestow extraordinary, unlimited, Divine intellect. Because only *You are eternally mighty,* so Your wisdom is eternal, infinite and infallible. Moreover, human intellect is weak and easily influenced by outside forces that distort the truth. Not so Divine intellect, because *You are holy* and separate from this world, You alone control and influence this world, while the world has no influence on You. Your Divine intellect cannot be corrupted."

◆§ Mind over Matter

The term דַּעַת, *intellect,* also connotes intellectual strength and fortitude shown through strong convictions and opinions not easily swayed. When one surrenders his intellectual advantage, he allows his emotions and physical desires to take control of his life's decision.

A tragic example of this was Esau. He was decapitated in front of the holy Cave of Machpelah and his head rolled inside next to the body of his brother Jacob. The rest of his body was buried elsewhere. This teaches that *intellectually* Esau was Jacob's equal and deserving of a position among the Patriarchs. Esau understood the truth as well as any of the *Avos*, but his convictions were weak and he allowed himself to go through life unbridled and untamed. Since his head and his body had nothing in common, they were separated and buried separately.

⊸§ Keep Your Head Above Water

The Talmud (*Kiddushin* 29a) rules that a father must teach his son Torah and a means of earning an honest, respectable livelihood. According to another opinion, he must also teach his son how to swim. The *Sochatchover Rebbe (Shem MiShmuel)* explained that the last two responsibilities are intertwined. When a father trains his son to earn a livelihood, he must warn him to apply to his career the fundamentals of swimming. The swimmer must know how to keep his body moving smoothly in the water while lifting his head above the surface to breathe. Similarly the father must caution his son: "Do your very best to succeed in your chosen field, but take care lest you become entirely submerged in your professional pursuits. Keep your head above your career and maintain scholarly and spiritual aspirations that point heavenward. Don't allow the affairs of your body to drown your mind."

⊸§ A Gift to Frail Man

וּמְלַמֵּד לָאֱנוֹשׁ בִּינָה — *And teach insight to a frail mortal.*

The term אֱנוֹשׁ denotes the weakness and frailty of man, especially the shortcomings and limitations of his mind, for he is destined to die and molder in the dust. Thus, when the Psalmist contemplates the awesome greatness of the Creator, he cries out, מָה אֱנוֹשׁ כִּי תִזְכְּרֶנּוּ, *What is the frail mortal that You should remember him? (Psalms 8:5).* Every time we exercise our mental powers we should sincerely thank God for endowing feeble finite mortals with this Divine gift.

⊸§ Between Intellect and Insight

The order of intellectual development is as follows: At birth, God endows man with basic human דַּעַת, *intellect.* The term חוֹנֵן, *graciously endow,* is used in reference to דַּעַת, *intellect,* because it is cognate with

חִנָּם, *free of charge*, implying that we are entirely undeserving of so generous and gracious a gift. בִּינָה, *insight*, is the next step and comes after one utilizes his basic intelligence to carefully study and examine any given subject. It is cognate with בִּנְיָן, *structure*, because as one delves into the intricate details of the subject, he perceives the underlying design and structure of all of its components. בִּינָה is an ongoing process of deepening and broadening one's comprehension. God is constantly teaching us new ways to approach our studies as He reveals new insights. Therefore, we refer to Him here as the מְלַמֵּד, *the* [constant] *Teacher*.

⋖§ The Force of Convictions

The word אֱנוֹשׁ is cognate with the Aramaic root אנשׁ, which means to weaken and dim. The Talmud (*Sanhedrin* 36a) describes how a recess of one day can dramatically alter a judge's opinion of a defendant. After a day's interruption the judge will recall the facts and figures that appear in the written record, but his feelings will not be the same and the original strength of his convictions will have somewhat diminished, because לִיבָּא דְּאִנְשֵׁי אַנְשֵׁי, *a man's heart forgets*.

It is בִּינָה, *insight*, that allows a person to delve deeply into the facts he studies; to become emotionally involved and to develop powerful, clear convictions. Without the perception of insight, all facts would be one dimensional, cold, and lifeless. The insight of בִּינָה breathes vitality into the data, because God, the Source of all life, is the מְלַמֵּד, *Teacher* of insight.

⋖§ Guard the Gift

Realizing that he is no more than a frail, earthly creature, man should take great care lest his behavior undermine his intellect. *Rabbi Yisrael Salanter* would say, "Even in our times, there are people upon whom God has bestowed marvelous mental abilities equal to those of the *Gaonim* who lived a thousand years ago. But מִדּוֹת רָעוֹת, *bad character traits*, dull their mental abilities."

Whenever he came to a town to deliver a talk, Reb Yisrael would post on the *shul's* door a list with dozens of sources that he would be using in his *shiur*. One Shabbos Reb Yisrael ascended to the *bimah* and asked the *shammas* to bring him the list. To his amazement, the references had been changed! Reb Yisrael turned white, and stood silently for several minutes. When his thoughts were settled, he delivered a deep discourse based on the new list of sources.

Reb Naftali Amsterdam recounted this incident and observed, "Don't think that Reb Yisrael needed even ten minutes to compose a new *drashah*. His abilities were beyond our comprehension; he could construct wonderful new *pilpulim* with lightning speed. But for those few minutes, Reb Yisrael was grappling with a difficult personal dilemma: Should he tell the congregation that he had forgotten his speech, and leave the *bimah* in shame, in order to conceal his amazing ability to construct a new *drashah* on the spot? On the other hand, if he left the *bimah* he would lose much of his influence, and his lifelong work to spread *mussar* would be jeopardized. This battle raged inside him for ten minutes until he clearly felt in the deepest recesses of his heart that his intentions were not for his own glory, to display his intellectual prowess, but dedicated to the service of God. Only then could he proceed with his lecture."

◅§ Aristotle's Folly

The famous Greek philosopher, Aristotle, is the perfect example of how the magnificent human intellect can be corrupted by mortal frailty. In his *Guide*, *Rambam* states that Aristotle reached the pinnacle of human understanding and came to the point where he was just one step beneath the level of prophecy. If so, asked *Rav Elchonon Wasserman*, why did the brilliant Aristotle fail to discover and recognize the existence of the One, True God? How could Aristotle be oblivious to a truth which is known to even the simple Jew? The answer is that Aristotle didn't want to see the truth, because truth makes many difficult and uncomfortable demands on the body. Aristotle was "bribed" by his desirous, complacent body and robbed of clear vision, as the Torah warns: *You shall accept no bribe, for the bribe blinds even the wise* (*Exodus* 23:8).

◅§ Treachery of the Mind

Beware of your mind for it can turn against you! The Midrash (*Yalkut Shimoni, Mishlei* 3) tells of a clever merchant who amassed a fortune, but because of his greed refused to give the tithes or share his wealth with others. God punished him and he was seized by a fit of madness. He took a stick and began to smash all the jugs and barrels in his warehouse. When one of his family members tried to restrain him, the merchant cried out, "Instead of stopping me, why don't you help me?" So the relative joined in the wild spree and together they destroyed all of the merchant's possessions.

The moral is that business acumen is a gift from God, but if you betray God, your mind will betray you and turn you into your own worst enemy. People spend a lifetime of toil amassing great fortunes, and in the end one miscalculation or a single bad investment wipes out the wealth they labored so hard to earn. Better to follow the advice of the wise King Solomon who said, *Trust in HASHEM with all your heart, and do not rely on your own understanding (Proverbs 3:5).*

◆§ Acquiring Wisdom

חָנֵּנוּ מֵאִתְּךָ דֵּעָה בִּינָה וְהַשְׂכֵּל — *Endow us graciously from Yourself with intellect, insight and wisdom.*

We ask God to endow us with Divine wisdom gradually, step by step. It is dangerous and futile to attempt to jump to advanced levels of wisdom without painstakingly mastering the preliminaries. The process is as follows: 1) דֵּעָה, *intellect,* gives us the capacity to learn basic facts. 2) בִּינָה, *insight,* is the ability to carefully dissect and examine the facts in order to understand their inner workings and composition. 3) הַשְׂכֵּל, *wisdom,* is the ability to glean information and lessons from past research and experience and apply them to new situations and problems. The initials of דֵּעָה, בִּינָה, שֵׂכֶל spell דְּבַשׁ, *honey,* implying that no experience can match the sweet delight of intellectual achievement.

Generally speaking, *intellect* and *insight* deal with the past — the absorption and analysis of concrete data and given facts. *Wisdom* is abstract, for it creates innovative ideas for the unseen future.

Intellect and *insight* focus on one subject at a time; they are building blocks of wisdom. Wisdom then puts them together, integrating and molding one's knowledge and experience to establish values, priorities, and procedures for dealing with all aspects of life. שֵׂכֶל, *wisdom,* is cognate with כָּל, *everything,* and שִׁכְלוּל, *perfection.* When we blend the units of knowledge into the totality of the intellectual experience, a broad, integrated world-view emerges, harmonious, balanced, and well adjusted. From the gift of שֵׂכֶל one derives many desirable personality traits: poise, tact, good taste, creativity — in short, the warm, personal touch that is the key to success. For this reason God exhorted Joshua to refine his mental abilities with Torah: כִּי אָז תַּצְלִיחַ אֶת דְּרָכֶךָ וְאָז תַּשְׂכִּיל —

For then you will be successful in your ways and then you will have acquired wisdom (Joshua 1:8). And of King David it says: וַיְהִי דָוִד לְכָל דְּרָכָו מַשְׂכִּיל וַה׳ עִמּוֹ, *And David succeeded in all his ways and* HASHEM *was with him (I Samuel 18:14).*

⋖§ The Foundation of Knowledge

According to the Sephardic liturgy this line reads: חָנֵּנוּ מֵאִתְּךָ חָכְמָה בִּינָה וָדָעַת, *Endow us graciously from Yourself with knowledge, insight, and intellect.* The term חָכְמָה, *knowledge,* may be used loosely as a general reference to all intellectual accomplishment, or it can be understood as pertaining to specific information and facts.

The fundamental requisite for all knowledge is the fear of God. This fact is repeated often throughout Scripture. King Solomon emphasized it in *Proverbs* (1:7): יִרְאַת ה׳ רֵאשִׁית דָּעַת, *The fear of* HASHEM *is the beginning of intellect,* and (9:10): תְּחִלַּת חָכְמָה יִרְאַת ה׳, *The beginning of knowledge is the fear of* HASHEM. The Sages (*Avos* 3:11) further note that when a scholar gives fear of God precedence over the pursuit of wisdom, his wisdom will endure, but when his pursuit of wisdom takes precedence over his fear of God, his wisdom will not endure.

One achieves fear of Hashem after he comes to the realization that God alone is holy and awesome. King David alluded to this by juxtaposing the two themes when he said, קָדוֹשׁ וְנוֹרָא שְׁמוֹ. רֵאשִׁית חָכְמָה יִרְאַת ה׳, *Holy and awesome is His Name. The beginning of wisdom is the fear of* HASHEM *(Psalms 111:9, 10).*

Perhaps the Ashkenazic version deletes mention of חָכְמָה in this blessing in order to call our attention to the fact that the starting point of knowledge is reverence and awe for God's Name, a concept already mentioned in the preceding blessing, *You are Holy and Your Name is Holy.*

⋖§ A Gift that Obligates

בָּרוּךְ אַתָּה ה׳ חוֹנֵן הַדָּעַת — *Blessed are You,* HASHEM, *gracious Giver of intellect.*

To the extent that one recognizes how graciously God has endowed him with intellect, he must use that gift for the proliferation of God's glory. "I know," said *Rav Yisrael Salanter,* "that I have the mental capacity of a thousand men, but because of that my obligation to serve Hashem is also that of a thousand men!"

Reb Yisrael's brilliance is shown in the following story: His son Yom Tov Lipman, an outstanding mechanical engineer, once visited him after an absence of a few years. "What have you innovated in the world?" asked R' Yisrael. His son replied that he had invented a small screw that tripled the productivity of a certain complex machine. R' Yisrael had his son draw him a plan of the entire machine with all its parts, without revealing the particular screw he had invented. R' Yisrael then studied the sketch for ten minutes, pointed to one of the screws, and said, "This is the screw that you invented."

The son later boasted to the university professors whom he taught, "What I worked on for years, my father found in a few minutes."

◄§ Gift from Heaven

Three special gifts were created for this world and he who is blessed with even one of them has merited the most exquisite delight. He who is blessed with wisdom has everything. He who is blessed with strength has everything. He who is blessed with wealth has everything. When is this so? Only when the recipient realizes that these are gifts from heaven and come by virtue of the Torah, otherwise the wisdom, strength, and wealth of flesh and blood are worthless, as it says, *Thus says HASHEM: "Let not the wise man glory in his wisdom, nor let the mighty warrior glory in his might, nor the rich man glory in his riches, but let him who seeks glory, glory in this, that he understands and knows Me"* (Jeremiah 9:22,23).

When blessings come from God, they will endure; if not, they will surely be terminated. Our Rabbis taught: Two very brilliant men arose upon the stage of history, Achitophel from the Jewish world and Balaam from the gentile world. In the end, though, their own brilliance brought about their downfall and doom. Why? Because they didn't recognize their blessing as a Divine gift from God, but rather saw it as something they had snatched and acquired for themselves! (*Bamidbar Rabbah* 22:6).

5

תְּשׁוּבָה / Repentance

הֲשִׁיבֵנוּ אָבִינוּ לְתוֹרָתֶךָ, וְקָרְבֵנוּ מַלְכֵּנוּ לַעֲבוֹדָתֶךָ, וְהַחֲזִירֵנוּ בִּתְשׁוּבָה שְׁלֵמָה לְפָנֶיךָ. בָּרוּךְ אַתָּה יהוה, הָרוֹצֶה בִּתְשׁוּבָה.

Bring us back, our Father, to Your Torah, and bring us near, our King, to Your service, and influence us to return in perfect repentance before You. Blessed are You, HASHEM, Who desires repentance.

❧ Wisdom Breeds Cognizance

If God fulfills one's request for intellect and insight, as expressed in the fourth blessing, it will inevitably result in the process of תְּשׁוּבָה, *repentance*, discussed in this fifth blessing. How can anyone who achieves intellectual honesty fail to detect his many shortcomings?

Even a person who does not uncover any new sins would have cause for perpetual penitence, because every new level of intellectual comprehension of one's earlier sins and shortcomings demands fresh repentance for them. The following incident illustrates this concept.

❧ The Cycle of Rediscovery

Rav Saadiah Gaon taught his disciples to examine their ways every day even if they felt certain they had not sinned. Rav Saadiah himself had adopted this practice after an enlightening experience.

Once, Rav Saadiah lodged with an innkeeper who was unaware of his illustrious guest's true identity. He put the Rav in a simple room and served him as he would any guest. When word circulated that the leader of the generation was passing through town, all the townsfolk flocked to the inn to glimpse Rav Saadiah. The innkeeper suddenly realized the greatness of his guest and approached the Rav, with tears streaming down his cheeks.

"Rebbi, please forgive me!"

"Forgive you? What have you done wrong? You treated me very well," he replied.

"Rebbi! I didn't know who you were! Believe me, had I know that the great Rav Saadiah Gaon was staying under my roof, I would have treated you like royalty!"

Hearing these sincere words, Rav Saadiah himself burst into tears. "From your words," he explained, "I now understand the extent of our obligation towards our King, Hashem. Previously, I felt I was serving Hashem well, but now I realize that I am lacking. Just as your service to me changes as you perceive my identity more clearly, so too should be my service of God. With each passing day, I discover new levels of God's kindness towards me. I realize that whatever respect and service I offered God yesterday was woefully insufficient, for had I known then what I know now about God, I would have served Him with even greater devotion and intensity. Life is indeed a constant cycle of rediscovery in which man sheds his relative ignorance of the past!"

⊷§ Five Is the Number of Repentance

The Talmud (*Menachos* 29b) teaches that God used the letters of the Hebrew alphabet as spiritual building blocks to create the world. The creation of the World to Come began with the letter י, *yud*, whereas the creation of this world began with the letter ה, *hei*.

The Talmud examines the form of the ה. It looks like a lobby with three walls, and with one side completely open. This indicates that God does not confine man to a life of Torah observance, but allows him free choice. He is free to obey or disobey God's will. But if he chooses to leave the safety of the Torah's spiritual and moral boundaries, he will lose his foothold and fall, as it were, through the bottom of the ה into the abyss.

Simultaneously, however, ה symbolizes God's readiness to forgive. God created the opportunity for a sinner to return to Him through תְּשׁוּבָה [*teshuvah*], *repentance*. That is why the left leg of the ה is not attached to the letter's roof. A small opening is left near the top, signifying that a space always remains open through which a repentant sinner can return and be drawn into ה׳, *Hashem*, again.

So powerful is *teshuvah* that God adorned the ה (as it is written in the Torah) with a תָּג, *crownlet*, as if to say, "If the sinner returns, I will bestow a crown upon him" (see ArtScroll, *The Wisdom of the Hebrew Alphabet*).

Furthermore, the letter ה has a numerical value of five, alluding to the Five Books of Moses which teach a person how to return to God.

Tur (*Orach Chaim* ch. 115) notes that this fifth blessing begins with the letter ה, *hei*, which has a numerical value of five, and it ends with a ה, as well. The sum of both letters is ten, which alludes to the Ten Days of Repentance, an especially auspicious time to return to God. Additionally, *Tur* observes that this blessing consists of fifteen words, which is exactly the number of words in numerous Scriptural verses that speak of repentance. Also, the number fifteen alludes to the Talmudic dictum (*Yoma* 86a) that repentance is so great that it soars heavenward until it reaches God's celestial throne. There are fourteen celestial levels beneath God's throne, which is on the fifteenth. The fifteen words of this blessing remind us of the fifteen heavenly heights scaled by genuine repentance.

◈§ Sin Sullies the Mind

הֲשִׁיבֵנוּ אָבִינוּ לְתוֹרָתֶךָ — *Bring us back, our Father, to Your Torah.*
In the preceding blessing we requested Divine wisdom and understanding. Now we express our awareness that God-given wisdom will not materialize out of thin air to be deposited effortlessly into our brain. Torah study is the vehicle through which God conveys His wisdom to the human mind.

It is virtually impossible, however, to comprehend Torah clearly if one's heart and mind are sullied with sin. The mind resembles a delicate mirror which reflects the light of the Divine intellect, and sin, like a scratch, distorts the image on the mirror's polished surface. The *Kotzker Rebbe* expressed this concept in much stronger terms: "Sin," he said, "is like thick mud, which clogs and jams the marvelous machinery of the human mind!"

Therefore we plead הֲשִׁיבֵנוּ, *Bring us back*, to purity through repentance so that we can study Torah properly.

At the same time, the only way to repent properly is via Torah study, as the prophet proclaimed: קְחוּ עִמָּכֶם דְּבָרִים וְשׁוּבוּ אֶל ה׳, *Take with you words, and return to HASHEM* (Hosea 14:2). The Midrash (*Shemos Rabbah* 38:3) observes: The only words which draw a Jew back to God are words of Torah!

◈§ Returning to the Source

הֲשִׁיבֵנוּ . . . לְתוֹרָתֶךָ — *Bring us back . . . to Your Torah,* is also a plea asking God to reawaken in us an instinctive, magnetic attraction to Torah. King David made a similar request when he said: חִשַּׁבְתִּי דְרָכָי וָאָשִׁיבָה רַגְלַי אֶל עֵדֹתֶיךָ, *I considered my ways, and brought my feet back to Your testimonies* (Psalms 119:59). *Yalkut Shimoni* (*Tehillim* #890) relates that King David said to the Holy One, Blessed is He: "Every day *I considered my ways* and planned my schedule, saying: 'Today I will travel to this place or I will visit that person's home.' However, when the time came to carry out my plans, *my feet* refused to take me to my planned destination. Instead they would turn back towards *Your testimonies* and propel me to the houses of prayer and study."

Although there was no sin involved in David's planned visits, he reconsidered after realizing that as the supreme leader, he set an example for his nation and the best thing he could do for himself and the Jewish people was to return to the source of Jewish life and strength — the

House of Torah study. Similarly, we pray for Divine guidance. "O, God, if our thoughts will pull us away from You, please tug at our hearts and lead our bodies back to where they belong!"

◆§ The Homing Instinct

Additionally, the plea הֲשִׁיבֵנוּ, *Bring us back*, reminds us that Torah study is never a *new* experience for any Jew. It is always a return to his roots, a repetition of an earlier encounter, for the Talmud (*Niddah* 30b) relates, an angel teaches each Jew the entire Torah while still an embryo in his mother's womb. This means that Torah is imprinted on our chromosomes and implanted in our genes, literally interwoven into the fabric of our being. Just before birth, the angel strikes the babe on the mouth, causing the Torah to disappear from his lips and recede into his sub-conscious. A Jew spends his lifetime studying the Torah texts in order to extract the Torah treasures buried within him. He can never really know himself until he knows the Torah. Without Torah, the Jew is estranged from himself, stumbling from one identity crisis to another, vainly sifting through alien cultures in order to discover his life's meaning.

For this reason, we cry out, הֲשִׁיבֵנוּ. . . לְתוֹרָתֶךָ, *Bring us back . . . to Your Torah* — imbue us with that homing instinct which brings the dove back to its nest and the Jew back to the core of his being.

◆§ A Reunion with Our Father

Tur (*Shulchan Aruch, Orach Chaim* 115) observes that only in this blessing of the *Amidah* and the next do we refer to God as אָבִינוּ, *our Father*. He explains that since here we are asking God to teach us His Torah, we must remind Him that He is our Father, and the *halachah* is that a father is obligated to teach his son the entire Torah!

Rabbi Chaim of Volozhin (*Nefesh HaChaim* II:1) points out that when referring to Torah study we call God אָבִינוּ, *our Father*, but in reference to *mitzvah* service, we give God the title מַלְכֵּנוּ, *our King*. The reason, he explains, is that only when the Jewish people study Torah are they considered בָּנִים לַמָּקוֹם, children of God, and God reveals the hidden secrets of the universe to them just as a father only reveals his most private matters to his beloved son.

However, any Jew who merely serves God through the performance of *mitzvos* is like a servant distantly fulfilling his master's commands.

Without Torah study a Jew will always feel far from God, removed as a lowly vassal from his sovereign king. [This explains why in reference to Torah we say הֲשִׁיבֵנוּ, *Bring us back*, all the way, a complete reunion, whereas in reference to *service* we merely say קָרְבֵנוּ, *Bring us near*.]

⊷§ Study Leads to Service

וְקָרְבֵנוּ מַלְכֵּנוּ לַעֲבוֹדָתֶךָ — *And bring us near, our King, to Your service.*

How can one be sure that he is studying Torah properly and has truly repented and returned to God? Proper Torah study should fill a person with profound reverence and passionate love for God. The dedicated student is overwhelmed by the awesome wisdom of the Almighty, Who in His Kindness has revealed to His people a glimpse of His unfathomable and infinite wisdom. The student earnestly seeks a way to demonstrate his gratitude to God, desperately yearning for some vehicle to cling to the Almighty. The natural result of Torah study is a desire to serve this King through *mitzvos*: גְּדוֹלָה לִמּוּד שֶׁמֵּבִיא לִידֵי מַעֲשֶׂה, Great is Torah study because it brings one to action.

Torah study is the ultimate encounter with God, because it binds the heart and mind to His intellect. But man also has a body, which must be elevated and consecrated to join the heart and mind. The body can only be bound to God through *mitzvah* performance.

⊷§ Harmony and Balance

וְהַחֲזִירֵנוּ בִּתְשׁוּבָה שְׁלֵמָה לְפָנֶיךָ — *And influence us to return in perfect repentance before You.*

After we commence the *teshuvah* process we pray that Hashem help us complete it, as our Sages assured us: הַבָּא לְטַהֵר מְסַיְעִין לוֹ, He who takes the initiative to purify himself will surely receive Divine assistance! (*Yoma* 38b).

What is תְּשׁוּבָה שְׁלֵמָה, *perfect repentance*? When the mind is purified through Torah study and the body is consecrated by *mitzvah* performance, a man achieves perfect harmony and balance because he is entirely in line with the Creator and all of His Creations.

Furthermore, *Chovos Halevavos* observes that just as fire and water cannot co-exist in one vessel, it is impossible for one's heart to harbor a desire for both physical and spiritual pleasure. Only when his physical drive is completely harnessed by the service of spiritual advancement can man attain *perfect repentance* and true peace of mind.

⋖§ Repentance from Love

Imperfect repentance is called תְּשׁוּבָה מִיִּרְאָה, *repentance motivated by fear*. The penitent does indeed regret his transgressions, but repents only because he fears Divine retribution. Sin is the ultimate act of selfishness, because the sinner is egocentric and places his own desires before the desires of the Almighty. He who repents out of fear remains egocentric, because his motivation to repent is essentially self-preservation.

Perfect repentance, on the other hand, is called תְּשׁוּבָה מֵאַהֲבָה, *repentance motivated by love*. Through intensive study, prayer and introspection, the penitent has achieved a new awareness of God's greatness and goodness, and his own insignificance and unworthiness. His heart throbs with a yearning to cleave to God and he longs to cleanse himself of any impurity which might cause God to keep him distant. His earlier sins now fill him with such revulsion that he determines to flee from his egocentric existence and makes God alone the focal point of his life. The very sins which once sullied this man now stimulate him to soar to the heights of purity and penitence. Therefore, those sins are now considered tantamount to *mitzvos*, good deeds!

This is תְּשׁוּבָה שְׁלֵמָה, *perfect repentance!*

⋖§ Uprooting the Source of Sin

Another definition of *perfect repentance*:

One who truly wishes to change his ways must dig beneath the surface to probe and discover the root of his transgression. Any sinful act is symptomatic of a deeper character flaw. One who gossips and speaks ill of his neighbor, for example, suffers from more than just a loose tongue; his actions result from having a heart filled with bitterness and malice. If he resolves merely to desist from *lashon hara*, this would constitute imperfect repentance, because he has not yet fully uprooted the problem. Only when he struggles with his cruel, insensitive nature and determines to fill his heart with love for every fellow Jew has he achieved penetrating and *perfect* repentance (*Rav Pinchos Aharon Weberman*).

⋖§ Search for God

בָּרוּךְ אַתָּה ה' הָרוֹצֶה בִּתְשׁוּבָה — *Blessed are You, HASHEM, Who desires repentance.*

Hashem's desire for us to return to Him is far more intense than we imagine, as shown by the following story: The Chassidic master, *Rabbi Mendele of Rimanov*, was once walking with his disciples when they encountered a weeping child. "We are playing hide-and-seek," the child cried. "I have hidden myself, but no one is trying to find me." Rabbi Mendele turned to his followers. "Now," he said, "can you not appreciate the distress of God, Who has concealed Himself in the universe, and commissioned man to search for and find Him? How painful it must be to God that people go their own ways and do not search for Him!"

∽§ Repentance Is Never Rejected

Manasseh, King of Judea, was arguably the most wicked ruler in Jewish history. From his righteous father, Hezekiah, he inherited a nation which reached the heights of piety and Torah scholarship. For twenty-two years, the depraved Manasseh dragged his people to the depths of idolatry and violence. Manasseh's hands were soaked with the blood of countless innocent victims, including his grandfather, Isaiah the prophet, who was killed by Manasseh's own sword.

Babylonian invaders eventually captured Manasseh and were burning him alive in a fiery cauldron, when Manasseh desperately turned back to the God of his fathers. The Jerusalem Talmud (*Sanhedrin* 10:9) relates that the celestial angels sealed all the gateways of heaven, refusing entry to the penitence of such a villain. But the Almighty Himself felt otherwise, and proclaimed, "If I reject Manasseh's repentance, it will discourage other worthier penitents!"

The Almighty, then, drilled a hole through His celestial throne, as it were, and made a new passageway through which Manasseh's penitence rose up to heaven. This shows how strongly God *"desires repentance."*

Shibbolei Halekket records the Midrash which states: When Reuben sinned with his father's concubine, Bilhah, he was condemned to die, but he repented and was granted life. At that moment the ministering angels chanted, "Blessed are You, HASHEM, Who desires repentance."

6

סְלִיחָה / Forgiveness

סְלַח לָנוּ אָבִֽינוּ כִּי חָטָֽאנוּ, מְחַל לָֽנוּ מַלְכֵּֽנוּ כִּי פָשָֽׁעְנוּ, כִּי
מוֹחֵל וְסוֹלֵֽחַ אָֽתָּה. בָּרוּךְ אַתָּה יהוה, חַנּוּן
הַמַּרְבֶּה לִסְלֹֽחַ.

Forgive us, our Father, for we have erred; pardon us, our King, for we have willfully sinned; for You pardon and forgive. Blessed are You, HASHEM, the gracious One Who forgives abundantly.

~§ Closeness to God

The ultimate purpose of prayer is to establish an intimate and meaningful relationship with our Father in Heaven. After repentance, accomplished in the fifth blessing, we seek to reestablish our closeness with God, Who loves us more than a parent, as King David said: *Though my father and my mother have forsaken me, Hashem will gather me in (Psalms 27:10).* Such a relationship with God is founded upon יִרְאַת שָׁמַיִם, *fear of Heaven.*

~§ Forgiveness and Fatherly Love

In his classic work בְּעִקְבוֹת הַיִּרְאָה, *In the Footsteps of Heavenly Fear,* Rabbi Avrohom Eliyahu Kaplan of the Berlin Rabbinical Seminary described a common, but false view of the God-fearing Jew. It imagines him to be a somber, unhappy person, bereft of joy or warmth, someone whose eyes are filled with constant terror, dreading the proverbial lightning bolt that may strike him as punishment for his sins.

In truth, however, a God-fearing person is like a father who carries his beloved, only son on his shoulders as he dances on *Simchas Torah.* The more the father dances, the stronger his love becomes. Even as these feelings of joy and love intensify in the father's heart, however, he feels fear and concern, as well, because he fears lest he slip and drop his precious child. Thus love for the child and fear for his welfare develop simultaneously.

The God-fearing man is similar. His face is radiant and smiling; his eyes shine and twinkle. He is serene and calm, content and secure. He feels cradled in God's protective embrace.

He has no fear save one: a constant concern that he may falter in his service of the Almighty, that he might disappoint God and betray His continual love and kindness. The more his love of God intensifies, the more he fears lest this unique relationship be harmed.

Because the Jewish ideal is that all Jews are God's children, we turn to Him three times a day and say סְלַח לָנוּ אָבִינוּ, *Forgive us, our Father,* lest we have made ourselves unworthy of Your fatherly love.

~§ The Symbolism of Six

This is the sixth blessing of the *Amidah,* and the sixth letter of the Hebrew alphabet is ו, *vav.* The letter is shaped like a hook, as indeed its

name וָו means *hook*. The letter *vav* is the prefix of conjunction [ן
הַחִבּוּר]; it unites manifold, even opposing concepts. Thus the number
six, which is represented by *vav*, implies a close relationship, because in
begging for forgiveness we ask God to renew the intimate relationship
we enjoyed with Him before we sinned.

⇜§ Pardon Follows Penitence

סְלַח לָנוּ אָבִינוּ כִּי חָטָאנוּ — *Forgive us, our Father, for we have erred.*

This plea for forgiveness follows our request for repentance. The
Talmud (*Megillah* 17b) teaches that this order is based upon the verse:
יַעֲזֹב רָשָׁע דַּרְכּוֹ וְאִישׁ אָוֶן מַחְשְׁבֹתָיו וְיָשֹׁב אֶל ה׳ וִירַחֲמֵהוּ וְאֶל אֱלֹהֵינוּ כִּי יַרְבֶּה
לִסְלוֹחַ, *Let the wicked forsake his way, and the man of crime, his
schemes; and let each repent unto Hashem, and He will have mercy
upon him, and unto our God for He will abundantly forgive* (Isaiah
55:7).

First, we repent, abandon our past sins, and commit ourselves to
improvement; only then can we sincerely ask God to forgive and
eradicate our misdeeds. One who asks for pardon *before* he stops
sinning is described as a טוֹבֵל וְשֶׁרֶץ בְּיָדוֹ, *one who immerses himself in
purifying waters while grasping an impure creature in his hand* (*Taanis*
16a). His immersion serves no purpose because he continues to
contaminate himself. So, too, one cannot expect forgiveness for sins that
he continues to commit or to harbor.

⇜§ A Father's Compassion

Tur (*Orach Chaim* 115) notes that in this blessing and the preceding
one God is called *our Father:* as we plead for mercy we remind God that
He is our Father, and a father's compassion is unsurpassed. As King
David said: כְּרַחֵם אָב עַל בָּנִים רִחַם ה׳ עַל יְרֵאָיו. כִּי הוּא יָדַע יִצְרֵנוּ זָכוּר כִּי עָפָר
אֲנָחְנוּ, *As merciful as a father to his children, so has Hashem shown
mercy to those who fear Him. For He knows our impulsive nature, He
remembers that we are dust* (Psalms 103:13,14).

God's mercy is not restricted to *those who fear him*, as we read: טוֹב ה׳
לַכֹּל וְרַחֲמָיו עַל כָּל מַעֲשָׂיו, *Hashem is good to all, and His mercies are on
all His creatures* (Psalms 145:9), but He cannot show it to those who
defy Him because continued success would only entrench them further
in their evil ways. We declare, therefore: "אָבִינוּ, *Our Father*, we
recognize Your authority as our Heavenly Parent. Because we stand in

reverence of Your Fatherhood and sincerely repent our sins, we dare to invoke Your Fatherly compassion and cry out, "סְלַח לָנוּ, *Forgive us!*"

Radak (comm. to *Psalms* 103:13) observes that no mercy is as intense as that of a father towards his child.

ᴥ Renewed Efforts

מְחַל לָנוּ מַלְכֵּנוּ כִּי פָשָׁעְנוּ — *Pardon us, our King, for we have willfully sinned.*

Yaaros Dvash explains that God is our loving Father and we are His children, but if we ignore His will, we allow the relationship to deteriorate. At first, the transgressions are considered to be mere חֲטָאִים, *unintentional errors*, and using the relatively casual term of סְלִיחָה, *forgiveness*, we ask God, *our Father*, to overlook them.

However, if the errant son fails to mend his ways, he gradually becomes defiant and commits פְּשָׁעִים, *willful sins*. Then, in order to move him toward repentance, God masks His Fatherly compassion and assumes the role of the stern מֶלֶךְ, *King*. Now the sinner must make a much more forceful plea and a more intense effort towards sincere penitence. He must ask for מְחִילָה, [complete] *pardon*.

ᴥ The Psychology of Sin

In *Shaarei Teshuvah* (1:23), *Rabbeinu Yonah* singles out *Psalm 51* as the פֶּרֶק הַתְּשׁוּבָה, *the Chapter of Repentance*, because it contains the principles of repentance. In it, David laments his conduct with Bath-sheba and confesses: כִּי פְשָׁעַי אֲנִי אֵדָע וְחַטָּאתִי נֶגְדִּי תָמִיד, *For I recognize my willful sins; and my error is before me always (Psalm 51:5).*

Rav Elya Lopian (*Lev Eliyahu* Vol. I, p. 286) explains David's approach towards his shortcomings. First he addresses his willful sins, acknowledging the wrongdoing and repenting sincerely — but he does not say that those sins are *before me always*. He does not linger on his past transgressions lest he become consumed by guilt. To dwell constantly on a willful sin can break a person's spirit, making him discouraged and depressed, and impeding his growth. However, in reference to חֲטָאִים, *errors*, the opposite is true. People tend to rationalize errors and to make light of them; therefore, David emphasized, *and my error is before me always*; because he knew that errors can lead to terrible transgressions, for if one feels no remorse over his errors, he may become insensitive to sin and come to defy God.

৵§ Confession and Re-awakening

It is customary to strike the left side of the chest, over the heart, with the right fist, while saying *we have erred*, and *we have willfully sinned*. These symbolic blows represent acknowledgment of our guilt and a confession of our failure to serve God properly. As the seat of passion and desire, the heart is the place where sins originate. Moreover, just as one knocks on a door to awaken a sleeper, so one taps his heart to arouse it from lethargy.

Furthermore, the Talmud (*Berachos* 7a) teaches that טוֹבָה מַרְדּוּת אַחַת בְּלִבּוֹ שֶׁל אָדָם מִמֵּאָה מַלְקִיּוֹת, *One [self-aroused] upheaval in a person's heart surpasses one hundred blows. Rashi* (ibid.) explains that the ultimate penitence is when a person's heart is filled with remorse over his sins. This will bring him to a level of humility and submission to God, which he could not attain even if he received "one hundred blows," in the form of misfortunes from external sources. When we ask God for forgiveness, therefore, we beat the heart to symbolize the need to arouse an internal upheaval in our hearts, for that is the most genuine form of contrition.

৵§ Priorities of Praise

כִּי מוֹחֵל וְסוֹלֵחַ אָתָּה — *For You pardon and forgive.*
In the first part of this blessing we mention casual סְלִיחָה, *forgiveness*, before intense מְחִילָה, *pardon*, because it is proper to make a lesser request before a greater one. At the conclusion of the blessing, however, in recounting God's praise, it is appropriate to give precedence to His greater attribute of [intense] *pardon* for defiant transgression, before mentioning His lesser attribute of *forgiveness* for less serious sins (*Iyun Tefillah*).

৵§ Only God Can Forgive

A common shortcoming is to accept flimsy excuses for our misdeeds. Recognizing this tendency to be overly lenient with ourselves, the *Kotzker Rebbe* identified it as a form of self-deception, and condemned it in the strongest terms: "Whoever studies Torah but does not exhaust himself, whoever sins and forgives himself, whoever prays today because he prayed yesterday — a totally wicked man is better than he!" If a wicked man knows he is wicked, he may repent someday. But someone who deludes himself into thinking he is righteous will never repent.

Therefore we say here: "For pardon and forgiveness I turn to *You* alone, O God — I will not forgive myself!"

⊸§ *Return to Grace*

בָּרוּךְ אַתָּה ה׳ חַנּוּן הַמַּרְבֶּה לִסְלוֹחַ — *Blessed are You, Hashem, the gracious One Who forgives abundantly.*

God treats us with exceptional compassion and grace. Not only does He forgive our sins, but he doesn't even harbor resentment or ill-will. Moreover, our very pleading for God's forgiveness arouses Him to look upon us with renewed favor and grace.

Rambam (*Hilchos Teshuvah* 7:6,7) eloquently describes this Divine grace:

> How great repentance is, for it draws a person close to the Divine Presence... even those who were very alienated. Yesterday the sinner was hateful in the eyes of God; repulsive, abhorrent, an abomination. And behold, today he repents and he is beloved, cherished, intimate, and endeared ... Yesterday [the sinner] was separated from God ... He cried out to God but was not answered ... The sinner performed *mitzvos* but God tore them up in his presence ... But today he is attached to the *Shechinah*. He cries out and is answered immediately ... He performs *mitzvos* and God accepts them graciously and with joy ... Furthermore, God yearns for penitents to constantly draw closer and closer.

7

גְּאוּלָה / Personal Salvation

רְאֵה בְעָנְיֵנוּ, וְרִיבָה רִיבֵנוּ, וּגְאָלֵנוּ מְהֵרָה לְמַעַן שְׁמֶךָ, כִּי גּוֹאֵל חָזָק אָתָּה. בָּרוּךְ אַתָּה יהוה, גּוֹאֵל יִשְׂרָאֵל.

Behold our affliction, take up our grievance, and redeem us speedily for Your Name's sake, for You are a powerful Redeemer. Blessed are You, HASHEM, Redeemer of Israel.

◄§ Redemption from Suffering

This blessing is a fervent plea for personal triumph over adversity; a petition to be released from the incessant perils and problems of everyday existence. We do not ask for a life without challenges and struggles, for such a life would lack meaning; rather we ask for relief in the areas of suffering and stress with which we feel we cannot cope. Some people feel trapped in a difficult marriage, others are shackled to an unsatisfying job. Some are crushed by financial burdens, others face deep trouble with the law. Everyone is under some sort of pressure. We turn to God and cry for help. "Forsake me not. Only You can soothe the pain. If You are with me, I am not alone; I will survive."

The Talmud (*Megillah* 17b) shows how this blessing fits into the order of the prayers. In the fourth blessing we asked for intellect and insight. Then we repented and asked for forgiveness, for redemption from the soul-paralysis of sin. Now, in this blessing, we plead for release from mental anguish and emotional pain (*Rashi*). Recognizing that many physical ailments are psychosomatic in origin, the physical manifestation of emotional distress, the Sages prescribed that before we ask for healing of the body in the eighth blessing, we first seek a cure for the ills of the spirit.

◄§ A Glimpse of the Final Struggle

The Talmud (*Megillah* 17b) explains that this blessing's position as number seven alludes to the future advent of the Messiah, which will be preceded by seven years of travail. In the seventh year, the pre-Messianic upheaval will reach its most dangerous stage and the world will totter on the brink of destruction. Then, the struggle will subside and an era of unsurpassed serenity and peace will unfold.

Not only does this blessing inspire us to look to the future, it also remind us to learn from our past. *Shibbolei Halekket* cites the Midrash, which teaches: The Redemption of the Children of Israel from the bondage of Egypt inspired the ministering angels to chant, "Blessed are You, HASHEM, Redeemer of Israel."

Thus, the number seven encourages us to think of the triumph of the past and the promise of the future, and thereby be encouraged in the present. It tells us, "Don't let adversity crush your spirit. Though you feel you are losing the battles of life, don't lose hope. One battle may be lost, but fortitude and faith can yet win the war. If the spirit remains strong, you will emerge victorious. And if your spirit feels weak, turn to God and He will give you strength."

In this vein we note that the seventh letter of the alphabet is זַיִן, *zayin*, which also means *weapon*. In this seventh blessing, we call upon God to *fight our battles* (רִיבָה רִיבֵנוּ) and to be our only זַיִן, *weapon*.

⊷ Part of the Whole

Our personal suffering is a direct offshoot of the collective, national suffering of the Jewish people in exile. The Midrash (*Eichah Rabbasi* 1:25, see also *Sanhedrin* 104b) relates that a certain widow who lived in Rabban Gamliel's neighborhood would weep bitterly over her plight. When Rabban Gamliel heard her cries in the night, he would arise and cry over the destruction of the Temple and the Jewish exile. *HaRav Mordechai Gifter* explains that Rabban Gamliel understood that the widow's personal woes were an outgrowth of Israel's general misfortune. When Israel is delivered collectively, all personal problems will be resolved as well.

For many years, *Rabbi Yoel Sirkis* could not arrange for the publication of *Bais Chadash*, his commentary on the *Tur Shulchan Aruch*. Whenever it was about to go to print, an unforeseen circumstance would arise and delay the printing. After many years of frustration, the rabbi, known as the *Bach*, was heartbroken. One midnight, as he grieved over his personal misfortune, he stopped and berated himself: "How selfish of me to weep over my personal problems when there is a far greater tragedy in the world, the calamity of Israel in Exile!" So the *Bach* took off his shoes like a mourner and recited *Tikkun Chatzos*, the midnight prayer for the Redemption of Israel.

Eventually, fatigue overcame the *Bach* and he fell asleep. A heavenly voice addressed him in a dream: "Know that for many years they have been displeased with you in heaven, because you became so engrossed in writing the *Bais Chadash* that you neglected the recital of *Tikkun Chatzos*. As great as Torah study is, one must never lose sight of the plight of the Jewish people. Tonight, for the first time in years you cried over the collective misery of God and Israel — so you have regained favor in heaven."

The very next morning, the publisher began printing the *Bais Chadash!*

The text of this blessing embodies the above concept. Although it addresses the personal suffering of the individual Jew, it speaks in terms of *national redemption*, because a Jew should never let his personal problems influence him to forget the problems of Israel. He should realize when the nation is redeemed all personal problems will be resolved as well.

▱§ Pay Attention to Those in Pain

רְאֵה בְעָנְיֵנוּ — *Behold our affliction.*

I know, O God, that You pay special attention to those who are in pain, as You took note of our Matriarch Leah, who felt rejected and forlorn. Hearing her prayers, You blessed her to become Jacob's most prolific wife. Leah acknowledged Your love and concern. When her first son was born, she named him רְאוּבֵן, *Reuben,* saying: כִּי רָאָה ה׳ בְּעָנְיִי, *For HASHEM has observed my affliction* (Genesis 29:32).

▱§ We Are Our Own Enemy

The root of עָנְיֵנוּ, *our affliction,* is עֹנִי, *poverty,* which alludes not only to material want, but to poverty of the spirit; our weak character and emotional inadequacy. Had we the courage to be honest with ourselves, we would admit that no one hurts us as much as we hurt ourselves. How often have we knowingly abused our bodies and our intelligence. How often have we surrendered to the delights of self-indulgence? How often have we failed to live up to our own high standards of conduct? We have only ourselves to blame for our failures and misfortunes. We are our own greatest enemies.

Of course other people victimize us, cheat us, wrong us; but the *Vilna Gaon* teaches that they are not our real enemies. When a person's conduct and character are perfect, it is virtually impossible for harm to come his way. The adversaries who cause us grief are agents dispatched by God to remind us of our failures and misdeeds. If we are wise we will first deal with the weakness and poor character within us, and then — *suffering* and *oppression* threatening from without will disappear.

⋖§ Only Complain to God

וְרִיבָה רִיבֵנוּ — *Take up our grievance* [lit. *fight our battles*].

The Talmud (*Gittin* 7a) relates that the Babylonian exilarch, Mar Ukva, was harassed by rebels who flouted his authority and insulted him personally. Although he could have turned them over to the government for punishment, Mar Ukva was reluctant to do so. He sought the advice of Rabbi Elazar who counseled him to call upon God to fight his battles. Basing himself on *Psalms* 37:7-9, Rabbi Elazar advised: "Be mute. Do not complain to your fellow man, but pray to God early in the day and again late in the evening, and He will cut off your enemies before you!"

⋖§ Prayer — Our Most Potent Weapon

Jacob was a powerful warrior, yet he knew that God, not man, wages war. Man's most potent weapon is prayer. On his death bed Jacob related that he conquered Shechem בְּחַרְבִּי וּבְקַשְׁתִּי, *with my sword and with my bow* (*Genesis* 48:22), which *Targum Onkelos* renders as בִּצְלוֹתִי וּבְבָעוּתִי, *with my prayer and with my supplication*. *Gur Aryeh* explains that the prayer of the righteous is likened to a 'sword' since it 'cuts' its way through the upper and lower worlds. Prayer is likened to a bow because just as an arrow's flight depends on the pressure exerted on the bow, so, too, a prayer's effectiveness depends on a person's degree of concentration and intent.

Meshech Chochmah explains the distinction between prayer, which is likened to a sword, and supplication, which is likened to a bow. The prescribed prayer, i.e., the *Shemoneh Esrei* prayer, which was composed by the Men of the Great Assembly, contains such inherent sanctity that it is not rendered ineffective by lack of *kavanah* [concentration]. Thus, *Shemoneh Esrei* is like a sharp sword that can cause injury even if it is not wielded with great force. A personal supplication, however, which an individual composes himself, is dependent on the degree of one's *kavanah* (cf. *Taanis* 8b). Consequently, such private prayers are like a bow and arrow; their effectiveness is in direct proportion to the degree of spiritual exertion with which one 'propels' them.

◄§ The Constant Battle

Life is a constant battle to curb our base desires. *Chovos Halevavos* (*Shaar Yichud Hamaaseh* 5) relates that a pious man once encountered a band of victorious soldiers returning from the battlefront. He said to them: "Be on guard! Although the battle you just concluded was fierce, it was a minor skirmish. The great war is about to begin — the incessant daily struggle between man and his Evil Inclination."

This constant struggle is really for our benefit, as the following incident illustrates:

Someone consulted the *Chofetz Chaim,* "My Evil Inclination does not give me any rest. What can I do?"

"That is for your good," replied the *Chofetz Chaim.* "We are in this world to overcome our forbidden impulses. By controlling our desires for evil, we elevate ourselves. The more difficult it is, the greater the merit" (*Michtevai Chofetz Chaim,* p. 97).

The Talmud (*Kiddushin* 30b) warns that we are locked in mortal combat with the Evil Inclination, which seeks to destroy us. "Man's Evil Inclination renews its fierce attack and attempts to overpower man every day. If not for God's assistance, man could never withstand the temptation of the Evil Inclination."

In recognition of the enormous danger that faces us daily, we must constantly renew our prayers to God, begging Him to protect us from the Evil Inclination.

◄§ To Shorten the Exile

וּגְאָלֵנוּ מְהֵרָה לְמַעַן שְׁמֶךָ — *And redeem us speedily for Your Name's sake.*

Israel's suffering is a desecration of the Name of God.

Although we recognize that Israel suffers because of its own sins, our enemies cannot claim that they are doing God's work, because they cause Israel to suffer more than is necessary. The Egyptians, for example, were punished for oppressing the Jews, even though God Himself had decreed suffering and slavery, because the Egyptians went far beyond God's decree. Because Israel suffered excessively under the cruel Egyptians, God reduced the exile from the prophesied total four hundred years to two hundred and ten. Similarly, we ask God to *redeem us speedily* now, because our tormentors are persecuting us excessively (*Etz Yosef*).

☙ Strength for the Weary of Spirit

כִּי גוֹאֵל חָזָק אָתָּה — *For You are a powerful Redeemer.*

God redeems by infusing us with His power. He strengthens our demoralized spirits and invigorates our weary bones. A popular folksaying goes: יְשׁוּעַת ה׳ כְּהֶרֶף עַיִן, *God's salvation comes as swiftly as the blink of the eye.* The word הֶרֶף can be rendered, "to release one's hold as a result of exhaustion." Often our eyes search for God's salvation. We wait and wait, and are filled with disappointment. But just at the moment of הֶרֶף עַיִן, i.e., when our eyes are closing from fatigue and frustration, that is precisely when Hashem appears and revitalizes us with a fresh dose of confidence and hope.

☙ Ongoing Redemption

בָּרוּךְ אַתָּה ה׳ גּוֹאֵל יִשְׂרָאֵל — *Blessed are You,* HASHEM, *Redeemer of Israel.*

Unlike the blessing preceding the *Amidah,* which refers to God as גָּאַל יִשְׂרָאֵל, *He Who redeemed Israel,* in the past, this blessing is in the present tense, which denotes ongoing action. God redeems us continually, on a daily, hourly, even minute-to-minute basis. He is prepared to help us with every problem, all the time. If we will only call on Him, God is ready to help us.

רְפוּאָה / Health and Healing

8

רְפָאֵנוּ יהוה וְנֵרָפֵא, הוֹשִׁיעֵנוּ וְנִוָּשֵׁעָה, כִּי תְהִלָּתֵנוּ
אָתָּה, וְהַעֲלֵה רְפוּאָה שְׁלֵמָה לְכָל מַכּוֹתֵינוּ, כִּי
אֵל מֶלֶךְ רוֹפֵא נֶאֱמָן וְרַחֲמָן אָתָּה. בָּרוּךְ אַתָּה יהוה, רוֹפֵא
חוֹלֵי עַמּוֹ יִשְׂרָאֵל.

Heal us, HASHEM — then we will be healed; save us — then
we will be saved, for You are our praise. Bring complete
recovery for all our ailments, for You are God, King, the
faithful and compassionate Healer. Blessed are You,
HASHEM, Who heals the sick of His people Israel.

☙ The Merit of Circumcision

In the seventh blessing we requested mental and emotional health — redemption from anguish and stress. Now we are ready to ask for physical well-being.

The Talmud (*Megillah* 17b) asks: "Why did the men of the Great Assembly establish the blessing for healing as the eighth one in the *Amidah*?" Because the בְּרִית מִילָה, *the Covenant of Circumcision*, is performed on the eight day, and because it is an operation which requires healing, they designated the blessing for healing as number eight. Indeed, the Midrash (quoted in *Shibbolei Halekket*) says: When the angel Raphael healed Abraham after his circumcision, the angels in heaven proclaimed: "Blessed are You, HASHEM, Who heals the sick of His people Israel."

The ability to heal the wounds and maladies of mankind is a great blessing that God bestowed upon the world in the merit of *bris milah*. Every successful healing process results directly from the healing of our Patriarch Abraham, the first person to undergo circumcision, and so we should keep him in mind whenever we recite this eighth blessing.

☙ When the Gateways to Heaven Are Open

The circumcision of an infant affords a most auspicious opportunity to pray for health. As the incision is made the baby wails. All the gateways to heaven open wide for this pure sound to rise before the Presence of the Almighty. The baby's suffering for God's sake arouses intense Divine compassion, and, as a result, God accepts all prayers and petitions favorably.

King David had the *mitzvah* of *milah* in mind when he composed the sixth Psalm and titled it עַל הַשְּׁמִינִית, *for the eighth* [day]. He says (verse 3): חָנֵּנִי ה' כִּי אֻמְלַל אָנִי, *Favor me, HASHEM, for I am circumcised* [אֻמְלַל is cognate with מָל, circumcised]; רְפָאֵנִי ה' כִּי נִבְהֲלוּ עֲצָמָי, *Heal me, HASHEM, for my bones shudder* [from the pain of circumcision]. And David acknowledged the power of the infant's weeping during the circumcision in the concluding verses of this psalm (verses 9-10): סוּרוּ מִמֶּנִּי כָּל פֹּעֲלֵי אָוֶן כִּי שָׁמַע ה' קוֹל בִּכְיִי. שָׁמַע ה' תְּחִנָּתִי ה' תְּפִלָּתִי יִקָּח, *Depart from me, all evildoers, for HASHEM has heard the sound of my weeping. HASHEM has heard my plea; HASHEM will accept my prayer* [based on *Drashos Olelos Ephraim* #415 and gloss of *Rav Eliyahu Gutmacher* to *Vilna Shas, Shabbos* 130a].

✑ Healing Is from Heaven

Maharal (*Ner Mitzvah*) demonstrates how the number seven symbolizes the heights of perfection and sanctity *within* the confines of nature, whereas the number eight stands for all that is לְמַעֲלָה מִן הַטֶבַע, *above the plane of nature.*

Abraham is called אָב לִשְׁמוֹנָה, *the father of eight*, because he was the first to perform *bris milah* on the eighth day (when circumcising his son, Isaac) and because he mastered the symbolism of eight, living a life of spiritual perfection.

By associating the power of רְפוּאָה, *healing*, with *bris milah* and the number eight, we are emphasizing that physical healing is actually a supernatural occurrence *above the plane of nature!*

Modern medicine appears to be the marvelous progeny of scientific research and technology. However, we should not be fooled by appearances, for the efficacy of even the most ultra-modern procedures derives from an other-wordly source.

✑ To Whom Do We Turn — God or Man?

The answer to this question is very complex, but we present here the major opinions on the subject. *Ramban* (Nachmanides) in his commentary on the Torah (*Leviticus* 26:11) states that when people are living Godly lives they have no need at all for doctors. In days of old when a pious person fell sick, he would not call a doctor for medical advice, but a prophet for spiritual advice. Those who follow the will of God are not limited by the laws of science and nature, but are controlled only by God's will. *Ramban* sums up his opinion in one pithy statement: מַה חֵלֶק לָרוֹפְאִים בְּבֵית עוֹשֵׂי רְצוֹן ה', *"What share do doctors have in the home of those who do God's will?"*

Rambam (Maimonides) takes an entirely different position (comm. to Mishnah, *Pesachim* chapter 4). He explains that medical care is a primary, basic human need, no different than eating or breathing. *Rambam* argues that malnutrition is a form of disease and constitutes a medical emergency. Only a madman would advise a starving man to rely on a miracle instead of eating. Similarly, only a fool would tell a sick man to decline medical attention and rely solely on God.

Michtav MeEliyahu (Part II, pp. 170-172) explains that *Ramban* and *Rambam* are discussing different people, on varying levels of faith.

Ramban is describing one who has reached the pinnacle of faith. He thinks about God constantly, and has relinquished to Him control of every aspect of his life. Since he turns to God for his every need, he should certainly turn only to God for a cure. *Rambam*, however, is addressing himself to the average person, who lives a normal, mainstream lifestyle. This man goes out to earn his livelihood and doesn't rely solely on God for all his needs. Such a person must turn to a doctor for his medical needs as well.

In short, when the deeply spiritual man falls ill he should reach out and grab a *Tehillim*; when the average man falls ill he should reach for his telephone and call his doctor.

Birkei Yosef (*Yoreh Deah* 331:2) rules that today no one has reached the level of *Ramban's* pious model.

Today one must not rely on miracles, and a sick person must conform to the natural order by calling on a physician to heal him. In fact, to depart from the general practice and claim greater merit than the many saints of previous generations who were cured by physicians is almost sinful. Not only does it smack of arrogance, but it places one's life in great jeopardy. Hence, one should adopt the ways of all men and be healed by physicians.

⋖§ Prayer for Success

Rashba (Responsa, Part I:413) warns that even though we must turn to doctors for medical treatment, we should place our hopes and confidence only in Hashem. The doctor and his medicine are merely tools in the hands of the Almighty, and we must beseech God to cure us through this doctor and this medicine (see *Responsa, Tzitz Eliezer*, Vol. 8:15).

Thus, this eighth blessing is relevant to one and all. Men of perfect piety and faith turn to God to cure them directly. The average person prays that God should cure him through His medical emissaries.

⋖§ The Prayer of a Talmid Chacham

The Talmud (*Bava Basra* 116a) teaches: If you have a sick person in your home, go to a Torah scholar and have him pray to God for mercy, as King Solomon said: *"When the King is infuriated He sends angels of death, but a wise man will pacify Him"* (*Proverbs* 16:14).

Meiri comments (ibid.) that one should never rely exclusively on another to pray for him; rather, "one should ask the Torah scholar to teach him how to pray, so that he himself can plead for God's mercy."

And today one should pray for God to send the right doctor to be His agent of healing.

✑§ A Doctor's Prayer

All medical practitioners should recite this blessing with special feeling and fervor. In a sense, every recitation of רְפָאֵנוּ is a renewal of their *spiritual* medical license, for unless a doctor feels that he is only God's agent he has no right to tamper with man, God's most majestic handiwork.

The Talmud teaches: טוב שֶׁבְּרוֹפְאִים לְגֵיהִנָּם, *The best of doctors will go to Gehenna* (*Kiddushin* 82a). The commentaries explain that this harsh condemnation applies only to the arrogant doctor who *thinks* he is the very best. Such a physician has absolute confidence in his own diagnosis and refuses to consult a colleague for a second opinion. Nor does he turn to God for help, and he feels no compunction to seek Divine permission to practice.

The blessing of רְפָאֵנוּ, which designates God as the Ultimate Healer, is repugnant to the haughty doctor and so he deletes it, or recites it without sincere intent. Now — for him — the original 18 benedictions are reduced to 17. For this reason the Talmud sarcastically refers to him as טוב, *the best*, because the numerical value of טוב is *seventeen*, alluding to the fact that this arrogant 'best' doctor recites only *seventeen* blessing in the *Amidah*.

✑§ A Permanent Cure

רְפָאֵנוּ ה' וְנֵרָפֵא — *Heal us, HASHEM — then we will be healed.*

In this blessing the Sages reformulate the personal request of the prophet who asked: רְפָאֵנִי ה' וְאֵרָפֵא הוֹשִׁיעֵנִי וְאִוָּשֵׁעָה כִּי תְהִלָּתִי אָתָּה, *Heal me, HASHEM — then I shall be healed; save me — then I shall be saved, for You are my praise* (*Jeremiah* 17:14).

Sometimes human beings or angels serve as God's agents to heal illness, but in that case the cure may be only partial or temporary. (Or the pain or other symptoms may be relieved while the illness itself remains — *Siach Yitzchok*.) But if God *Himself* undertakes to cure the patient, we are confident that it will not be a temporary or a partial measure: *then we will be healed* (*Etz Yosef* from *Zohar*).

Another interpretation: רְפָאֵנוּ ה', *Heal us, HASHEM,* from preexisting conditions and ailments; וְנֵרָפֵא, *and keep us healthy* — immunize and protect us from future illness (*Tefillah L'David; Buchacz*). Similarly, the Talmud (*Shabbos* 32b) teaches: "A healthy person should always pray that he does not get sick, because once sickness strikes he must have great merit to regain his health."

Rabbeinu Bachaya observes that the Torah sanctions one human being to heal another with the two words וְרַפֹּא יְרַפֵּא, *and He shall surely heal (Exodus* 21:19). In both words the middle letter of the verb root רפא is pronounced as the harsh-sounding פ, *peh,* suggesting that medical treatment is often harsh and extremely painful, for the dot or point inside the פ, *peh,* alludes to the pricking and cutting doctors do with their needles, syringes, and scalpels. Therefore, the text of the *Amidah* follows Jeremiah's plea רְפָאֵנוּ, in which the soft, undotted פ, *pheh,* sound is used, signifying that God's cures are gentle, sensitive and painless.

◈§ Sensitivity of Healers

The Steipler Gaon was sorely distressed by the minority of doctors and other health care professionals who are insensitive to their patients. Such people, he felt, actually endangered their patients' health. This anguish inspired the Steipler to interpret וְרַפֹּא יְרַפֵּא in a novel way: "*May God heal us from the doctors!*"

One of the worst offenses committed by insensitive doctors is that they give up hope on a patient and fill the patient's heart with helplessness and gloom, as illustrated in the following story:

Rebbitzin Rivkah, the wife of Reb Shmuel of Lubavitch, developed such a serious lung condition that her doctors declared her case to be beyond hope.

Her father-in-law, Reb Menachem Mendel of Lubavitch, heard this and said: "On the verse וְרַפֹּא יְרַפֵּא, *and he shall surely heal,* the Sages of the Talmud comment, 'from this we learn that the Torah permits a doctor to heal.' *This* is what the Torah permits — but when it comes to pronouncing the opposite verdict, God forbid, that is no affair of his at all."

In view of her weakened physical condition, he instructed her to eat a breakfast of bread and butter every morning immediately after washing her hands when she woke up — without observing the usual order of first saying her morning prayers — and gave her his blessing for long life. After some time she decided to allow his instruction to lapse, and told her father-in-law that she now hurried through the morning prayer, and immediately after that sat down to breakfast. "It is better to eat in order to be able to pray," he said, "than to pray in order to be able to eat.

~§ Inner Healing

הוֹשִׁיעֵנוּ וְנִוָּשֵׁעָה — *Save us — then we will be saved*."

In this blessing we request spiritual salvation and growth. When a person leads a holy life he is surrounded by a sacred aura which insulates him from any sickness or harm. When one is afflicted by physical ailment it is *often* a symptom of spiritual failure.

The Hebrew word for a sick person, חוֹלֶה, is cognate with the word חוּל, which means *unholy* or *profane*. The term חוּל is related to the word חָלָל, *vacuum; emptiness* — implying that where there is a void of sanctity, physical debilitation and illness inevitable ensue. The Hebrew word for health, בְּרִיאוּת, is cognate with בְּרִיאָה, *creation*, implying that a person will be healthy when he lives up to what God created him to be.

Therefore we ask God, הוֹשִׁיעֵנוּ, *save us*, from *spiritual* failure and then נִוָּשֵׁעָה, *we will be saved*, from *medical* problems (see *Tefillah L'David*).

Another interpretation: A tragic reality is that sometimes the cure administered to the patient turn out to be more dangerous than his original ailments, because many medicines produce devastating side effects. Therefore we ask God not only to cure us but also to *save us* from adverse side effects.

The *Novominsker Rebbe zt"l* said that this is what the Psalmist had in mind when he said: יִשְׁלַח דְּבָרוֹ וְיִרְפָּאֵם וִימַלֵּט מִשְּׁחִיתוֹתָם, *He dispatched His word and cured them, and rescued them from devastation* (*Psalms* 107:20), i.e., when one is cured by the word of God he is rescued from side effects.

~§ Passionate Praise Purifies and Heals

כִּי תְהִלָּתֵנוּ אָתָּה — *for You are our praise.*

This phrase is based on the words of the prophet Jeremiah (17:14) who asked God to heal him: כִּי תְהִלָּתִי אָתָּה, *for You are my praise*. The request is puzzling: What does praising God have to do with good health?

King Solomon gives us an insight into the relationship in *Proverbs* (27:21) where he teaches: מַצְרֵף לַכֶּסֶף וְכוּר לַזָּהָב וְאִישׁ לְפִי מַהֲלָלוֹ, *A refining pot for silver, a crucible for gold, and a man according to his praise.*

This means that just as a fiery crucible refines metal and removes its dross, similarly, a person who prays with fervor and passion is aflame with love and praise for God. This holy spiritual fire purifies the soul, purges the character and cleanses the body of all its physical ailments. Thus we pray: "*Heal us, Hashem...* because we are aflame with Your praises, which should completely purify and cure us!"

Yet another relationship between praise and health is suggested by King Solomon in *Song of Songs* (2:5), where he declares: כִּי חוֹלַת אַהֲבָה אָנִי, *For I am sick with love* [for my beloved God].

The Midrash (*Shir HaShirim Rabbah* 2:14) states: The House of Israel declares: "Master of the universe! We know that all of the sicknesses with which you afflict us are only meant to bring us closer to You. We are literally 'love-sick' because you make us suffer with illness in order to arouse our fervent prayers and love!"

Therefore in our daily prayers we plead: "*Heal us, Hashem!* You need not make us sick in order for us to love and praise You — *You are our praise* already and we promise to continue praising You in good health. You afflict only those who are indifferent to you — we promise not to forget you!"

King Solomon compiled a work called סֶפֶר הָרְפוּאוֹת, *The Book of Cures*, which contains a cure for every malady. *Rav Nachman of Breslav (Likkutei Maharan)* says that Solomon intertwined all these cures in *Song of Songs,* so if a person wishes to effect a cure, he should fervently recite the entire Song of Songs before dawn. (See *Taamei Haminhagim* p. 556).

⫸ When a Cure Is Complete

וְהַעֲלֵה רְפוּאָה שְׁלֵמָה לְכָל מַכּוֹתֵינוּ — *bring 'complete' recovery for all our ailments.*

In this blessing, we pray for a *full* recovery, thereby acknowledging that God is a Healer of a higher order, for when God participates in the healing process the cure is permanent and the ailment never returns. But when man cures on his own, the cure is temporary and illness may recur (*Zohar Vayikra*).

Rav Yaakov Lorberbaum of Lisa teaches that when man attempts to heal on his own the ailment is not really cured, it is merely transferred from one person to another [and it can eventually return to the first patient]. But when God heals, everyone's health improves because not only is this illness obliterated, but a measure of sickness disappears from the world (*Nachlas Yaakov* quoted in *Taamei Haminhagim* p. 42). We keep this concept in mind when we recite these words, *"and bring complete recovery for all of our ailments."* as the Sages teach, "There is no sickness in the entire world which has no cure" (*Midrash Tanchuma; Noach* §8).

⊷§ The Master Healer

כִּי קֵל מֶלֶךְ רוֹפֵא — *For You are God, King, the Healer.*

The title מֶלֶךְ, *King*, appears only rarely in the blessings of the *Amidah*. It appears here to emphasis that even though men are licensed to practice medicine they should never forget that the Master and King of all healers is God Himself.

Moreover, *Zohar* (*Parshas Shelach*) teaches that sickness results when the accusing angels denounce a person for his sins before the Heavenly Tribunal and he is condemned to suffer. But when the sick person repents and accepts God as his King, all is forgiven. Indeed, when the penitent asks for health so he can study Torah and perform *mitzvos*, the accusing angels themselves proclaim: "Make way for this servant of the King!"

One should never lose sight of the fact that God Himself participates in every successful healing procedure. It is the Almighty who literally holds the doctor's hand and guides his heart. King David said of the sick man: ה' יִסְעָדֶנּוּ עַל עֶרֶשׂ דְּוָי, *Hashem will fortify him on the bed of misery* (*Psalms* 41:4). From this verse the Talmud (*Shabbos* 12) derives that God personally supplies the invalid with strength and reinforces his vigor and will to live. Consequently, we know that the שְׁכִינָה, *Divine Presence*, rests at the head of every sick person. A visitor may not sit on the sick man's bed, therefore, for in doing so he would be acting irreverently towards the *Shechinah*, which rests on the sick bed.

Birkei Yosef (*Yoreh Deah* §336) points out that the numerical value of שְׁכִינָה, *Divine Presence*, is 385, which equals that of the phrase רוֹפֵא חִנָּם, *He Who heals for no fee.*

◌§ Painless Compassion

רוֹפֵא נֶאֱמָן וְרַחֲמָן אָתָּה — *You are the faithful and compassionate Healer.*

The human healer often cannot enjoy the luxury of being softhearted and compassionate. If the patient requires a crippling amputation, harsh chemotherapy, or a painful surgical procedure, the doctor cannot say, "My compassion for you won't let me cause you so much pain — we will forego the procedure!" Some say that this is the meaning of the Mishnah (*Kiddushin* 82a) which states: טוֹב שֶׁבָּרוֹפְאִים לְגֵיהִנָּם, *the best of doctors will go to Gehenna,* i.e., if a doctor is too good-hearted and "mercifully" fails to administer painful medical treatment where necessary — he is condemned to severe punishment. Thus if a doctor is to be נֶאֱמָן, *faithful,* to his medical ethics, he cannot always be רַחֲמָן, (overly) *compassionate.*

But Hashem, the Creator of all flesh, can cure mercifully without surgery, medicine, or any pain. With one Divine command, the illness can vanish in a manner which is both *faithful* and *compassionate.*

◌§ Angels of Illness — God's Loyal Agents

The Talmud (*Avodah Zarah* 55a) relates the story of a philosopher named Zunin who asked Rabbi Akiva: "I know and you know that idols are false and helpless, but how do we explain the phenomenon that sometimes sick and crippled people visit a pagan shrine and emerge entirely recovered?" Rabbi Akiva answered with a parable. Once there was a scrupulously honest man whose neighbors would deposit money with him for safekeeping without witnesses. However, one man cast aspersions on his honesty and insisted that two witnesses be present whenever he deposited money. Once he forgot and deposited money with the honest person without witnesses. The honest person's wife saw an opportunity for revenge and suggested to her husband, "When he comes to collect his deposit, let's frighten him and deny that he gave us anything. After all, he has no witnesses now to disprove us!" The honest husband rejected this trick. "Just because this man mistreats us, should we forfeit our precious trait of scrupulous honesty?"

"Similarly," continued Rabbi Akiva, "It is God Himself Who dispatches the angels of suffering and sickness. As they set out on their missions, God adjures each angel as follows: "Swear that you will enter this man only at the specified time and that you will leave him on a certain hour, but only if he is treated by the particular doctor who administers a specific medicine and none other."

The faithful angel swears to fulfill his mission without fail, but when the exact time comes for him to depart, he finds himself in a quandary — because at that moment the sick man decided to seek a miraculous cure at a pagan temple. The angel reasons: "To punish this fool who abandoned God, I should not leave. On the other hand, just because this fool betrayed God, should I violate my solemn oath?" So even as this sinner is bowing to an idol, the faithful angel of sickness departs, and the idol appears to have effected a miracle cure.

Rabbi Yochanan said that this concept explains the verse which describes heavenly afflictions as חֳלָיִם רָעִים וְנֶאֱמָנִים, *hurtful and faithful maladies* (*Deuteronomy* 28:59), i.e., illnesses are hurtful in their mission to punish, but faithful to their oath to obey God's orders.

Maharsha (ibid.) explains that undoubtedly if the sick man repents his sins and prays sincerely, God's mercy will be aroused and He will nullify the vow of the angel of suffering, so that he will forsake the invalid long before the time specified in his oath. Thus, God can cure suffering in one of two ways. If the patient fails to repent, then the Divinely ordained suffering must run its full course, at which time God will assume His role of רוֹפֵא נֶאֱמָן, *faithful Healer*, and cause His angels to depart at the pre-ordained time. However, if the patient learns from his suffering and repents, then God immediately acts as רוֹפֵא רַחֲמָן, *the compassionate Healer*, and sends an instant cure.

✑§ Israel's Privilege

בָּרוּךְ אַתָּה ה׳ רוֹפֵא חוֹלֵי עַמּוֹ יִשְׂרָאֵל — *Blessed are You, HASHEM, Who heals the sick of His people Israel.*

Hashem's healing is not restricted to Jews, as we acknowledge in the conclusion of the *Asher Yatzar* prayer: בָּרוּךְ אַתָּה ה׳ רוֹפֵא כָל בָּשָׂר וּמַפְלִיא לַעֲשׂוֹת, *Blessed are You, HASHEM, Who heals all flesh and acts wondrously*. However, God promised to give special attention to the health of His Chosen People. As they fled from Egypt and entered the treacherous and parched Wilderness, God said: *"If you will carefully listen to HASHEM, your God, and do what is upright in His eyes, heed all of His commandments and obey all His decrees, then I will not afflict you with any of the maladies that I brought upon Egypt; for I am HASHEM, your Healer"* (*Exodus* 15:26).

Tur (Orach Chaim 11b) notes that there are twenty-seven words in this eighth blessing of רְפָאֵנוּ. By this number, the Men of the Great Assembly alluded to many things:

☐ The aforementioned verse (*Exodus* 15:26) wherein God promises to be the Healer of the Jewish people, contains twenty-seven words;

☐ There are twenty-seven verses in *Genesis* 17, the chapter which introduces the *mitzvah* of *milah* to Abraham and his descendants, and, as stated above, the themes of healing and *bris milah* are intertwined;

☐ There are twenty-seven letters in the verse כִּי חַיִּים הֵם לְמֹצְאֵיהֶם וּלְכָל בְּשָׂרוֹ מַרְפֵּא, *For they [words of Torah] are life to those who find them, and a healing to all their flesh* (*Proverbs* 4:22); for flesh find its cure in the merit of Torah and *mitzvos*.

Siddur Chassidei Ashkenaz lists numerous themes that are reflected in the number twenty-seven — most significantly the fact that there are twenty-seven letters in the Hebrew alphabet with which the Torah is written (twenty-two regular letters, and five variations used at the end of a word). This reminds us that by virtue of dedication to the fundamentals of Torah will the flesh be healed.

Similarly, we pray for Divine guidance. ''O, God, if our thoughts pull us away from You, please tug on our heartstrings and pull us back to where our hearts and bodies belong!''

9

בִּרְכַּת הַשָּׁנִים / Year of Prosperity

בָּרֵךְ עָלֵינוּ יהוה אֱלֹהֵינוּ אֶת הַשָּׁנָה הַזֹּאת וְאֶת כָּל מִינֵי
תְבוּאָתָהּ לְטוֹבָה, וְתֵן (בְּרָכָה / טַל וּמָטָר לִבְרָכָה)
עַל פְּנֵי הָאֲדָמָה, וְשַׂבְּעֵנוּ מִטּוּבֶךָ, וּבָרֵךְ שְׁנָתֵנוּ כַּשָּׁנִים
הַטּוֹבוֹת. בָּרוּךְ אַתָּה יהוה, מְבָרֵךְ הַשָּׁנִים.

Bless on our behalf – O HASHEM, our God – this year and
all its kinds of crops for the best, and give (blessing / dew
and rain for a blessing) on the face of the earth, and satisfy
us from Your bounty, and bless our year like the best years.
Blessed are You, HASHEM, Who blesses the years.

After asking for physical health in the eighth blessing, we now request financial health in this ninth blessing. The Talmud (*Megillah* 17b) explains that the Men of the Great Assembly purposely made this blessing number nine to correspond to the prayer in the ninth chapter of the Book of Psalms: *Break the strength of the wicked* (*Psalms* 10:15) [see ensuing paragraph for clarification]. There, David condemns the unscrupulous manipulators who drive up food prices in order to reap fabulous profits at the expense of the impoverished masses. Similarly, in this blessing we ask God to provide us with a trouble-free livelihood.

[Originally, chapters 1 and 2 of Psalms were one chapter, so that the verse cited by the Sages was in chapter 9. Later, the first chapter was split, so that the above verse is now in chapter 10. See *Rashi* and *Tos.* to *Megillah* 17b. The reason for splitting the first Psalm into two parts is discussed at length in the commentary to the meditation after the *Amidah*, יִהְיוּ לְרָצוֹן אִמְרֵי פִי, *May the words of my mouth find favor.*]

Furthermore, we request that God grant us true prosperity, not false prosperity. Sharp upturns in the business cycle may inflate property values, launch corporate takeovers, and cause stock prices to skyrocket. Unscrupulous speculators may take advantage of this situation to drive up optimism to unrealistic levels. Suddenly, everyone is investing in stocks, junk bonds, and real estate, and it seems as if instant wealth is within anyone's reach. Then the bubble bursts and countless investors and innocent bystanders are the victims of yet another recession. To help prevent this scenario, we beseech God to protect us from the false prosperity created by selfish manipulators. We desire lasting prosperity which can only come as a gift from God.

◆§ *Nine Represents Goodness*

Interestingly, the ninth letter in the Hebrew alphabet is ט, *tes*, and the first ט that appears in the Torah is in the word טוֹב, *good* (*Genesis* 1:4). This demonstrates that the letter ט and the number nine represent goodness. The Talmud teaches that if one sees the letter ט in a dream, it is a good sign (*Bava Kamma* 55a; *Rashi*). During the six days of creation, God evaluated each day's accomplishments and pronounced judgment on it: וַיַּרְא אֱלֹקִים כִּי טוֹב, *God saw that it was good* (*Genesis* 1:12). Therefore, in this *ninth* blessing we ask God to bestow upon us the goodness which He invested in creation.

We realize that this goodness will not come overnight. God's blessings often emerge gradually, like a baby emerging from its mother's womb after *nine* months of gestation. We have patience, because God's gift of true, enduring prosperity is worth the wait.

◆§ Annual Bounty

בָּרֵךְ עָלֵינוּ ה' אֱלֹהֵינוּ אֶת הַשָּׁנָה הַזֹּאת — *Bless on our behalf — O HASHEM, our God — this year.*

In this blessing we ask for prosperity for *this year*, because one's wealth is determined on an annual basis. As the Talmud (*Beitzah* 16b) teaches, "All of a person's food and sustenance for the coming year is Divinely decreed on Rosh Hashanah."

Nevertheless, we continue to pray for our sustenance every day of the year because our allotment can be withheld for a variety of sins. During the course of the year, God reviews every man's actions and spiritual level and may issue new decrees of poverty and suffering against the man who on Rosh Hashanah was bountifully blessed. In addition, the *Baal Shem Tov* teaches that every day God decides how much pleasure and satisfaction each person will derive from the possessions that he already has, and so we must constantly pray for *daily* satisfaction.

◆§ Living in the Present

The emphasis on הַשָּׁנָה הַזֹּאת, *this year*, serves to remind one of the importance of living in the present. Often we are overwhelmed and intimidated by the realities of the present and seek refuge in fantasies about the future. This blessing urges us to live in the present and plan for the immediate future.

A master of the Mussar movement, *Rav Yosef Yoizel Horowitz, the Alter of Novardok*, would say: "Even the worst present is far more beautiful than the brightest future." He also said, "A person must relinquish all of his tomorrows for one today, lest he come to relinquish all of his todays for one tomorrow."

✑§ Enjoy Today!

The Talmud (*Eruvin* 54a) teaches us a wonderful and extremely useful lesson: "Grab and eat! Grab and drink! — For this world resembles a wedding banquet." *Rashi* (ibid.) explains this as a vivid allegory. Just as the wedding feast is fleeting — one day there is food for everyone and the next day there is nothing — so, too, our time on this world is very short. If God bestows financial means upon us, we should use it for worthwhile purposes immediately, because who knows what tomorrow brings. Certainly, it should not be squandered on unnecessary luxuries, but we all have certain pressing needs that we are tempted to push off because we are afraid to spend too much money. This is the wrong attitude. It is often wrong to deprive oneself now in order to put away a nest egg for the proverbial "rainy day." God, Who sent you this money today, has enough and can take care of your future as well. Hoarding is a sign of insecurity, as the Talmud (*Sotah* 48b) teaches: "He who has bread in his basket today but worries, 'What will I eat tomorrow?' — that is a man of meager faith." Can we imagine how many lives were not saved, institutions not built, children's lives not improved, because people were afraid to dip into their "rainy day accounts"?

✑§ Secure Lines of Supply

וְאֶת כָּל מִינֵי תְבוּאָתָהּ לְטוֹבָה — *And all its kinds of crops for the best.*

The Talmud (*Menachos* 103b) illustrates that a person is considered financially secure only when he owns land that can produce enough crops to sustain all his needs (see *Maharsha* ibid.). This is shown in the Torah portion that describes the travails that await the Jewish people if they forsake God. It says: וְהָיוּ חַיֶּיךָ תְּלָאִים לְךָ מִנֶּגֶד, *And your life shall hang in doubt before you* (Deut. 28:66). This verse refers to the man who purchases a year's supply of wheat but is still concerned about wheat for the next year.

וּפָחַדְתָּ לַיְלָה וְיוֹמָם, *And you shall be fearful night and day* (ibid.). This verse describes the man who buys wheat for this week while worrying about next week.

וְלֹא תַאֲמִין בְּחַיֶּיךָ, *And you shall have no faith in your life* (ibid.). This verse refers to the man who depends on the baker to supply his daily needs.

We therefore ask God to constantly bless our *own* crops which can provide a more secure and reliable source of sustenance.

We request that God not only give us sustenance, but also peace of mind in obtaining it. Let us enjoy job security, and not be anxious about our careers and our future. Let us enjoy the comfortable assurance that our supply lines are open and unthreatened by shortages.

In some countries people may earn fine incomes, but their money does them no good because the shelves in the stores are empty. People spend long, miserable days enduring endless lines just to purchase the basic staples of life. Some countries have an abundance of one product and an utter dearth of another essential item. For this reason, we pray for *all kinds of crops*, at all times, for all people.

◄§ A Year's Sustenance

The Mishnah (*Peah* 8) establishes that a person with two hundred *zuz* or more is ineligible for the agricultural gifts given to the poor. The commentaries (*Rav; Rash; Rosh*) explain that the Rabbis calculated that two hundred *zuz* was sufficient to cover all of a person's basic expenses for one year. Therefore, even if a person had 199 *zuz* (which is also the numerical value of צְדָקָה, *charity*), he is below the established poverty level and may take gifts as one of the poor. From this it is clear that the Torah's standard for financial security is one full year's sustenance in hand.

◄§ Attitude Is Everything

Rabbi Yitzchak Blazer (*Kochvei Ohr* 11) notes an apparent contradiction between two Talmudic statements. On the one hand the Talmud (*Menachos* 103b) states that even a person with an entire year's supply of wheat is cursed if he is insecure about the following year. On the other hand the Talmud (*Yoma* 76a) teaches that God rationed the manna to the Jews in the wilderness on a daily basis for just that reason — so that they should feel no security for the future and turn their hearts to Him. And the manna was considered a blessing!

This dichotomy can be understood by analyzing a person's attitude. A person who develops a sense of security in God is delighted that God provides for him anew each and every day. As long as he has bread in his basket today, he does not give a thought to what he will eat tomorrow. But the man who does not recognize God as the source of his sustenance will be consumed by anxiety even if he has an entire year's supply, because he is already worrying about next year.

✌§ Global Prosperity

וְתֵן בְּרָכָה עַל פְּנֵי הָאֲדָמָה — *And give a blessing on the face of the earth.*

The term "on the face of the earth" can be interpreted several ways. It can refer to the entire globe and denote that we are asking for world-wide prosperity, not merely personal or local bounty. We recognize that the fortunes of all mankind are related and one should not be able to enjoy personal abundance if elsewhere others are suffering.

The Talmud (*Taanis* 24b) illustrates this idea with the story of the pious Tanna, Rabbi Chanina ben Dosa, who was journeying on the open road when suddenly he found himself being drenched by a cloudburst. He prayed: "Master of the universe! All the world is comfortable in their homes while Chanina is suffering!" Immediately, the downpour stopped. After reaching the safety of his home, Rabbi Chanina turned to God again and cried out: "Master of the universe! The whole world is suffering for lack of vital rain while Chanina is home in comfort!" Immediately, the life-giving rains resumed.

✌§ Don't Devour Your Hereafter

By requesting a blessing *"on the face of the earth"* one keeps in mind to ask only for prosperity that comes from this world. No one should want to prematurely receive some of the reward which is stored up for eternal enjoyment in the Hereafter.

The Midrash (*Shemos Rabbah* 52:3) tells how Rabbi Shimon Bar Yochai's students were impressed by a former student who had made a fortune in the business world. Rabbi Shimon brought the entire student body to a valley and cried out, "Valley! Valley! Give forth dinars of gold!" The valley instantly filled with gold coins. The rabbi turned to his disciples and said, "If it is wealth that you want, take all the gold you desire. But remember, whoever takes from here is taking from his portion in the World to Come!"

Similarly, the Talmud (*Taanis* 24b) relates how the merit of Rabbi Chanina ben Dosa brought sustenance to the entire world, yet he himself lived in grinding poverty. One day the harsh deprivation stirred Rabbi Chanina's devoted but desperate wife, and she pleaded with her husband to pray to God for livelihood. Reluctantly the *tzaddik* prayed and was answered by a wondrous hand that reached down from heaven and gave Chanina a solid-gold table leg! Afterwards, Chanina had a dream in which he saw all the *tzaddikim* in the World to Come seated at sturdy three-legged tables, while he and his wife were sitting at a table with only two legs. When he awoke, Rabbi Chanina explained to his wife that it was their Divine destiny to serve God in destitution in this world, so that their future portion would be enhanced. If they requested wealth in this world they would receive it, but it would be taken from their share in the World to Come. They would be transforming spiritual bliss into material blessing. At his wife's suggestion, Rabbi Chanina prayed that heaven retrieve the golden leg, and it was restored to their heavenly table.

Accordingly, in this prayer we take care to emphasize that we certainly want blessings of prosperity, but want them to come *on the face of the earth* — from a source in this world, and *not* from our share in the World to Come.

◄§ Sustenance at the Source

Another interpretation of *"a blessing on the face of the earth"* is that the blessing should be close to home, on the nearby plot which faces us. As King Solomon said: יְהִי מְקוֹרְךָ בָרוּךְ, *May your fountainhead be blessed* (Proverbs 5:18), to which the Midrash comments, "Fortunate is the man whose livelihood comes from his own hometown."

Chovos Halevavos tells the tale of a saintly man who traveled to a distant land seeking a livelihood. He arrived at a city whose inhabitants were idol worshipers. "Fools!" he rebuked them. "Why do you worship helpless images of wood and stone? Join me and worship the living, all-powerful God who feeds and supports all of mankind!"

The pagans retorted, "Your own actions contradict your words! If indeed your God supports all men at all times and in all places, then why did you jeopardize your life by traveling so far to seek your fortune? You should have stayed home and let your God provide for you there!"

Upon hearing their reproach, the pious man immediately resolved never to leave his land again in order to search for sustenance. *Tehillas Hashem* comments that this is what King David had in mind when he advised, *"Trust in HASHEM and do good; dwell in your own homeland and be sustained by your faith"* (Psalms 37:3).

~s Blessings from Paradise

Finally, "the face of the earth" may be interpreted as a reference to the Land of Israel. When God exiled him from the Garden of Eden, Cain said, *"Behold, You have banished me this day from the face of the earth"* (Genesis 4:14). The *Vilna Gaon* (*Aderes Eliyahu*) comments that God designed the earth to parallel the shape of the human body. The body has 248 limbs, and the earth has many corresponding protrusions, inclines and indentations. The body has 365 sinews and veins, and the earth has corresponding channels and streams. The blessing and bounty which God infuses into the earth resembles the soul which is infused into the body. Just as the soul enters the body via the nostrils, so does God's bounty flow down to earth via the "face of the earth," which is the Garden of Eden, and the Holy Land of Israel. Therefore, we pray to God to *"send a blessing on the face of the earth,"* i.e. send it through the Paradise of Eden and from there it will radiate all over the globe via *Eretz Yisrael*.

~s Nourishment for the Soul

וְשַׂבְּעֵנוּ מִטּוּבֶךְ — *And satisfy us from Your bounty.*

Yaaros Dvash elaborates: Food acquired in a dishonest manner is devoid of the holiness which nourishes the soul. We therefore ask God to satisfy us from *His* bounty, not from earnings to which we are not entitled.

~s Faith and Long Life

The Talmud (*Sotah* 47b) describes how toward the end of the Second Commonwealth, "As the number of people who depended on gifts increased, the days of life became fewer, and the length of years was shortened, as it says, *he who hates gifts shall live* (Proverbs 15:27)." Accordingly, we pray that Hashem bless us with sustenance directly from His hands, so that we should not be tempted to depend on gifts that will shorten our years and diminish our quality of life.

~s The Side Effect of Success

We ask for prosperity with utmost caution and trepidation, as success can easily be a curse, for the perils of prosperity are many:

One: Prosperity can easily lead to arrogance, as the Torah warns: *"Take care ... lest you eat and are contented and build fine homes in which to live, and your herds and flocks multiply and your silver and gold increase and your heart grows proud and you forget HASHEM, your God ... and you say in your heart, 'My power and the might of my hand have gotten me this wealth' "* (*Deut.* 8:11-17).

Two: Property must be maintained and protected, a laborious and pressing burden as the Mishnah (*Avos* 2:8) teaches: מַרְבֶּה נְכָסִים מַרְבֶּה דְאָגָה, *He who increases his possessions increases his worries.* And as King Solomon observed: *The sleep of the [poor] laborer is sweet, whether he eats little or much; but the prosperity of the rich man prevents him from restful sleep* (*Ecclesiastes* 5:11).

In this vein, a penniless beggar once said to his mighty king, "Your majesty, you are much needier than I, for I need very little to satisfy my beggarly wants, while you need so much to live on your royal scale!"

Three: The greatest hazard of prosperity is that it fosters insatiable greed. As the *Vilna Gaon* observed: "Materialism is like saltwater — the more you drink, the thirstier you become!" The Midrash (*Koheles Rabbah* 1:34) also teaches: No man leaves this world having amassed half of his desires. If he has one hundred, he desires two hundred. If he succeeds in acquiring two hundred, he wants four hundred, as it says: *He who loves money shall never be satisfied with money* (*Ecclesiastes* 5:9).

With all these potential dangers in mind we pray to God: *Satisfy us from Your bounty.* We can be content only when we realize that the source of our success is You, not our own efforts. If we humbly appreciate that all of our blessings are the fruits of God's generosity, we will experience no negative side effects, as King Solomon said: בִּרְכַּת ה' הִיא תַעֲשִׁיר וְלֹא יוֹסִף עֶצֶב עִמָּה, *The bounty of HASHEM — it truly enriches — and He adds no sorrow to it* (*Proverbs* 10:22).

⋈§ *A Glimpse of Future Goodness*

The Torah relates that when Abraham died, he was זָקֵן וְשָׂבֵעַ, *old and satisfied* (*Genesis* 25:8). *Ramban* (*Comm.* ibid.) observes that Abraham was unique because, ordinarily, men as wealthy as he are never satisfied; the more they have the more they want. Abraham and all the righteous people who emulate him, however, are filled with a yearning to know

God and merit a special blessing. The Midrash (*Bereishis Rabbah* 62:2) says: "The Holy One, Blessed is He, shows the righteous in this world the blissful reward that He is destined to give them in the World to Come, and their souls are filled with contentment and they peacefully slip into the slumber of death."

Thus we pray that God will *satisfy us* with a glimpse of the bounty He has reserved for us in the Hereafter, removing from our hearts all excessive desires for this world.

⋘ The Source of Blessing

The version endorsed by *Rabbeinu Asher* (*Rosh*) and other authorities is וְשַׂבְּעֵנוּ מִטּוּבֶךְ [see *Mishnah Berurah, Orach Chaim* 117]. However, many commentaries, including the *Vilna Gaon*, rule that this phrase should be וְשַׂבְּעֵנוּ מִטּוּבָה, *and satisfy us from 'its' goodness*, meaning the goodness of the Land of Israel. [See explanation of "*a blessing on the face of the earth*" based on words of the *Vilna Gaon*.] This idea that *Eretz Yisrael* is the source of global bounty is consonant with the teaching of *Ramban* in the introduction to his commentary on the Torah. There, he cites the Rabbinic tradition that King Solomon successfully cultivated every type of fruit, vegetable and plant in Jerusalem; even exotic and rare spices thrived in his gardens. This accomplishment defied all established rules of agriculture, for many plants only grow in certain regions.

Ramban explains that at Creation, God first invested Jerusalem with the substances necessary to produce all the fruits of the earth. Then He disseminated those substances throughout the world, meaning that all the nutrients found anywhere in the earth emanate from Zion. If the soil of one area of the world is suited to a particular fruit, it is because that land has a "pipeline," as it were, from Jerusalem feeding it the necessary ingredients for that fruit. In his wisdom, Solomon was able to locate the exact spot in Jerusalem where each vein of fertility began; thus he successfully grew every plant on its respective site [see *Tosafos Rabbeinu Peretz, Pesachim* 8b].

Bach (comm. to *Tur, Orach Chaim* ch. 28) describes how God spreads His sanctity throughout the world via the fruits of *Eretz Yisrael*. He fills them with holy sparks which sanctify those who eat them!

◆§ A Constant Flow

וּבָרֵךְ שְׁנָתֵנוּ כַּשָּׁנִים הַטּוֹבוֹת — *And bless our year like the best years.*

We ask for a blessing which is apportioned evenly throughout the year. What good is a financial windfall at the end of the year, if a cash-flow crisis has already bankrupted the business at the beginning of the year? Of what value is a bumper crop at the year's start, if cataclysmic weather conditions destroy it later? Thus we pray for a year of constant blessing like the *best years*, i.e. those that were blessed from beginning to end.

◆§ A Timely Return

בָּרוּךְ אַתָּה ה' מְבָרֵךְ הַשָּׁנִים — *Blessed are You, HASHEM, Who blesses the years.*

People often invest enormous amounts of time, money and energy into a venture that fails to produce a return for a long time. Even when the investors finally realize a profit, their initial frustration and disappointment may make them wonder whether the final profit was worth all their grief. When God blesses someone's endeavors, he realizes a timely return, within a reasonable amount of time, such as a year, and enjoys the satisfaction of seeing his property flourish. Such was the case with our Patriarch Isaac, of whom it is written: *And Isaac planted in that land and received in that year a hundredfold, for HASHEM blessed him* (Genesis 26:12). *Shibbolei Halekket* quotes the Midrash that when the ministering angels saw Isaac's bounty they chanted, "Blessed are you, HASHEM, Who blesses the years."

10

קִבּוּץ גָּלֻיּוֹת / Ingathering of Exiles

תְּקַע בְּשׁוֹפָר גָּדוֹל לְחֵרוּתֵנוּ, וְשָׂא נֵס לְקַבֵּץ גָּלֻיּוֹתֵינוּ, וְקַבְּצֵנוּ יַחַד מֵאַרְבַּע כַּנְפוֹת הָאָרֶץ. בָּרוּךְ אַתָּה יהוה, מְקַבֵּץ נִדְחֵי עַמּוֹ יִשְׂרָאֵל.

Sound the great shofar for our freedom, raise the banner to gather our exiles and gather us together from the four corners of the earth. Blessed are You, HASHEM, Who gathers in the dispersed of His people Israel.

⋞ Return and Bounty

Throughout its two thousand-year exile, the Jewish people have always remained faithful to their homeland, *Eretz Yisrael*, and in turn, the Holy Land has been loyal to the Jews. Over the last nineteen centuries, many conquering invaders have attempted to strike roots in our land, but she has rejected them all, preferring instead to let the desolation of its once fertile fields and valleys reflect the heaviness of Israel's exiled heart.

The bond of loyalty that links the land to her true owners is reflected in the order of the *Amidah*. In the ninth blessing we ask God to shower His blessing on the Holy Land and from there to spread the bounty throughout the world. We immediately follow with this tenth blessing — an entreaty for the ingathering of exiles — because, as *Megillah* 17b teaches, it is inconceivable that *Eretz Yisrael* should give forth her bounty unless her children return to her soil. This concept is based on the prophecy of Ezekiel (36:8) who said: *"You mountains of Israel sprout your branches and give forth your fruit to My people Israel, for they are close to returning."*

Rabbi Abba taught (*Sanhedrin* 98a): There is no more obvious sign of the final redemption than the flowering of Israel's hills. If the Land of Israel ceases her mourning, it is because her children are returning home.

⋞ Ten Symbolizes Sanctity and Unity

The request to return to *Eretz Yisrael* is appropriately placed in the tenth blessing because the unique nature of the land is bound to this number. *Rambam* writes (*Hilchos Beis Habechirah* 7:12), "The holiness of *Eretz Yisrael* surpasses that of all other places in the world, and in *Eretz Yisrael* itself there are ten levels of sanctity" (based on *Mishnah Keilim* 1:6).

Additionally, the tenth letter of the Hebrew alphabet, י, *yud*, is the smallest letter and consists of a single component. Thus the tiny *yud* symbolizes humility, the essential component of national unity. When the Jews allow the bounty of the land to fill them with pride, their arrogance leads to divisive quarrels which tear the nation apart. But when Jews allow themselves to be influenced by the special tenfold sanctity of the Holy Land, they are humbled by God's Presence, which fuses them into indivisible solidarity. For this reason the Divine Presence rests only upon a quorum of ten men, a *minyan*, because anything less than ten is considered a mere fragment, while ten is a complete unit.

Consequently, the number ten is appropriate when praying for reunification of the scattered and estranged exiles of Israel. In this vein, *Shibbolei Halekket*, quoting the Midrash, says that when Jacob came to Egypt and Joseph was reunited with his brothers, the ministering angels said, "Blessed are You, HASHEM, Who gathers in the dispersed of His people Israel." Only nine brothers participated in the malicious sale of Joseph, since Reuben and Benjamin were absent. So when the nine estranged brothers reconciled with Joseph, they became ten.

ᴇ§ *The Historic Horn*

תְּקַע בְּשׁוֹפָר גָּדוֹל לְחֵרוּתֵנוּ — *Sound the great shofar for our freedom.*

What is the great *shofar*? The ram that Abraham sacrificed in place of his son, Isaac, had two horns that were to play historic roles. The smaller, left horn was sounded at Mount Sinai when God revealed Himself and gave the Torah to Israel. The larger, right one will be sounded by God when the time comes to redeem the exiles of Israel (*Pirkei d'Rabbi Eliezer* Chapter 31).

The prophet Isaiah foretells this great event. *And it shall come to pass on that day that a great shofar shall be sounded and they shall return, those who were lost in the land of Ashur and the outcasts in the land of Egypt, and they shall bow down to HASHEM on His holy mountain, in Jerusalem* (Isaiah 27:13).

ᴇ§ *Repentance and Redemption*

Nothing stirs the soul as powerfully as the *shofar's* blast. *Rambam* explains that the *shofar* cries out figuratively, "Awake, O sleepers, from your sleep! Arouse yourselves, O slumberers, from your slumber! Scrutinize your deeds and return with contrition! Remember your Creator! Those of you who have forgotten the truth in the futilities of the times and have let all your years elapse in futility and emptiness... peer into your souls, improve your ways and your deeds. Each of you should abandon his evil ways and bad thoughts" (*Hilchos Teshuvah* 3:4).

The Tenth Blessing / 155

The sounding of the *shofar* prior to redemption conforms with *Rambam's* principle: The Torah guarantees that the Jewish people are destined to return to God at the end of the exile period and their repentance will lead to immediate redemption (ibid. 7:5).

⋑ Two Types of Exiled Jews

וְשָׂא נֵס לְקַבֵּץ גָּלֻיּוֹתֵינוּ — *Raise the banner to gather our exiles.*

There are two steps toward complete redemption, because there are two types of exiled Jews. For some Jews, the signal received from the initial blast will be sufficient to arouse them and they will return immediately. *Meshech Chochmah* (*Deuteronomy* 30:3) observes that these Jews always feel like strangers in the lands of exile, never fully adapting to their host countries. They yearn for an opportunity to return home, and even the faint sound of the *shofar* heard from a distance is enough to cause them to return to their homeland.

The sound of the *shofar* may well be an allegorical reference to the voice of God which speaks within the soul. The devout will hear the call and follow their homing instinct to be among the first who return.

Other Jews, however, will not be moved until they see a clear signal, one that will make a powerful visual impact. *Meshech Chochmah* describes this group, the majority of whom are very comfortable in exile and call it home. They dread the privations of the primitive undeveloped Holy Land. Prosperity has dulled their senses, so they are oblivious to the *shofar* sounds which call them homeward. For them we ask God to *raise the banner*, to display unmistakable, visible evidence as it says, *And it shall come to pass on that day that HASHEM will stretch out His hand again, a second time, to recover the remnant of His people that shall be left over from Ashur and from Egypt. . . and He shall raise a banner for the nations and shall assemble the outcasts of Israel and gather together the dispersed of Judah from the four corners of the earth* (Isaiah 11:11,12).

⋑ Miraculous Redemption

The *Munkatcher Rebbe, Rav Chaim Elazar Shapiro,* translates the word נֵס as *miracle* and explains that the real ingathering of exiles cannot take place through conventional, political, or military means.

The Jewish people will return permanently to its land only through overt, Divine action which we pray for and await with patient faith (*Darkei Chaim V'Sholom* p. 54).

⋙ Rising to New Heights

The prayer *Raise the banner to gather our exiles* alludes to the fact that the spiritual status of each Jew will rise dramatically upon returning to the Holy Land. The Talmud (*Kesubos* 75a) quotes *Psalms* (87:5): וּלְצִיּוֹן יֵאָמַר אִישׁ וְאִישׁ יֻלַּד בָּהּ, *But of Zion it can be said: "Man after man was born in her."*

The Talmud explains the double term אִישׁ וְאִישׁ [lit. *a man and a man*] to mean that the inhabitants of the Holy Land are twice as great as those of other countries. The example of R' Yirmiah is cited. When he lived in Babylon, he was an inferior student who failed to fully comprehend his lessons, but when he moved to *Eretz Yisrael*, his talents developed so fast that he quickly surpassed his former associates who remained in Babylon.

Rashi (comm. to *Kesubos* 75a) explains this verse as a prophecy for the future. In the Messianic era, all the empires and nations of the world will appreciate those people born in Zion, and whenever they identify a native of Zion stranded in exile, they will eagerly escort him home.

⋙ Yearn to Return to Zion

The Talmud (*Kesubos* 75a) also says that the double term אִישׁ וְאִישׁ teaches that two types of people can be called children of Zion: the person who was actually born there and the one who always yearned to live there.

At the time of the British mandate over Palestine, the authorities were very strict about immigration, and limited the number of Jews who entered the Land. However, any Jew who declared that he had been born in Palestine was exempt from the quota system and was given permission to reenter.

Once, a group of desperate Jews contacted Rav Yosef Chaim Sonnenfeld, the leading Rabbi in Jerusalem. They were foreign born, and the only way they could possibly enter *Eretz Yisrael* was by declaring that they were born there. Although the Rav was a scrupulously honest man, he permitted them to make this declaration. "The Talmud teaches that both the man born in Zion and the man who yearns to live there equally deserve to be called children of Zion," he explained (*Ha'ish al Hachomah*, vol. II, p. 154).

While reciting this prayer for the ingathering of the exiles, therefore, it is very important to yearn for our homeland. The very expression of longing for Zion can effect a wondrous transformation in a Jew.

⋙ Out of Diversity, Harmony!

וְקַבְּצֵנוּ יַחַד מֵאַרְבַּע כַּנְפוֹת הָאָרֶץ — *And gather us together from the four corners of the earth.*

It would be insufficient for God to simply *gather us* physically; we must also be יַחַד, *together*, spiritually and ideologically, to prevent the redemption from disintegrating because of discord, just as the current exile was caused by disunity and hatred. Despite our different customs and attitudes which developed in the various places of exile, and despite our diverse features and languages which evolved throughout the four corners of the globe, we pray that Hashem will help us overcome these differences so that we can rebuild a unified Jewish nation (*Rav Avigdor Miller, "Praise My Soul"*).

The Talmud (*Taanis* 31a) describes this ultimate harmony and unification: Rabbi Elazar said that in the future the righteous will form a circle around the Holy One, Blessed is He, in the Garden of Eden, and each will point to Him proclaiming, "Behold, this is our God, we placed our hopes in Him and He saved us" (*Isaiah* 25:9).

Rabbi Akiva Eiger explains that in this world of diversity, and especially in the exile, it is difficult to detect the common thread that binds all righteous Jews. Vast differences in customs, dress and liturgy separate the *Sephardi* from the *Ashkenazi*, the *chassid* from the *misnagged*, the kabbalist from the student of *mussar*. Physically, Yemenite Jews hardly look like their European brothers.

For this reason, God will demonstrate that all these diverse elements were truly united all along by a brotherhood of common belief. Every *tzaddik* will take up a different position around the circle, no two positions exactly alike. In fact, each person will be diametrically opposite the one on the other side. Nevertheless, all will be united by a common focal point at the center of the circle. They will proclaim: "Our differences are merely superficial, our means and methods of preserving our traditions vary, and we have different approaches from where we start; but our final goal is one and the same. The essence of our lives is the service of God."

◂§ Solidarity Through Torah

Maharal writes that the Torah shares the history of the Jewish people. At Sinai, all Jews were united in perfect harmony כְּאִישׁ אֶחָד בְּלֵב אֶחָד, *as one person with one heart* (*Rashi, Exodus* 19:2). Similarly, the Torah they received was completely organized and arranged for them. No search was necessary to find answers to any questions. But as the Jews became dispersed, the Torah followed suit, becoming progressively disorganized, a process the Talmud (*Shabbos* 138b) foretells will end in the chaotic pre-Messianic era when the Jews will be scattered across the earth and, likewise, it will be impossible to find one clear, undisputed, halachic ruling that will be accepted universally.

The only way the Jewish people can turn the tide of discord and dispersion is to follow the advice of our Sages: אָמַר רַבִּי חֲנִינָא: אֵין הַגָּלֻיּוֹת מִתְכַּנְּסוֹת אֶלָּא בִּזְכוּת לִמּוּד הַמִּשְׁנָיוֹת, *Rabbi Chanina taught: The exiles will be assembled only by virtue of the study of the Mishnah* (*Yalkut Shimoni, Hoshea* #8). When Jews rally around the banner of organized Torah study, they will be ready to behold the banner of redemption.

◂§ Ingathering of hte Castaways

בָּרוּךְ אַתָּה ה' מְקַבֵּץ נִדְחֵי עַמּוֹ יִשְׂרָאֵל — *Blessed are You, HASHEM, Who gathers in the dispersed of His people Israel.*

The word נִדָּח means one who is lost, castaway, abandoned. This blessing says that even the most estranged Jew in the most remote corner of the globe will be summoned homeward. Even those who don't know they are Jewish will stir. According to many Sages in the Mishnah and Talmud (*Sanhedrin* 110b), even the ten lost tribes who seem to have disappeared forever will return to Israel.

Indeed, even before the future ingathering of the exiles, God constantly reaches out to save those who seem to have "dropped out" of the ranks of Israel, as we read: *The Lord does not take away life, rather He devises means to prevent the abandoned from remaining abandoned* [לְבִלְתִּי יִדַּח מִמֶּנּוּ נִדָּח] (*II Samuel* 14:14).

We mourn for the Jews who are estranged from their roots. We never despair for their return to the fold and we pray for them in the words of King David, *"I have strayed like a lost sheep — seek out Your servant"* (*Psalms* 119:176).

11
דִּין / Restoration of Justice

הָשִׁיבָה שׁוֹפְטֵינוּ כְּבָרִאשׁוֹנָה, וְיוֹעֲצֵינוּ כְּבַתְּחִלָּה, וְהָסֵר מִמֶּנּוּ יָגוֹן וַאֲנָחָה, וּמְלוֹךְ עָלֵינוּ אַתָּה יהוה לְבַדְּךָ בְּחֶסֶד וּבְרַחֲמִים, וְצַדְּקֵנוּ בַּמִּשְׁפָּט. בָּרוּךְ אַתָּה יהוה, מֶלֶךְ אוֹהֵב צְדָקָה וּמִשְׁפָּט.

Restore our judges as in earliest times and our counselors as at first; remove from us sorrow and groan; and reign over us – You, HASHEM, alone – with kindness and compassion, and justify us through judgment. Blessed are You, HASHEM, the King Who loves righteousness and judgment.

◦§ Fearless Justice

The Talmud (*Megillah* 17b) observes that following the ingathering of exiles, the justice system will be re-established in Israel. Corruption and perversion of justice was one of the main causes of our people's decay and banishment. As the Talmud (*Shabbos* 118b) graphically describes, the judges of the Temple era were afraid of powerful and influential litigants and twisted the law in their favor.

The Torah's qualifications for judges include not only wisdom and honesty, but fearlessness. The judge trembles only before God; no mortal can intimidate him. Therefore, when Jewish society is renewed in the future, steps must be taken to rebuild a justice system that will not be undermined again.

◦§ Eleven Fundamentals

We pray for integrity and justice in the eleventh blessing because the number eleven is closely identified with the themes of honesty and decency. The Talmud (*Makkos* 24a) teaches that although six hundred and thirteen *mitzvos* were given at Sinai, the leaders of every generation have the right to place special emphasis on certain commands according to the needs of the times. In this manner, David stressed *eleven* principles of conduct בֵּין אָדָם לַחֲבֵרוֹ, improving man's relationship with his fellow man. All *eleven* principles are examples of לִפְנִים מִשּׁוּרַת הַדִּין, *acting beyond the letter of the law*, i.e., conducting oneself above the minimum requirements of the Torah. In *Psalms* 15:5, David describes the righteous man who follows these eleven fundamentals, the last of which is, "...*he takes no bribe against the innocent.*" The Talmud (ibid.) says this phrase describes the judge who is scrupulous in avoiding the slightest trace of what might be construed as a bribe.

Rabbi Ishmael ben Yose personified this level of extreme honesty, as the following incident shows (*Kesubos* 105b): Rabbi Ishmael ben Yose employed a sharecropper who brought him a basket of fruits every Friday as payment. Once, the sharecropper brought the fruits on Thursday, prompting Rabbi Ishmael to question the early payment. The sharecropper explained that he had to appear before Rabbi Ishmael's court that day anyway and, therefore, brought the basket with him. Rabbi Ishmael refused to accept the fruits even though they were his.

He believed that the small amount of gratitude he would feel from receiving his payment a day early might slightly influence him in favor of the sharecropper, and as such would constitute bribery.

The eleventh blessing of the *Amidah* reminds us to pray for the restoration of judges who embody all eleven fundamentals of honesty outlined by King David.

ৼ Eleven Basic Texts

Additionally, the *Vilna Gaon* (comm. to *Proverbs* 16:4) notes that the essence of the Written Law is the Five Books of Moses, while the essence of the Oral Law is the Six Orders of the Mishnah — a total of eleven works which a scholar must master before he can be appointed a judge. After the judge has mastered the entire Torah which is embodied in these eleven core texts he can fully uphold the eleven principles of conduct set forth by King David.

ৼ Return to Integrity

הָשִׁיבָה שׁוֹפְטֵינוּ כְּבָרִאשׁוֹנָה — *Restore our judges as in earliest times.*

Rabbi Yose ben Elisha taught: If you see a generation which is plagued with many miseries and catastrophes, go out and investigate the judges of Israel, because all tragedies which befall the world are caused by the corrupt judges of Israel! ... God's holy spirit will never return to rest upon the Jewish people until the corrupt judges and law-enforcement officers are eradicated! (*Shabbos* 139a).

The Talmud goes on to describe the sorry state of the judicial system during the First Temple era: Judges accepted bribes and twisted their decisions. Men of influence paid handsomely to have their dishonest and unqualified relatives appointed to the bench. Even Torah scholars used their prestige to help their ignorant relatives acquire judgeships. These perverse scholars would then instruct their inept relatives on how to appear well versed in the law. Lawyers trained their clients to employ deception and double talk. Powerful bailiffs of the court extorted money from weak litigants and court clerks forged deeds and documents. The entire system was a corrupt shambles.

Isaiah laments: *How has the faithful city become a harlot? It had been filled with justice, righteousness lodged in it; but now — murderers!* (*Isaiah* 1:21). Isaiah then tells how God Almighty promises to purge the city of its crooked leaders and only after the city is completely cleansed, וְאָשִׁיבָה שֹׁפְטַיִךְ כְּבָרִאשֹׁנָה וְיֹעֲצַיִךְ כְּבַתְּחִלָּה... , 'And I shall restore your judges as in earliest times and your counselors as at first.' Isaiah continues: *Afterwards you shall be called the city of righteousness, the faithful city. Zion shall be redeemed with justice and those who return to her, with righteousness (Isaiah 1:26, 27).* This redemption is what we desire when we pray, *Restore our judges as in earliest times.*

✒ The Sanhedrin System

The Talmud (*Sanhedrin* 88b) records Rabbi Yose's teaching that originally no major disputes divided the people of Israel. There was a rigid judicial system that operated as follows: The highest body of law was the Sanhedrin of seventy-one members which convened in the לִשְׁכַּת הַגָּזִית, *the Chamber of Hewn Stone*, inside the Temple building. In addition, there were two high courts composed of twenty-three members each. One convened at the lower gate, the entranceway to the Temple Mount, and the other convened at the upper gate, the entranceway to the Temple Courtyard. Additionally, other courts of twenty-three members were established in every city throughout the Land of Israel.

Any time a question arose anywhere in Israel, it would first be referred to a local court. If none of the local courts could resolve the matter, the query was taken to the court at the entrance of the Temple Mount. If this court could not settle the question, it was sent to the court at the entrance of the Temple Courtyard. If this court was also unsuccessful, the matter was brought before the Supreme Court, the Sanhedrin of seventy-one which did not recess until the question was decided.

In later years, however, Roman persecution undermined the comprehensive Torah-education system which had been established. As ignorance increased, many disciples of Hillel and Shammai (the leaders of the generation) could not study nor prepare themselves adequately to serve as Israel's judges. As a result, the system slowly declined, leading to many disputes which were never resolved satisfactorily.

✒ Self-Judgment

One should be aware that judgment is not confined to the courtroom, but is a process that occurs continually within the human heart. Rabbi Yose HaGallili taught: Righteous people are controlled by the judgment of their Good Inclination, while the wicked are controlled by the judgment of their Evil Impulse. Ordinary, ambivalent people are controlled by the judgments of both [and they invoke Divine assistance to help them decide in favor of the judgment of their Good Inclination] (*Berachos* 61b).

In the course of normal human existence we are constantly confronted with sets of options that demand decisions based on our sound judgment and solid values. The *Kotzker Rebbe* explained that the verse, *Judges and law enforcement officers shall you appoint for yourself in all your gates* (*Deuteronomy* 16:18), is also directed at each individual person. It instructs: Be a judge over yourself and enforce the values you have accepted as true and binding. Always be completely honest with yourself, and accept no "bribes" to be lenient in self-evaluation.

In the initial, embryonic stage of human development, the unborn child in its mother's womb is under the exclusive influence of angelic, spiritual forces which inculcate it with the Good Inclination (*Niddah* 30b). The Evil Impulse sets in only after the child's birth (*Sanhedrin* 91b). Therefore we pray, *Restore our judges as in earliest times*, as it was in our embryonic stage when only the Good Inclination affected our judgment and we were all righteous. Help us today to make proper decisions and value judgments.

This interpretation could explain a puzzling inconsistency in the wording of this blessing. When asking for the restoration of judges we say כְּבָרִאשׁוֹנָה, *as in earliest times*, but in reference to the reappearance of counselors we say כְּבַתְּחִלָה, *as at first* [see comm. of *Malbim, Genesis* 1:1]. The reason for this change is that the first request refers to our personal lives; we ask to be as righteous as we were *in earliest times* of our embryonic stage. The second petition refers to the history of our nation which enjoyed the leadership and guidance of the best counselors *at first*.

⊸§ *Personalized Guidance*

וְיוֹעֲצֵינוּ כְּבַתְּחִלָה — *And our counselors as at first.*

Our counselors refers to the authentic prophets who offered wise advice in both spiritual and temporal affairs (*Olas Tamid*).

The *Vilna Gaon* (comm. to *Proverbs* 16:4) explains that just as no two people are physically identical, so too God gives each person a unique mission on earth. In days of old, a prophet could study a person's facial features and identify from them the nature of that person's soul and its designated course in life. Moreover, a person who erred and strayed into sin could go to the Temple in Jerusalem where the priests would conduct an in-depth spiritual analysis and offer him advice on how to repent and improve.

After the destruction of the Temple, however, prophecy ceased. Yet, the Talmud (*Bava Basra* 12B) teaches that the Jewish people still enjoys the advice of Torah sages, and, in truth, חָכָם עָדִיף מִנָּבִיא, *a wise man is preferable to a prophet;* the insight and perception of the scholar surpass that of a prophet in certain ways. Therefore, one should make every effort to designate a Torah scholar as his guide and advisor for life.

✦§ Each Generation and Its Judges

King Solomon, in his wisdom, counseled *not* to compare the leaders of our times to the great leaders of early times. *Do not say, "Why was it that the earlier days were better than these?' For you are not asking wisely in this matter* (Ecclesiastes 7:10). The Talmud (*Rosh Hashanah* 25b) further states that even an ordinary person who is legitimately appointed as the leader of the Jewish people is to be considered like the greatest of the great, and his rulings must be accepted unquestionably.

In light of this, our request for a restoration of judges and leaders as in days of old appears to be inappropriate. In reality, though, it is not. The Talmud only demands an acceptance of authority, ruling that it is incumbent upon every generation to defer to the sovereignty of its leaders with total dedication and obedience. This is because every leader merits Divine assistance which guides his decisions and judgment. However, even if all leaders are equal in *authority* they are unequal in *ability*. The Talmud notes that some leaders are very simple and some extraordinary. The greater the knowledge, piety and ability of the leader, the more he is able to educate and elevate the people both scholastically and spiritually. This superiority is what we pray for.

✦§ Fatherly Leadership

In this blessing we also express our desire for strong and sensitive leaders, who stand at the helms of our communities.

When Moshe, the first leader of the Jewish nation, asked God to appoint the proper person to assume his position, he said: *Master of the universe, each person's disposition is known to You, and they are not similar. Appoint a leader who will be able to tolerate each one according to his disposition* (Rashi, Numbers 27:16). Hashem responded that Moshe's disciple, Joshua, was best suited for leadership because he is אִישׁ אֲשֶׁר רוּחַ בּוֹ, *a man within whom there is spirit* (Numbers 27:18), meaning he is capable of adapting himself to every individual's personality (*Rashi*, ibid.).

Rav Chaim Shmulevitz zt"l (*Discourses, Parshas Shoftim*) explains that a leader or advisor can achieve this degree of tolerance only if he considers each and every person as his own child. Only then can he cope with everyone's individual needs, characteristics, and idiosyncrasies, the way a father relates to each of his children as disparate as they may be.

ঙ্গ The Advisor's Role

The Mishnah (*Avos* 2:8) teaches: מַרְבֶּה עֵצָה מַרְבֶּה תְבוּנָה, *The more counsel, the more understanding.* Rabbi Chaim of Volozhin (*Ruach Chaim* ibid.) quotes the popular saying, "Ask for advice and then follow your own opinion." Then why bother to seek out advice in the first place? Because when someone asks for advice it doesn't mean that he wants someone to make up his mind for him. Rather he seeks advice in order to gain a better perspective of the issue at hand. When plagued by a difficulty, people often develop tunnel vision, limiting them to a narrow approach to the problem. They need outside advice, a different perspective. Still, each advisor can only give his personal assessment of the dilemma, and therefore, one must seek the advice of many to perceive the full scope of the problem and assess the situation from many different angles. Only then can one properly consider and evaluate all his options and arrive at a final conclusion.

We ask Hashem, therefore, to send us advisors who are sincerely interested in our welfare and are not out to promote their own personal interests. Secondly, we want advisors who do not attempt to force their opinions upon us, arguing קַבְּלוּ דַעְתִּי, *accept my opinion.* We request broad-minded, considerate, skilled counselors who will help us arrive at our own best conclusions.

~§ No Justice, No Joy

וְהָסֵר מִמֶּנּוּ יָגוֹן וַאֲנָחָה — *Remove from us sorrow and groan.*

This phraseology is unique to this blessing of the *Amidah*. Despite our suffering, we do not ask God to heal us, redeem us, or forgive us, in order to *remove our sorrow and groan*. This teaches us that injustice crushes the human spirit in a way that no other misfortune does. Nothing is more frustrating than to be the victim of crime or violence and to have no recourse. Even worse is to be condemned or chastised by a judge who is known to be corrupt.

Injustice drives away all joy, as the Talmud (*Sotah* 48a) teaches: When the Sanhedrin [and the entire justice system which depended on it] was dismantled, all singing ceased from the places of feasting, as the verse states, *The elders are gone from the gate* [where the courts convened], *the young men from their music. Gone is the joy of our hearts, our dancing has turned into mourning* (*Lamentations* 5:14-15).

~§ Tempering Justice with Leniency

וּמְלוֹךְ עָלֵינוּ אַתָּה ה׳ לְבַדְּךָ בְּחֶסֶד וּבְרַחֲמִים — *And reign over us — You, HASHEM, alone — with kindness and compassion.*

Mortal judges are often compelled to issue overly harsh verdicts as a warning to intimidate lawbreakers. Strictness and severity are often signs of insecurity, because the judge fears that leniency and compassion will be misconstrued as weakness and doubt. These concerns do not apply to God. He can judge with kindness and compassion, without undermining His universal authority in any way.

~§ Leaders — Not Idols

Although we ask for judges, leaders and counselors, we wish to avoid one of the dangerous pitfalls which strong leadership often creates — excessive admiration. The function of the Jewish leader is to draw the people closer to God and influence them to be even more dependent on Him. Unfortunately, foolish people often come to idolize these leaders. They rely so much on their leaders that they either forget about Hashem, or they are not afraid to sin because they are confident their leaders will pray on their behalf and absolve them.

The *Kotzker Rebbe* says that Moshe understood this when he interceded on behalf of the Israelites who had just sinned by worshiping the Golden Calf. He prayed, *Blot me out of Your book, I beg of You* (*Exodus* 32:32). The *Kotzker* explains Moshe's request with a parable of the *Dubner Maggid*:

The prime minister's young nephew was a habitual lawbreaker, and the uncle had to intercede constantly on the young man's behalf to beg the king's pardon. The youth's latest crime, however, was so offensive that the prime minister was ashamed to approach the king and plead for leniency. Yet, he loved his nephew and wanted to save him from the severe punishment that awaited him. So, he went to the king and said, "My nephew sins because he relies on me to intercede for him, but if he knew that I could no longer serve as his go-between, he would stop behaving so objectionably. I therefore request that you remove me from my position."

◄§ Judge Others Favorably

וְצַדְּקֵנוּ בַּמִּשְׁפָּט — *And justify us through judgment.*

Judgment is an action that takes place constantly in our own hearts and minds. Whenever we observe our fellow men and women, we are evaluating and judging their actions. Accordingly, the Torah rules: בְּצֶדֶק תִּשְׁפֹּט עֲמִיתֶךָ, *You shall judge your fellow man with righteousness* (*Leviticus* 19:15). This verse obligates us to give someone else the benefit of the doubt when we see him performing an action that could be interpreted unfavorably (see *Chofetz Chaim*, chapter three, for complete details of this law).

If we commit ourselves to judging other favorably, surely all others — both God and man — will reciprocate and *justify us through judgment.*

The *Baal Shem Tov* teaches that it is virtually impossible for one Jew to see another Jew sinning unless the observer himself is guilty of the very same sin. God causes him to witness the transgression so he should see how ugly his own ways are.

Maharil Diskin develops this idea even further. God says to the sinner, "I won't judge you; I'll let you judge yourself. I will allow you to see someone performing a sin similar to your own, and the way you judge him is how you shall be judged yourself. If you condemn the other sinner harshly, I shall judge you harshly. If you look upon the other sinner with compassion, I shall judge you with compassion." This is why the Mishnah (*Avos* 1:6) urges: וֶהֱוֵי דָן אֶת כָּל הָאָדָם לְכַף זְכוּת, *and judge everyone favorably*, for only then can we hope that God will acquit us in judgment.

◆§ No One Is Above the Law

בָּרוּךְ אַתָּה ה׳ מֶלֶךְ אוֹהֵב צְדָקָה וּמִשְׁפָּט — *Blessed are You, HASHEM, the King Who loves righteousness and judgment*.

The commentaries note two anomalies in this blessing. First, this is the only concluding statement in the *Amidah* that mentions God's sovereignty as מֶלֶךְ, *king*. Second, nowhere else does it say that God *loves* what He does. He is not described as the King Who loves to cure or loves to forgive or loves to redeem; but here we say that He loves righteousness and judgment.

Abudraham marshals a number of Scriptural sources to demonstrate that, indeed, God does have a special *love* of justice [because it is one of the three pillars which supports the world (*Avos* 1:18)]. And King David said, וְעֹז מֶלֶךְ מִשְׁפָּט אָהֵב, *Mighty is the King Who loves justice* (*Psalms* 99:4), to which *Midrash Shocher Tov* comments: A ruler who wields great power often considers himself to be above the law, and tends to abuse his power for his own advantages. Not so, the Holy One, Blessed is He, Who really *loves justice* and uses His Divine power to enforce the strict letter of the law for everyone.

Sefer HaChinuch (*Mitzvah* #491) observes that God wants us, the Jewish people, to love justice, and for this reason we are commanded to appoint strict judges over every community. At first, we will reluctantly obey their verdicts and directives out of fear. Through habit, however, we will develop an abiding respect and deep love of the law. The more we abide by the law, the more we will love God. In turn, He will love us and shower us with His bounty; and then God will rejoice with all His handiwork!

◆§ Justice and Charity

God's love of צְדָקָה וּמִשְׁפָּט, *righteousness and judgment*, is shown through the example of King David about whom Scripture says: וַיְהִי דָוִד עֹשֶׂה מִשְׁפָּט וּצְדָקָה לְכָל עַמּוֹ, *And David executed judgment and righteousness for all his people* (*II Samuel* 8:15). The Talmud

(*Sanhedrin* 6b) explains that if a rich man and a poor man came before him, David would first execute strict justice and render an honest decision, even if it went against the pauper. Afterwards he would consider the dire straits of the poor man and supply him with charity, so that he might meet his obligations.

⋖§ Never Shirk Leadership

Abudraham quotes *Rabbi Yechiel ben Asher* (the son of *Rosh*) who cites another verse showing how God's kingship and His love of justice are intertwined. מֶלֶךְ בְּמִשְׁפָּט יַעֲמִיד אָרֶץ וְאִישׁ תְּרוּמוֹת יֶהֶרְסֶנָּה, *Through justice the king establishes the land; but he who stands aloof overthrows it* (*Proverbs* 29:4).

Midrash Tanchuma (*Parshas Mishpatim*) uses this verse to show that God demands that everyone participate in administering justice in the world. In this verse King Solomon criticizes the man who possesses Torah leadership qualities, but holds himself aloof and says, "Why should I get involved in community problems? My soul is at peace; I am serene; why burden myself with settling the quarrels and arguments of others?" This man destroys the world!

The Midrash tells of Rav Assi who was on his deathbed. His nephew approached and saw his illustrious uncle crying bitterly. "Uncle, why do you weep?" he asked. "You spent your life well, involved exclusively in teaching Torah and performing acts of charity. Above all, you never wasted your time getting involved in settling disputes and never let yourself assume the time-consuming task of community leadership." Rav Assi replied, "My son, this is exactly what I am crying about! I fear that the Heavenly Tribunal will take me to task for shirking my responsibility, because I was capable of judging and counseling the Jewish people but failed to do so!"

⋖§ God Joins the Judges

It is written, in *Psalms* (82:1): אֱלֹהִים נִצָּב בַּעֲדַת אֵל בְּקֶרֶב אֱלֹהִים יִשְׁפֹּט, *God stands in the assembly of God; in the midst of the judges, He shall judge.* This means that when magistrates assemble for deliberation, God pays very close attention to their decisions (*Radak*) in order to determine if they are inspired by a quest for equity and truth (*Rashi*).

Moreover, notes *Sforno*, God grants the righteous judge Divine perception which helps him to discover the truth. Indeed, *Ramban* (*Deuteronomy* 19:19) assures that God will never allow a genuinely righteous judge to be deceived by false witnesses. In addition, the Talmud (*Sanhedrin* 7a) teaches that the scrupulously honest judge causes the spirit of God to descend upon the entire congregation of Israel.

In summation, *Shibbolei Halekket* quotes the Midrash that when Hashem commanded Moses: *Now these are the judgments that you shall set before them* (*Exodus* 21:1), the ministering angels chanted, "Blessed are You, HASHEM, the King Who loves righteousness and judgment."

12

בִּרְכַּת הַמִּינִים / Against Heretics

וְלַמַּלְשִׁינִים אַל תְּהִי תִקְוָה, וְכָל הָרִשְׁעָה כְּרֶגַע
תֹּאבֵד, וְכָל אֹיְבֶיךָ מְהֵרָה יִכָּרֵתוּ,
וְהַזֵּדִים מְהֵרָה תְעַקֵּר וּתְשַׁבֵּר וּתְמַגֵּר וְתַכְנִיעַ בִּמְהֵרָה
בְיָמֵינוּ. בָּרוּךְ אַתָּה יהוה, שׁוֹבֵר אֹיְבִים וּמַכְנִיעַ זֵדִים.

And for slanderers let there be no hope; and may all
wickedness perish in an instant; and may all Your
enemies be cut down speedily. May You speedily uproot,
smash, cast down, and humble the wanton sinners –
speedily in our days. Blessed are You, HASHEM, Who breaks
enemies and humbles wanton sinners.

✎§ Outcome of Justice

The Talmud (*Megillah* 17b) explains that when the judicial system is restored, its primary goal will be to eradicate the evil influences that threaten Jewish life. This sequence is foretold by Isaiah who describes the renewal of the legal system, after which he says: *The destruction of the transgressors and sinners shall be together, and those who forsake* HASHEM *shall be utterly consumed (Isaiah 1:26-28).*

✎§ A Response to the Times

This blessing is unique, as it was not part of the original eighteen blessings of the *Amidah* composed by the Men of the Great Assembly. Rather, it was instituted five hundred years later by the great *yeshivah* in Yavneh, under the leadership of Rabban Gamliel II, after the destruction of the Second Temple. The blessing was composed in response to the threats made upon tradition by such heretical Jewish sects as the Sadducees, Boethusians, Essenes, and the early Christians. These groups made every attempt to lead Jews astray through example and persuasion. Heretical Jews turned against their mother religion with malicious fury when their missionary overtures were rejected. They used their considerable political power to harshly oppress observant Jews and slander them to the anti-Semitic Roman government. They informed against their Jewish brethren and brought torture and death to thousands.

Under ordinary circumstances, it would not be the Jewish way to ask God to destroy our enemies; we would rather that they be inspired to repent. The Talmud (*Berachos* 7a) relates how a heretical Sadducee caused great anguish and grief to Rabbi Yehoshua ben Levi. Finally, the Sadducee's harassment became so unbearable that the Rabbi decided to pray for his destruction at the specific moment in the day when God's anger is kindled against sinners. Just as that moment neared, the Rabbi fell asleep and missed his opportunity. He correctly interpreted this as a sign that God did not look favorably upon such prayers, as it is written: *And His mercies are upon all His creatures (Psalms 145:9)*, and *Causing punishment is not good for a righteous man (Proverbs 17:26)*.

In this extremely dangerous atmosphere, however, with the future of the Jewish nation at stake, Rabban Gamliel felt the urgent need to compose a prayer against the heretics and informers. As *Rambam* (*Hilchos Tefillah* 2:1) records: In the days of Rabban Gamliel, there was a dramatic increase in the number of heretics in Israel who persecuted the Jews and made every attempt to seduce them away from God. When Rabban Gamliel recognized this as the greatest of all possible human needs [the need to preserve the true faith], he and his court introduced this blessing. He went so far as to incorporate it into the *Shemoneh Esrei* so that it would be universally accepted and repeated thrice daily, impressing the danger upon the populace.

◄§ Prophetic Composition

When Rabban Gamliel determined that this blessing had to be composed, he arose in his *yeshivah* in Yavneh and addressed the sages: "Is there anyone who knows how to compose a benediction against the heretics?" Only Shmuel HaKattan volunteered to accept this task (*Berachos* 28b).

The *Brisker Rav* observes that no one else was qualified because only an inspired prophet can invest each word and letter of the *Amidah* with eternal, universal meaning (*Nefesh HaChaim* II, 13). The Men of Great Assembly, who originally composed the *Amidah*, had prophets in their ranks, but in the days of Rabban Gamliel, prophecy had disappeared. The Talmud (*Sanhedrin* 11a) teaches, however, that even in his time, certain exceptional men merited brief periods of prophetic inspiration. Shmuel HaKattan was one of them and thus had the ability to compose an additional blessing for the *Amidah*. *Pnei Yehoshua* (*Berachos* 28b) adds that Shmuel HaKattan was the only sage who knew how to combine the numbers of words and letters of *Shemoneh Esrei* so they would have an impact on every part of the cosmos (as explained in the Overview to this volume).

◄§ With Malice Toward None

The Mishnah (*Avos* 4:24) teaches: Shmuel HaKattan said, "*When your enemy falls do not rejoice, and when he stumbles do not allow your heart to be glad; lest HASHEM see this and it will be evil in His eyes, and He will turn His anger away from him [toward you]*" (Proverbs 24:17,18).

This teaching is not an original statement, but a verbatim quote of two verses from *Proverbs*. If the Mishnah records them as the teaching of the humble Shmuel HaKattan, it is evidently because these verses were constantly on his lips and ever present in his heart and mind, the perfect expression of his personal credo and lifelong principle.

When it became necessary to compose this prayer, only a man who bore no trace of personal animosity could set its words. In prayer before God, there is no room for personal vindictiveness or malicious hatred. Only Shmuel "the Little One", humble and unassuming, was capable — the man who could not rejoice if a personal enemy fell. His words of prayer flowed from a pure love of his people, a concern for their safety, and a desire to protect their faith. Additionally, in his extraordinary humility, Shmuel HaKattan followed the example of our Patriarch Abraham who demonstrates how humble surrender is a prerequisite of prayer.

◄§ *Twelve — The Number of Endurance*

This blessing is number twelve to remind us that the reason we pray for the eradication of traitors and heretics is to protect the overall structure of the Jewish people, which is defined in terms of twelve tribes. That Israel was destined to comprise exactly twelve tribes (see *Rashi, Genesis* 29:21,34) is not an arbitrary number, but parallels the twelve constellations and the twelve months of the year (*Ramban, Deuteronomy* 33:8).

The Talmud (*Bava Basra* 115b) states a tradition that no tribe will even be wiped out. *Ramban* (*Sefer Hageulah Shaar* I) offers at least eight proofs that the Ten Lost Tribes will return. The Mishnah (*Sanhedrin* 110b) records a dispute between R' Elazar, who believes the lost tribes will return, and R' Akiva, who says that they will not. *Rashi* and *R' David Bonfils* (ibid.) explain that even R' Akiva gave up hope only for the wicked and unrepentant of the Ten Tribes. For those who return to God there is always hope.

Thus the number twelve recalls the essential bond between every Jew and his people. Although treachery and apostasy can sever it, sincere repentance can always mend it.

Most prayerbook texts follow the new version of this blessing, which omits certain terms that could be found offensive by gentile censors and critics (see *Siddur Otzar Hatefillos*). For instance, today we say, וְכָל הָרִשְׁעָה כְּרֶגַע תֹּאבֵד, *and may all wickedness perish in an instant*, whereas the old version has וְכָל הַמִּינִים, *let all heretics [perish]*. Christian censors claimed that the term מִין was really an acronym for מַאֲמִינֵי יֵשׁוּ נוֹצְרִי, *believers in Yeshu [Jesus] the Nazarene*, and claimed that Jews were praying for their destruction. Therefore, the word was changed.

Another phrase in the old version reads, וּמַלְכוּת זָדוֹן מְהֵרָה תְעַקֵּר, *May You speedily uproot the evil government*. For the obvious reason, government censors required that this be changed to וְהַזֵּדִים מְהֵרָה תְעַקֵּר, *may You speedily uproot the wanton sinners*.

The new version contains twenty-seven words. *Tur*, however, (*Orach Chaim* 118) says that his version was composed of twenty-nine words, symbolizing the heretic who denies the authenticity of the Torah, which is written with the *twenty-two* regular letters, five final letters, and is comprised of *two* parts — the Written Law and the Oral Law (22 + 5 + 2 = 29).

⊸§ *Plots Foiled; Hopes Dashed*

וְלַמַּלְשִׁינִים אַל תְּהִי תִקְוָה — *And for slanderers let there be no hope.*

Informers slander us to the tyrannical gentile governments to curry favor and earn rewards from the rich and the powerful. We pray that their hopes be dashed and their plans foiled (*Rav Avrohom ben HaGra*).

Ordinarily, God is every man's hope, as the prophet says, מִקְוֵה יִשְׂרָאֵל מוֹשִׁיעוֹ בְּעֵת צָרָה, *O Hope of Israel, its Savior in time of distress* (*Jeremiah* 14:8); but not for informers, who are enemies of God. *Rabbi Yehudah ben Yakar* cites the Midrash (*Shemos Rabbah* 19:5) which teaches that after death all heretics and informers will fall into hell, but will rely on our Patriarch Abraham to rescue them by virtue of their circumcisions (see *Eruvin* 19b). The Holy One, Blessed is He, however, will frustrate them by sending down ministering angels to mask their circumcisions. Their hope disintegrates as they are devoured by the fires of Gehinnom.

◆§ Sins, Not Sinners

וְכָל הָרִשְׁעָה כְּרֶגַע תֹּאבֵד — *And may all wickedness perish in an instant.*

The *Vilna Gaon* cites the Talmud (*Berachos* 10a), which relates that evildoers in Rabbi Meir's neighborhood vexed him sorely and he wanted to pray for their death. But his wife, Beruriah, asked him, "How can you justify such a prayer? The verse in *Psalms* (104:35) says only יִתַּמּוּ חַטָּאִים מִן הָאָרֶץ, *May sins be eliminated from the earth.* The verse doesn't say יִתַּמּוּ חוֹטְאִים, *may 'sinners' be eliminated.* Rather the phrase is spelled יִתַּמּוּ חַטָּאִים without a *vav*, which can be read חַטָּאִים, meaning *may 'sins' be eliminated.* This means that our hope should not be that sinners should be struck down, but that they should be inspired to repent. When they abandon their deplorable behavior their wickedness will be eliminated." Accepting his wife's argument, Rabbi Meir prayed that the evildoers repent, and his request was granted. Here too, explains the *Vilna Gaon*, we pray for *wickedness to perish*, so that the wicked will repent and eradicate their own sins (*Iyun Tefillah*). [We are permitted to pray for the personal destruction only of incorrigible heretics and missionaries for whom there is no hope of repentance, as the Talmud (*Yoma* 81a) teaches, "Whoever causes the masses to sin will not be afforded the opportunity to repent."]

Maharsha (comm. to *Berachos* 10a) asks: How could Rabbi Meir ask God to make the evildoers repent? Doesn't this contradict the principle that God never interferes with a person's free will and does not force anyone to do either good or bad? *Rav Moshe Feinstein (Igros Moshe, Orach Chaim* Vol. IV, 40:13) explains that Rabbi Meir prayed only that God give the sinners very favorable *opportunities* to repent, by exposing them to righteous men who would talk to and inspire them. Thus, the final decision on whether or not to repent always rests with the sinners.

◆§ The Moment of Divine Wrath

כְּרֶגַע תֹּאבֵד — *Perish in an instant.*

There is one precise moment every day when God displays wrath at evildoers. Throughout the day God views the world through מִדַּת הָרַחֲמִים, *the Divine Attribute of Mercy*, making allowances for human shortcomings. But for one moment each day, He views the world as it

178 / Shemoneh Esrei

really should be — if people would only choose to discipline themselves in accordance with the Divine will. At that moment, God views the world according to מִדַּת הַדִּין, *the Divine Attribute of Strict Justice*, and His wrath is kindled by mankind's defiance of His will. King David alluded to this instant in *Psalms* (7:12) when he said, אֱלֹהִים שׁוֹפֵט צַדִּיק וְאֵל זֹעֵם בְּכָל יוֹם, *God is the righteous judge, and God is angered every day*. The Talmud (*Berachos* 7a) asks: And how do we know that this anger lasts only a moment? For it is written: כִּי רֶגַע בְּאַפּוֹ, *For His anger endures but an instant* (*Psalms* 30:6). The Talmud then explains that this *instant* equals 1/58,888 of an hour. Furthermore, no living creature could compute precisely when this instant occurs, except for Balaam the wicked prophet, who attempted to curse the Jews at precisely that moment of Divine wrath. In this blessing we ask God to judge and condemn heretics in that moment of intense fury.

⋗§ *Defending the Torah's Honor*

וְכָל אֹיְבֶיךָ מְהֵרָה יִכָּרֵתוּ — *And may all Your enemies be cut down speedily.*

The litmus test of how much a person loves God is his attitude toward the enemies of God. If an observant Jew sees others trampling God's law and is indifferent to this sacrilege, his genuine devotion to God is suspect.

This idea was emphasized by King David in many places. He said, אֹהֲבֵי ה' שִׂנְאוּ רָע, *O lovers of HASHEM, despise evil!* (*Psalms* 97:10) and asked, *Those who hate You, HASHEM — do I not hate them? And do I not quarrel with those who rise up against You? I despise them with the utmost hatred, I regard them as my own enemies! Search me, O God, and know my heart, test me, and know my thoughts!* (*Psalms* 139:21-23).

Tur advises a person not to allow anyone to deter him from performing *mitzvos*, not even those who mock and humiliate him for his piety (*Orach Chaim* 1). *Mishnah Berurah* (ibid.) explains that if sinners mock him privately, he should ignore them. But if heretics publicly degrade *mitzvos* and disgrace *mitzvah* observers in an attempt to change the overall observance of the community, it is imperative to stop them. If peaceful persuasion fails, one must fight them with every available resource, as King David said, *Do I not quarrel with those who rise up against You?*

Tanya (*Likkutei Amarim* ch. 32) emphasizes that this total hatred is reserved exclusively for the heretics who have completely severed themselves from God. In dealing with sinners who *do* believe in God, however, one should hate only their sins while continuing to love them for the good that is in them, in the hope that this love and compassion will influence the sinners to repent.

⊷§ Divine Love

Rambam elaborates that if a Jew sees another Jew knowingly commit a transgression, the observer is obligated to hate the sinner until he repents. Nevertheless, if the observant Jew finds the sinner struggling to load or unload his donkey or in any type of danger, he must immediately come to his assistance, because God is very concerned for the welfare of every Jew. Anyone who believes in God and accepts the fundamentals of His Torah is beloved by Him, for God has no desire to destroy the sinner. Rather, He yearns for him to abandon his evil ways and repent (*Hilchos Rotzeach* 13:14).

It is a great *mitzvah* to reach out and draw sinners back into our congregation. In fact, the Hebrew term for congregation, צִבּוּר, is an acronym for צַדִּיקִים בֵּינוֹנִים וּרְשָׁעִים, *righteous, average, and wicked*. All three components have a place.

The Torah teaches (*Exodus* 30:34) that in the Temple the *ketores* [incense] was made up of eleven aromatic ingredients. Ten of these had a pleasing fragrance while the eleventh, *chelbenah* [galbanum], gave off a very bad odor. *Rashi* (ibid., based on *Kereisus* 6b) observes that incense symbolizes the congregation of Israel, with the malodorous *chelbenah* representing its sinners. We learn from this that any prayer service on a fast day which fails to include the presence of at least one sinner will not find favor in God's eyes (see *Shulchan Aruch, Orach Chaim*, chapters 55 and 619; *Tur* and *Beis Yosef*).

⊷§ The Faces of Evil

וְהַזֵּדִים מְהֵרָה תְעַקֵּר וּתְשַׁבֵּר וּתְמַגֵּר וְתַכְנִיעַ בִּמְהֵרָה בְיָמֵינוּ — *May You speedily uproot, smash, cast down, and humble the wanton sinners — speedily in our days.*

We repeat our wish for the absolute eradication of all heretic evildoers, reminding us too that we must dig beneath the surface of our own sins and penetrate the source of evil which is the יֵצֶר הָרַע, *the Evil Impulse*. The Talmud (*Sukkah* 52) teaches that the Evil Impulse manifests itself in many different ways and is called by a variety of names, seven in all. God called it *evil*. Moses called it *stubbornness of heart*. David called it *impure*. Solomon called it *enemy*. Isaiah called it *stumbling block*. Ezekiel called it *heart of stone*. Joel called it *hidden one*.

Sometimes the Evil Impulse causes us to be cold, insensitive and indifferent, both to the will of God and to the needs of our fellow man. Our hearts become like hard rock, which must be smashed and ground into fine sand. Or the Evil Impulse can cause the opposite effect. It can ignite our hearts with flaming passion and lust. In that case, advises the Talmud, the Evil Impulse is like a red-hot iron which must explode in order to dissipate its intense heat.

When we recite these words of the *Amidah*, it is an appropriate and auspicious time to ask God to protect us from our own deadliest enemy, the Evil Impulse. We pray that God should strengthen us to overcome our adversary and release us from his lethal grip.

⋖§ A Chance to Return

בָּרוּךְ אַתָּה ה' שׁוֹבֵר אֹיְבִים וּמַכְנִיעַ זֵדִים — *Blessed are You, HASHEM, Who breaks enemies and humbles wanton sinners.*

The *enemies* are the heretics who abandoned Judaism and make every effort to lead others astray. There is no hope for their return, so they must be broken and completely destroyed. The *wanton sinners*, however, are not enemies of the faith, but rather captives of their Evil Impulse that incites them to rebel against the Torah and God's will. We pray that they be humbled and their Evil Impulse subdued, so that they will repent their sinful ways (*Iyun Tefillah*).

According to the Midrash quoted by *Shibbolei Halekket*, when the Egyptians drowned in the Sea of Reeds, the ministering angels chanted, "Blessed are You, HASHEM, Who breaks enemies and humbles wanton sinners." Although the entire Egyptian army was destroyed because of its thorough wickedness, surprisingly, God detected a spark of hope in its leader, Pharaoh. God saved him from drowning in the sea. Humble and contrite, Pharaoh repented and described the wonders of God to the world. Thus, the miracle at the Sea of Reeds portrayed how the *enemies* of God *were broken* while the *wanton sinner* was *humbled*.

13

צַדִּיקִים / The Righteous

עַל הַצַּדִּיקִים וְעַל הַחֲסִידִים, וְעַל זִקְנֵי עַמְּךָ בֵּית
יִשְׂרָאֵל, וְעַל פְּלֵיטַת סוֹפְרֵיהֶם, וְעַל
גֵּרֵי הַצֶּדֶק וְעָלֵינוּ, יֶהֱמוּ רַחֲמֶיךָ יהוה אֱלֹהֵינוּ, וְתֵן שָׂכָר טוֹב
לְכָל הַבּוֹטְחִים בְּשִׁמְךָ בֶּאֱמֶת, וְשִׂים חֶלְקֵנוּ עִמָּהֶם לְעוֹלָם,
וְלֹא נֵבוֹשׁ כִּי בְךָ בָּטָחְנוּ. בָּרוּךְ אַתָּה יהוה, מִשְׁעָן וּמִבְטָח
לַצַּדִּיקִים.

On the righteous, on the devout, on the elders of Your
people the Family of Israel, on the remnant of their
scholars, on the righteous converts and on ourselves — may
Your compassion be aroused, HASHEM, our God, and give
goodly reward to all who sincerely believe in Your Name. Put
our lot with them forever, and we will not feel ashamed, for
we trust in You. Blessed are You, HASHEM, Mainstay and
Assurance of the righteous.

⋞ Reassurance

The Talmud (*Megillah* 17b) explains that this blessing follows the preceding one because after the wicked are obliterated, the glory of the righteous soars. As the Almighty foretold: *All the pride of the wicked I shall cut down; exalted shall be the pride of the righteous (Psalms 75:11).*

This blessing is a source of encouragement and inspiration in times of adversity. God assures the righteous that even if they experience failure and misfortune their setbacks are only temporary, for He continues to be close to them. Even as they fall, God is with the righteous so that He can cause them to rise to new heights. Accordingly, *Shibbolei Halekket* cites in the Midrash that when God reassured Jacob and said, "*I shall descend with you down to Egypt, and I shall also surely bring you up, and Joseph shall place his hand on your eyes*" (*Genesis* 46:4), the ministering angels chanted, "Blessed are You, HASHEM, Mainstay and Assurance of the righteous."

⋞ The Source of All Blessings

Yaaros Dvash exhorts us to pray with fervor for the welfare of righteous men because we are dependent upon them, as King Solomon said: וְצַדִּיק יְסוֹד עוֹלָם, *and the righteous man is the foundation of the world (Proverbs 10:25).* As long as righteous men and Torah scholars exist in the world, there will be blessings, goodness, and life in the world.

A supplicant may ask that his prayers be answered in merit of the righteous. This is based on the Talmud (*Bava Metzia* 84b) which relates how sixty sailors once gave Rabbi Elazar ben Shimon a gift of sixty chests filled with treasure. *Rashi* explains that while at sea a huge storm threatened to capsize their ship. The sailors begged God to save them in the merit of the pious Rabbi Elazar ben Shimon, and the sea was calmed. When the sailors docked, they went to his house with gifts to show him their appreciation.

⋞ The Breath of Jewish Life

The Roman governor, Turnus Rufus, conspired to murder Rabban Gamliel, the leader of Israel, but a benevolent Roman noble informed the rabbi of the peril via a coded message saying: "The master of the nose is in danger!" *Maharsha* (ibid.) explains that the entire Jewish nation resembles the human body, and each Jew has his own mission, as each bodily organ has a specific function. God breathed life into Adam's nostrils, and continues to inhale vital air through man's nose. Similarly, God breathes the spirit of life and holy energy into the Jewish nation via their righteous leaders, who thereby resemble the nose. In this vein, Scripture speaks of King Josiah as, *The breath of our nostrils, the anointed of HASHEM . . . under his shadow we shall live among the nations* (*Lamentations* 4:20).

⊷§ The Power of a Tzaddik's Prayer

An adjunct to belief in God is that He responds to the prayers of the righteous, whose deeds and thoughts conform completely with His will. All the forces of nature are subservient to such a *tzaddik* and submit to his prayers (*Sefer HaIkarim*, IV:22, 41).

Ramban emphasizes that the person who seeks God must seek the company of the *tzaddikim* who are closest to God, and whose prayers He deeply desires (*Exodus* 18:15; *Deuteronomy* 33:1).

The *Vilna Gaon* observes that every prayer of the *tzaddik* is heard because God is very close to him, as close as the ear is to the mouth (*Proverbs* 15:29).

Although, *Rashi* teaches that a sick person's prayer for himself is the most effective prayer of all, and is the first to be answered (*Genesis* 21:17), *Maharsha* (*Berachos* 34b) notes that sometimes a *tzaddik's* prayer is accepted as readily by God. Thus, based on the Talmud (*Bava Basra* 116a and *Taanis* 8a), *Rama* (*Yoreh De'ah* 335:10) rules that when someone in the family falls ill, his relatives should go to the outstanding Torah scholar in the city and ask him to pray on behalf of the patient.

Mabit (*Beis Elokim, Shaar Hayesodos* ch. 22) states that the power of the *tzaddik* surpasses that of the ministering angels, because angels lack freedom of choice, but the *tzaddik* obeys God of his own free will, despite temptations to the contrary. God reciprocates by fulfilling the *tzaddik's* wishes.

Rav Yonasan Eibeschutz writes that the prayers of the Jewish people are drawn to the pure prayers of the *tzaddikim* and cling to them. As the *tzaddik's* prayers ascend, the gateway of heaven opens for them, and the prayers of all Israel enter with them (*Yaaros Dvash* part I, sermon 9).

Based on the above, *Chasam Sofer* (gloss to *Orach Chaim* 102) advises that one stand at the side of the *tzaddik* as he prays for thus it will be of great assistance to the acceptance of one's petition.

►§ *Numerology*

Tur (Orach Chaim 118) notes that this blessing is unique in that it contains all of the letters of the Hebrew alphabet. This indicates that Hashem should treat us compassionately in the merit of the righteous scholars who immerse themselves in the study of the Torah that is written with these letters.

This is the thirteenth blessing of the *Amidah* because in it we beseech God, "May Your compassion be aroused," and God's compassion is composed of the Thirteen Attributes of Mercy.

Moreover, the numerical value of אַהֲבָה, *love*, is thirteen, as is the value of אֶחָד, *one*. This symbolizes that when we arouse our love for God, Who is the One and only God, His compassion will be aroused toward us.

►§ *Motivated by Fear and Love*

עַל הַצַּדִּיקִים וְעַל הַחֲסִידִים — *On the righteous, on the devout.*

Most commentaries explain that the list of those we pray for is in ascending order of prominence (see *Siddur Beis Yaakov,* by *Rav Yaakov Emden*). First we pray for the righteous צַדִּיק who scrupulously follows the letter of the law, then we pray for the welfare of the devout חָסִיד who goes beyond the letter of the law. In this sense, the righteous *tzaddik* is motivated by יִרְאָה, *fear* of punishment, so he does only what is necessary to avoid transgression. The devout *chassid*, however, is motivated by intense אַהֲבָה, *love* of God and will do everything in his power to give God pleasure (*Mesillas Yesharim* chapter 18).

Certainly both of these categories describe people who have attained high levels of Torah scholarship, without which it is impossible to serve God properly. As *Rambam* clearly explains (*Hilchos Issurei Biah* 14:3), one cannot be a צַדִּיק גָּמוּר, *a fully righteous person,* unless he has acquired [Torah] wisdom so that he can understand and perform the *mitzvos* properly.

►§ *Command Responsibility*

וְעַל זִקְנֵי עַמְּךָ בֵּית יִשְׂרָאֵל — *On the elders of Your people the Family of Israel.*

Rabbi Yehudah ben Yakar explains: The elders are a level above the *righteous* and the *devout*, who are essentially private citizens and have not accepted responsibility for the Congregation of Israel. The elders, however, deserve special consideration and respect because they accepted the responsibility of leadership in the Jewish community. Examples of such communal positions are: 1) A *shaliach tzibbur* who regularly leads the congregation in prayer. 2) A *gabbai* who is a trustee over community concerns such as charity collection or synagogue administration. 3) A rabbinical judge who renders legal decisions for the community and generally oversees its spiritual and social welfare.

The Talmud (*Kiddushin* 32b) says that the Hebrew word זָקֵן, *elder*, is an acronym for זֶה קָנָה חָכְמָה, *he has acquired wisdom*. Unless he is well versed in Torah, one is not qualified to be an "elder" of the Jewish community.

⋟ Qualities of Leadership

Rabbi Yehudah ben Yakar emphasizes that the key to real leadership is עַרְבוּת, *acceptance of responsibility for others*, as the Midrash (*Shemos Rabbah* 27:9) says:

As long as a Torah student studies privately he does not have to become involved in communal affairs, and will not be punished for his abstention. But once he is appointed to a position of leadership and has donned the mantle of authority, he cannot be preoccupied with personal affairs. From then on, every community problem is his personal responsibility. If someone complains that he has been wronged, the leader must act or be punished for his indifference. The Holy One, Blessed is He, cries out to the community leader, "You have entered the ring to fight. Before you enter you can still cancel the match, but once you are in the ring you must fight. Either vanquish the problem at hand or the problem will vanquish you."

⋟ Counsel of Elders

The Midrash (*Vayikra Rabbah* 11:80) states: Rabbi Akiva taught that the Jewish nation is compared to a bird. Just as a bird cannot fly without wings, so too the Jewish people are immobilized and incapable of action without the counsel of their elders. Likewise the Talmud (*Nedarim* 40a) observes: If youngsters tell you to build while elders advise you to demolish, take care to heed the counsel of the elders and ignore the youngsters, because the "building" of youngsters is actually destruction, while the "demolition" of elders is truly constructive.

◆§ Geriatric Care

Rabbi Yehudah ben Yakar notes that we should also pray for the welfare of *all* elderly people who are sick or frail and require special Divine care and assistance. For this reason, King David prayed, *Do not cast me off in time of old age, when my strength fails, forsake me not* (*Psalms* 71:9).

Midrash Tanchuma (*Mikeitz* 10) states: A person should always pray that in his old age his eyes should continue to see, his mouth should continue to eat, and his feet should continue to walk.

וְעַל פְּלֵיטַת סוֹפְרֵיהֶם — *On the remnant of their scholars.*

Rabbi Yehudah ben Yakar says that these are the outstanding Torah scholars who guide the entire Jewish world. The Talmud (*Nedarim* 49b) instructs us to pray for their welfare every day of the year because they toil in Torah which weakens them physically, and they are susceptible to illness (see *Sanhedrin* 26b and *Ran* ad loc.). *Rashi* (ibid.) explains that the Talmud is specifically referring to this phrase, *on the remnant of their scholars.*

◆§ The Transmitters

The leading Torah scholars of the generation are charged with the most essential and difficult task of all. They not merely teach Torah, they transmit the entire Oral Tradition from previous generations to the present one without the slightest deviation, so that the Torah teachings of today are linked to the unbroken chain of tradition reaching all the way back to Moses at Mount Sinai. *Rambam* in the *Introduction to Mishneh Torah* demonstrates how in every generation there is a select group of individuals who are the בַּעֲלֵי מְסוֹרָה, *the masters of tradition.* They receive the traditions of the past generations and pass it on to the present and future generations. That is why we refer to them as פְּלֵיטַת סוֹפְרֵיהֶם, *the remnant of their scholars,* because these transmitters *remain* past their generation, transferring Torah to the present one.

๙ Order and Organization

The word סוֹפֵר commonly refers to the scribe who writes sacred Scriptural texts. Historically, however, the title *Sofer* was bestowed only upon the greatest scholars who toiled to transmit Torah from generation to generation. As a rule, the Jewish nation descends spiritually, as it grows farther and farther away from the Revelation and giving of the Torah at Mount Sinai. Thus, while earlier generations could grasp and retain vast amounts of Torah knowledge, later generations have more limited spiritual capacities and are more easily overwhelmed by the mass of Torah literature which is handed over to them. For this reason, the transmitters facilitated Torah study by organizing Torah topics into orderly sections. Through the Mishnah and the Gemara, interrelated subjects were identified and grouped together, and the laws of the various divisions were carefully counted and numbered. This organization made it easier to perceive Torah as a cohesive unit and to memorize its laws.

Therefore, observes the Jerusalem Talmud (*Shekalim* 5:1), the teachers were called סוֹפְרִים, literally *counters*, as they prepared lists such as "the thirty-nine categories of Sabbath labor" and "the four prime categories of damage" (see *Kiddushin* 30a and *Tosafos* s.v. נקראו סופרים).

We pray, therefore, for the dedicated Torah leaders of our generation who have accepted the burden of making Torah accessible to the masses. We are grateful to them for clarifying, simplifying, and amplifying our ancient traditions in terms and concepts that are appropriate for these times, while meticulously preserving the absolute authenticity of our tradition.

Finally, *Etz Yosef* notes that *melamdim*, elementary school teachers, are also included in the title *Sofrim*, because they introduce their charges to holy *sefarim*, books, and devote their lives to giving their young pupils a firm grounding in the essentials of Judaism. We pray for them now in appreciation of their dedicated service.

๙ The Baal Teshuvah

In the Sephardic version of the *Siddur*, this text reads וְעַל פְּלֵיטַת בֵּית סוֹפְרֵיהֶם, *on the remnant* [lit. *those who escaped*] *of the academy of their scholars.* Rav Yehudah ben Yakar explains that this is a reference to

בַּעֲלֵי תְּשׁוּבָה, *penitents*, who escaped from homes and schools that were under the influence of non-Jewish scholars and teachers. The term פלט, *escape*, is used in reference to one who was on the verge of sinning, but escaped at the last moment by virtue of exerting great effort and fear of Heaven (see *Sanhedrin* 19b in reference to פַּלְטִי בֶּן לַיְשׁ). We pray that God continue to strengthen these penitents in their sincere efforts to avoid sin.

◂§ Concern for All

וְעַל גֵּרֵי הַצֶּדֶק — *On the righteous converts.*
 While we pray for the welfare of the Jewish leaders who are on the top of our social order, we must never forget to respect even the most recent converts to Judaism who are just entering the social structure. We therefore pray for the converts here, following the Scriptural example in *Leviticus* (19:32-33) which juxtaposes elders and converts: *Honor the presence of the elder ... And if a convert should dwell in your land do not wrong him (Beis Yosef, Tur Orach Chaim* 118).

◂§ Strangers on Earth

Maharal (Gevuros Hashem, chapter 9) explains that a common bond links the convert to the dedicated elder and Torah scholar; they all feel like strangers in a foreign environment. The convert recognized the truth of God and Torah, and felt like a stranger in his gentile surroundings; therefore, he converted to be closer to the source of truth. Similarly, the Torah scholar recognizes that his essence is his intellect, not his body; he feels that his mind and spirit are aliens in this mundane, material world. Estranged from the physical world, the scholar is drawn to the world of Torah study where his heart and mind feel at home.

◂§ Righteous Converts

We pray for the גֵּרֵי הַצֶּדֶק, *righteous converts*, who convert because they come to believe in the righteousness of God and His eternal Torah. Judaism, however, had always been plagued by what the Talmud calls גֵּרִים גְּרוּרִים, *'drag-along' converts*, who convert for selfish, ulterior motives and become a burden and even a scourge to the Jewish people. At the very dawn of Jewish history, with the Exodus from Egypt, hundreds of thousands of insincere converts jumped on our triumphant 'band wagon' and attached themselves to the Jewish people like a סַפַּחַת, a *skin disease* (*Kiddushin* 70b). This group, known collectively as the עֵרֶב רַב, *the mixed multitude,* was the source of all of Israel's woes. They inspired the construction of the Golden Calf and they incited the Jews to complain and rebel against God time and again. The *Vilna Gaon* (*Even Shlaimah,* Chapter 11) reveals that all the heretics and wicked Jews throughout the ages are the descendants of this group and that they will proliferate and rise to power in the era preceding the Messiah, causing tremendous harm to the righteous.

Therefore, in this blessing for the welfare of the righteous we pray only for the righteous converts, and have in mind to reject and condemn false, insincere converts.

✌ *At Mount Sinai*

Count Valentin Potocki, a member of the Lithuanian aristocracy, was studying for the priesthood in Vilna when he recognized the truth of Judaism. Secretly, he converted and adopted the name Avraham ben Avraham. Discovered by the Roman Catholic Church, he was condemned to be burnt at the stake for heresy against the church, a fate he gladly accepted as an opportunity to publicly sanctify God's Name. However, Avraham ben Avraham sent word to his mentor, the *Vilna Gaon,* that only one thing troubled him. Since a convert is like a newborn child, and he had not married, he had no relatives in the world to mourn for him. The *Gaon* responded that he had nothing to worry about because God Himself is the Father of all righteous converts and the Almighty Himself would mourn for him. Who could have a closer relative?

The second day of Shavuos marks the *yahrzeit* of Avraham ben Avraham. The *Chofetz Chaim* would note the occasion every year with the following insight: Our Rabbis taught that before God offered the Torah to the Jews, He first offered it to all the gentile nations, who refused it. However, the truth is that there were some individual gentiles who shouted that they did want the Torah, but their voices and opinions were drowned out by the vast dissenting majority. The righteous converts of all generations are descendants of those few gentiles.

Similarly, the Talmud (*Shabbos* 146a) teaches that the souls of all the righteous gentiles who were destined to convert in future generations gathered at Mount Sinai when the Torah was given and were eternally purified and elevated by the experience.

◆§ Identify with the Righteous

וְעָלֵינוּ — *And on ourselves.*

We identify ourselves with the righteous to remind us that the mission of every Jew is to become a *tzaddik*. One must strive to maximize his potential and behave as righteously as possible. But at the same time, no matter how much one has accomplished, he must always be concerned that he is not really as righteous as he thinks. This is as the Talmud (*Niddah* 30b) teaches: Before the infant is allowed to leave its mother's womb, the angels command:

> "Swear that you will be righteous and not wicked, and even if the entire world tells you that you are righteous, look upon yourself as wicked. Always bear in mind that the Holy One, Blessed is He, is pure and His ministering angels are pure, and the soul that He has given you is pure. If you safeguard it in purity, it will be good for you. If not, I will take it back from you." The righteous man who fulfills his prenatal oath is referred to as, *He whose hands are clean and whose heart is pure, who has not sworn by My soul in vain, nor has he taken an oath deceitfully* (Psalms 24:4).

Malbim explains that this "oath" is allegorical, describing the ethical and moral instincts which are deeply ingrained in the fiber of the Jewish character, impelling the Jew toward righteousness with the binding force of an oath.

◆§ Torah Arouses Divine Compassion

יֶהֱמוּ (נָא) רַחֲמֶיךָ ה׳ אֱלֹקֵינוּ — *May Your compassion (please) be aroused, HASHEM, our God.*

Some texts add the word נָא, *please. Eliyahu Rabbah* notes that *Tur* and *Kol Bo* state that this blessing contains exactly forty-two words, implying that they delete the extra word נָא, *please,* as do *Rambam* and *Abudraham* (*Anaf Yosef*).

Forty-two is the numerical value of the word בָּם as in the phrase

וְדִבַּרְתָּ בָּם, *and you shall converse in them*, meaning the words of Torah (*Deuteronomy* 6:7). The first letter of בָּם alludes to the Written Torah, which begins with the letter ב of בְּרֵאשִׁית, *In the beginning*, and the second letter alludes to the Oral Torah, which commences with Tractate *Berachos*, beginning with the letter מ of מֵאֵימָתַי, *When do we begin?*

Thus, the forty-two words of this blessing allude to the fact that one can only be a truly devout and righteous scholar if he masters both the Written and Oral Torahs.

◄§ Spiritual Rewards

וְתֵן שָׂכָר טוֹב לְכָל הַבּוֹטְחִים בְּשִׁמְךָ בֶּאֱמֶת — *And give goodly reward to all who sincerely trust in Your Name.*

In order to be in the category of צַדִּיקִים וְחֲסִידִים, *righteous and devout*, simple אֱמוּנָה, *belief* in God, is not enough. One must have absolute בִּטָּחוֹן, *trust* in the Almighty, and complete faith that He alone is in control of every detail of life and nothing happens anywhere against His will. *Trust* is *belief* translated into action, meaning that one is not content with abstract belief, but conducts himself accordingly in his business and other practical affairs. *Ramban* formulated this axiom of faith: כָּל הַבּוֹטֵחַ מַאֲמִין וְלֹא כָּל הַמַאֲמִין בּוֹטֵחַ, *Everyone who trusts surely believes, but not everyone who believes, trusts.*

However, this request for God to *grant goodly reward* to those who trust in Him appears to contradict a different dictum of our Sages who taught: "Be not like servants who serve their master for the sake of receiving a reward" (*Avos* 1:3). It must be understood, therefore, that the Mishnah in *Avos* frowns on a request for *material* reward in return for Divine service. But certainly we may ask for *spiritual* rewards. Indeed, spiritual growth and intensified faith in God is the very purpose of Divine service.

◄§ Even Today

Why do we have to pray that God reward the righteous? Is it not self-evident that God will give the righteous their due?

Rabbi Moshe Leib of Sasov explained that this prayer is to remind us that there are virtuous people who are so selfless that they never pray for their own needs. We therefore intercede for them.

How refreshing it is to know that our Sages had to formulate this prayer because there actually are people on this earth who do not think at all of their own needs and are concerned only with the needs and wants of others. Since this prayer has been preserved today, we have every right to believe that even today such wonderful people exist.

The Sages tell us that in each generation there are at least thirty-six truly righteous people. In an age where there is so much self-centeredness and self-indulgence, it is refreshing to know this. But more important, if this degree of selflessness is attainable even today, why should we all not aspire to it? "Place our share with them," says the prayer, "that we may become like them" (*Rabbi A.J. Twerski, Living Each Day*).

◆§ *The Power of Trust*

King David says, 'קַוֵּה אֶל ה׳ חֲזַק וְיַאֲמֵץ לִבֶּךְ וְקַוֵּה אֶל ה, *Place confidence in HASHEM, strengthen yourself and He will give you courage; and place confidence in HASHEM (Psalms 27:14).* HaRav Yitzchak Zev HaLevi Soloveitchik, the Brisker Rav, explains this repetition in the light of a statement by Chovos Halevavos (Shaar Habitachon), who describes בִּטָחוֹן, *trust* in Hashem, as the most wonderful experience life has to offer, far surpassing all earthly fortunes. Since trusting in Hashem is such a vital *mitzvah*, it deserves a proportionately great reward, and this world can offer nothing as great as *trust* itself. Thus, King David declares, *If you place confidence in HASHEM,* your reward will be that God will strengthen your heart to achieve even higher levels of intense faith and you will *place* [ever more] *confidence in HASHEM.* We therefore request שָׂכָר טוֹב, *goodly reward,* meaning spiritual reward, which is intensified trust and confidence in Hashem.

Chazon Ish, in *Emunah U'Vitachon 2:1,* takes great pains to correct the common misconception that בִּטָחוֹן, *trust,* means the conviction that God will fulfill all the wishes of believers. On the contrary, trust does not imply that God is hostage to fulfill the wishes of the pious. What it does mean is that one believes that every aspect of life is controlled by God and events take only the course He ordains, even though man would have wanted another result. *Chazon Ish,* however, offers a final assurance: Those who place *all* of their trust in Hashem will merit a special kindness — that *His* wish will be to fulfill *their* wish, "and a holy spirit will fill their hearts with a mighty surge of confidence, assuring them that indeed, God will save!" (ibid. 2:7).

◆§ Trust Is for Everyone

Ramban (*Ha'Emunah V'haBitachon*, chapter 1) makes an important observation. King David said, בְּטַח בַּה' וַעֲשֵׂה טוֹב, *Trust in HASHEM and do good* (*Psalms* 37:3). First, King David advises to *trust*, then *do good*, emphasizing that even a sinner who has yet to *do good* can still trust that God will assist even those unworthy of His kindness. Whether you are righteous or not, *trust in HASHEM.* Then, after the all-merciful God has responded favorably to your sincere trust, show Him your appreciation — repent and *do good!* Accordingly, we ask God to *grant goodly reward* to *all* who sincerely trust in His Name, even the unrighteous.

◆§ Sincerity Is the Key

There is a condition, though: They must be among those בּוֹטְחִים בְּשִׁמְךָ בֶּאֱמֶת, *who sincerely* (lit. *truly*) *believe in Your Name.* As it says, 'קָרוֹב ה לְכָל קֹרְאָיו, *HASHEM is close to all who call upon Him. . .* (*Psalms* 145:18). If so, why do many prayers go unanswered? Because, the verse continues, God is close only לְכֹל אֲשֶׁר יִקְרָאֻהוּ בֶאֱמֶת, *to all who call upon Him sincerely.* God answers those who address Him with complete and unswerving confidence. If a man "hedges his bets," so to speak, and places his hopes for salvation on other forces *in addition*, he cannot be considered one who calls upon God בֶּאֱמֶת, *in truth.*

◆§ Children Are the Best Reward

The *Radziner Rebbe* wondered why the *Amidah*, which expresses numerous wishes and needs, does not mention one of the most essential human desires — the yearning to have children. The Rebbe speculated that the words of this prayer allude to children and we should keep that in mind when we plead וְתֵן שָׂכָר טוֹב, *and give goodly reward*, for no reward is better than children. As King David said, *Behold! Children are the heritage of HASHEM, the fruit of the womb is a reward* (*Psalms* 127:3) (quoted in *Massas Kappai* by Rav Dovid Cohen).

◆§ Cling to Torah Scholars

וְשִׂים חֶלְקֵנוּ עִמָּהֶם לְעוֹלָם — *Put our lot with them forever.*
Rambam teaches (*Hilchos De'os* 6:2):
It is a Scriptural *mitzvah* to keep close company with Torah masters

and their disciples in order to learn from their ways. The Torah commands: וּבוֹ תִדְבָּק, *And you shall cling tightly to Him* (*Deuteronomy* 10:20). Is it then possible to actually cling unto God Himself? Our Sages explained that the only way to fulfill this *mitzvah* is to cling to Torah scholars and their students. Therefore a person should make every effort to marry the daughter of a Torah scholar, to marry his daughter to a Torah scholar, to eat and drink with Torah scholars, to do business with Torah scholars, and to be involved with them in every way possible.

◆§ An Eternal Partnership

It is known that one who supports Torah scholars in this world will be privileged to sit next to them in the World to Come. Even if he is illiterate and can't read the *Aleph-Beis*, he will study alongside scholars. *Rabbi Yaakov Kamenetsky zt"l* explained this phenomenon based on the Talmud (*Niddah* 30b) which states that every Jewish child learns the entire Torah in his mother's womb. At birth an angel strikes the infant's lips and the Torah leaves his memory and recedes into his subconscious mind. Thus, every Jew, scholar and simpleton alike, possesses a reservoir of Torah wisdom. The scholar extracts Torah knowledge from the inner recesses of his mind while he is in this world. The reward of the man who supports the scholar is that he will be privileged to retrieve his internal fund of Torah wisdom in the World to Come, where he will be the scholar's Torah-study partner for eternity.

◆§ God Guarantees

וְלֹא נֵבוֹשׁ כִּי בְךָ בָּטָחְנוּ — *And we will not feel ashamed, for we trust in You.*

One who puts his faith in people feels ashamed, because he is shown to be helpless on his own. But one who puts his trust in God experiences no shame at all, because no one can accomplish anything without God's help (*Dover Shalom*).

Moreover, if a person makes a commitment to others and genuinely relies on God to help him honor his commitment, Hashem will surely help and not allow him to suffer the shame of failure. This concept is found in the Talmud (*Chullin* 84b), which teaches that a person should never spend more for his clothes than he can afford, even if it means buying inexpensive, simple clothes. But when outfitting his wife and children, he should assure that they are clothed with dignity, even if he must borrow money to cover the costs (see *Maharsha* ibid.). What guarantee does he have that he will be able to repay the loan? The Talmud states that he can rely on God Himself as guarantor: שֶׁהֵן תְּלוּיִין בּוֹ וְהוּא תָּלוּי בְּמִי שֶׁאָמַר וְהָיָה הָעוֹלָם, *because his family is dependent on him, and he is dependent on He Who spoke and the world came into being!*

◄§ *Future Shame*

According to the Sephardic liturgy the text reads: וּלְעוֹלָם לֹא נֵבוֹשׁ כִּי בְךָ בָּטָחְנוּ, *And for eternity we will not feel ashamed, for we trust in You.* This alludes to the teachings of our Rabbis (*Sotah* 48a,b) that on the Day of Judgment, God will take to task even the most righteous and devout people, because, although they had faith in Him, it was incomplete and they should have attained a more perfect trust. While they will nevertheless enjoy eternal bliss, it will be marred by the shame they will feel upon realizing that they could have achieved more.

The Talmud elaborates: When the Temple was destroyed, men of faith ceased to exist, as it says, *Save me, HASHEM, for the devout are no more, for truthful men have vanished from mankind* (Psalms 12:2). Rabbi Yitzchak comments that this refers to men who sincerely believe in the Holy One, Blessed is He. *Rashi* explains that these men place their faith in God alone, rely on Him, and never worry about any loss. They readily give away their money for the sake of enhancing and beautifying a *mitzvah*, for charity, or for Sabbath and festival expenses. As we learned: Rabbi Eliezer the Great says, "He who has bread in his basket [for today] and asks, 'What will I eat tomorrow?' is a man of limited faith" (*Sotah* 48a,b).

◄§ *Future Shock*

Chovos Halevavos (*Shaar Hakniyah*) warns that in the future many people who consider themselves righteous will be shocked to find out otherwise. The Heavenly Tribunal will open the record book of their deeds. First the list of *mitzvos* and merits will be checked and these people will be astounded to find that all the pages of the ledger are blank! The shock will be even greater when the record of transgressions shows a long list of heinous sins which the defendants are sure they never committed. The Tribunal will explain that this is the harsh penalty for those who speak *lashon hara*, hurtful gossip and slander. When one speaks badly of someone else, he is stripped of his hard-earned *mitzvos*, which are then transferred to the victim of the gossip, while all the sins of the victim are transferred to the man who slandered him. We pray, therefore, that our trust in Hashem intensify so that we do not slip into the sin of slander, which brings with it eternal humiliation (see *Chofetz Chaim, Shmiras Halashon, Shaar Hazechirah*, chapter 4).

◆§ Total Reliance

בָּרוּךְ אַתָּה ה׳ מִשְׁעָן וּמִבְטָח לַצַּדִּיקִים — *Blessed are You, HASHEM, Mainstay and Assurance of the righteous.*

God is the מִבְטָח, *Assurance,* of the righteous, so they can rest assured that eventually their faith will be requited and they will see the salvation of God. But meanwhile they are suffering; how will they persevere through the troubles of the present? Once again God is at their side and He is their מִשְׁעָן, *Mainstay,* Who fortifies them with the power to endure adversity (*Rav Avraham ben HaGra*).

King David counseled: *Cast your burden upon HASHEM and He will sustain You, He will never allow the righteous to falter (Psalms 55:23).* Thus, God is the מִשְׁעָן, *Mainstay* (lit. *cane* or *crutch*), Who does not allow the righteous to falter or err. Additionally, He is the מִבְטָח, *Assurance,* upon whom they can cast all their burdens and problems and be assured of a solution. The cardinal rule of successful prayer is that its efficacy depends upon how completely a person relies on Hashem.

◆§ Dependence Disturbs Prayers

Even the prayers of the most righteous *tzaddikim* can be disturbed by the slightest trace of dependence on other people. *Rav Yechezkel Halberstam of Shiniva*, the son of Rav Chaim Sanzer, was one of the Chassidic masters of the late nineteenth century. The following stories relate the *Shiniva Rebbe's* complete dependence upon God during his journey to *Eretz Yisrael.*

It is said that just before he set out on the trip, one of his *chassidim* presented him with a promissory note for several thousand rubles, saying, "No doubt the Rebbe will be in need of funds. With this note, the bank in Constantinople will give you whatever you need." When R' Yechezkel arrived in Constantinople, he felt that he could not pray properly, and traced the disturbance to the note, which was interfering with his concentration. He immediately took it out from his pocket and tore it up, so as not to be relying in any way on flesh and blood. After that he was again able to pray with full devotion as he was accustomed.

A similar incident occurred on board ship. R' Yechezkel made the acquaintance of a certain wealthy Jew. The latter, wishing to help the Rebbe, gave him his business card on which he had written the addresses of certain high officials in *Eretz Yisrael* who could help R' Yechezkel, if necessary. A short while after taking the card, the Rebbe began to feel that as long as it was in his pocket he could not think with his usual clarity. Again, the solution was not difficult. It was only a few steps to the edge of the boat, where, without hesitation, R' Yechezkel dropped the card into the water.

⊷§ Trust Is the Key to Sincere Prayer

Rav Nachman of Breslav emphasized that a person who depends on others will never pray properly. If he feels that his livelihood depends on his employer, he won't turn to God with his whole heart. If he is insecure and needs other people for emotional support, his prayer is easily diluted. Such a person may fervently sway or clap his hands during prayer in order to impress those upon whom he depends for his livelihood or for his sense of importance. The person who depends upon mortal man for anything will find it very difficult to pray, because he is incessantly plagued by a host of insincere motives that limit his prayers' effectiveness. In preparation for prayer, therefore, this person must learn to concentrate and place all his hopes and trust in God (*Likkutei Eitzos* 66:3).

14

בִּנְיַן יְרוּשָׁלַיִם /

Rebuilding Jerusalem

וְלִירוּשָׁלַיִם עִירְךָ בְּרַחֲמִים תָּשׁוּב, וְתִשְׁכּוֹן בְּתוֹכָהּ
כַּאֲשֶׁר דִּבַּרְתָּ, וּבְנֵה אוֹתָהּ בְּקָרוֹב בְּיָמֵינוּ
בִּנְיַן עוֹלָם, וְכִסֵּא דָוִד מְהֵרָה לְתוֹכָהּ תָּכִין. בָּרוּךְ אַתָּה
יהוה, בּוֹנֵה יְרוּשָׁלָיִם.

And to Jerusalem, Your city, may You return in compassion, and may You rest within it, as You have spoken. May You rebuild it soon in our days as an eternal structure, and may You speedily establish the throne of David within it. Blessed are You, HASHEM, the Builder of Jerusalem.

Ideals of Excellence

In the previous blessing we asked that the prestige and influence of the righteous be restored, prompting the Talmud (*Megillah* 17b) to assert: "And where will the righteous reach the height of their glory? Only in the holy city of Jerusalem!" As the Psalmist sang: שַׁאֲלוּ שְׁלוֹם יְרוּשָׁלָיִם יִשְׁלָיוּ אֹהֲבָיִךְ, *Pray for the peace of Jerusalem; those who love you will be serene* (*Psalms* 122:6).

The very name of this city demonstrates that it embodies the values beloved by the righteous, יְרוּשָׁלַיִם being a contraction of the words יִרְאָה, *fear* [of Heaven], and שָׁלֵם, *perfect* [peace and harmony among men]. Thus, the capital of *Eretz Yisrael* represents the ideals of both *spiritual* and *social* excellence. (See *Bereishis Rabbah* 56:10 and comm. of *Rav Yehudah ben Yakar*.)

Gateway to Heaven

The Talmud (*Kiddushin* 69a) states that Jerusalem is the highest spot on earth. This must be understood, of course, in a spiritual sense. Jerusalem is the point on the globe that is closest to heaven, enabling the soul to soar to the loftiest heights (see *Maharsha* ibid.).

Pirkei d'Rabbi Eliezer (chapter 35) teaches: Whoever prays in Jerusalem is considered to be standing in prayer before God's Throne of Glory, for the gateway to Heaven is in Jerusalem, and the gates are always open so the Almighty can hear our prayers. This is why the Talmud (*Berachos* 30a) rules that one should direct his body and heart towards Jerusalem when he prays, as this city [because of the Holy Temple within it] is תֵּל שֶׁכָּל פִּיוֹת פּוֹנִים לוֹ, *the hill toward which all mouths are turned [in prayer]*.

Fairest of Sites, Joy of All the Earth

"Ten measures of beauty were allotted to the world. Jerusalem took nine, leaving one for the rest of the world" (*Kiddushin* 49b).

"Whoever did not see Jerusalem in her glory never saw a beautiful city in all his days" (*Sukkah* 51b).

Undoubtedly, Jerusalem in her glory was a model of architectural brilliance and aesthetic perfection. The Talmud (*Bava Kamma* 82b) lists a number of restrictions enforced in the city in order to protect her flawless beauty and pure environment. The real beauty of Jerusalem, however, was that she beautified her inhabitants and visitors and afforded spiritual revitalization. Numerous Psalms extol the praises of this city; in one of them we read: *Great is HASHEM and much praised in the city of our God, Mount of His Holiness. Fairest of sites, joy of all the earth, Mount Zion . . . (Psalms 48:2-3).*

Any man who arrived in the city downcast and deeply troubled by the burden of his sins went to the Temple. There, he sacrificed a sin- or guilt-offering, absolving him of his sins, and left feeling cleansed and brimming with joy. On a larger scale, the communal sacrifices of the Temple were a source of blessing for all of Israel and the entire world (*Rashi*).

Furthermore, the sacred atmosphere of Jerusalem is conducive to producing scholars of the highest caliber, who can then go forth to guide the entire world towards truth — the epitome of joy (*Sforno*). When the Sages first established a system of public Torah education for youngsters, they wanted the central school to be in Jerusalem. They knew that if the children witnessed the dedication of the Priests to their Temple service and sensed the sanctity that envelops the city, they would advance tremendously in their studies, fulfilling the verse: *From Zion, Torah goes forth (Isaiah 2:3) (Bava Basra 21a; Tosafos* s.v. כי מציון).

Moreover, no melancholy or depressed spirits were tolerated in this city of joy. The Midrash (*Shemos Rabbah* 52:5) relates that outside of Jerusalem was a large rock called כִּיפָּה שֶׁל חֶשְׁבּוֹנוֹת, *Rock of Calculations*. Whenever a person needed to analyze his financial affairs he would have to leave the city and make his computations at this rock, lest his account prove unfavorable, causing him anguish which cannot be tolerated in Jerusalem, *joy of all the earth.*

The city of Jerusalem was a beacon of light for the entire world (*Bereishis Rabbah* 59:8) but the light was dimmed with the Temple's destruction. Only when the Temple is rebuilt will the original radiance return, and God will rejoice as He fills Jerusalem with happiness (*Shemos Rabbah* 52:4).

⊸§ *City of Brotherhood and Peace*

King David extolled Jerusalem: יְרוּשָׁלַיִם הַבְּנוּיָה כְּעִיר שֶׁחֻבְּרָה לָּה יַחְדָּו, *The built-up Jerusalem is like a city that is united together (Psalms*

122:3). Jerusalem served as a unifying social force. Pilgrims from all the tribes and cities of Israel converged upon Jerusalem for the festivals. They were young and old, rich and poor, learned and ignorant — from all stations and walks of life. Throughout the year, these groups were separated by distance as well as social barriers; but during each festival, Jerusalem transformed them. The city was חֶבְרָה, *integrated and united*; it made all Jews into חֲבֵרִים, *comrades*, who embraced each other as parts of one indivisible nation (based on *Yerushalmi, Chagigah* 3:6).

The Talmud (*Bava Kamma* 82b; *Yoma* 13a) even cites an opinion that all of the territory in the Land of Israel was divided among the tribes, except for Jerusalem, which remained the property of the entire nation. Thus the city was truly *united together* because it was collectively owned by everyone.

As a city, Jerusalem was different from any other. Generally, cities are no more than clusters of buildings, where masses of people settle together for the sake of security or commercial convenience. When the urban multitude increases, the significance of the individual decreases. As the individual grows ever more dependent upon the services and culture of the masses, his personal stature is diminished, for his own worth and personal ability have less effect on society. This situation tends to breed friction and animosity in the metropolis and polarize its citizens.

This was not the case in Jerusalem, where every Jew experienced a personal encounter with God. This encounter was a dramatic revelation which demonstrated to every man the special, Divine nature of his soul. The crowds of pilgrims that converged upon the city helped to enhance this realization of individuality rather than detract from it. Every additional pilgrim gave further evidence to the diversity and uniqueness of God's creations. Thus, the proliferation of the masses heightened the individual's self-esteem and lifted his spirits. This fostered brotherhood and unity in Jerusalem, which came to be known as the city of peace, the city that is united together.

◆§ Yearning: The Key to Redemption

Sefer Chareidim notes that the Jews were evicted from Jerusalem and the rest of the Holy Land because they wearied of living in such close proximity to God and despised His constant scrutiny. Consequently, we can return only if we make a complete turnaround and genuinely yearn for an intimate bond with God through living in His Presence. As King David sang, *You will arise and show Zion mercy, for it is time to favor her, for the appointed time has come. For Your servants have desired her stones and cherished her dust* (Psalms 102:14,15).

The Talmud (*Kesubos* 112a) describes the amazing love the Rabbis expressed toward the Land of Israel: Rabbi Abba would kiss the rocks of Acre to show his deep affection. Rabbi Chanina would smooth out the roadways of Israel, repairing anything which was not in order so that there would be no cause for complaint about the highways of his beloved land (*Rashi*).

Rabbi Ammi and Rabbi Assi took great pains to assure their comfort in *Eretz Yisrael* so that they would never be tempted to complain about its climate and living conditions. In the summer, they made sure to stay cool. When the sun started to beat down on the place where they were learning, they quickly moved to the comfortable shade. In the winter, they got up from the cold shadows to sit and learn in the warm sun.

Rav Chiya bar Gamda would roll around in the dust of *Eretz Yisrael* to comply with this verse, *For Your servants have desired her stones and cherished her dust*.

Similarly, when Sir Moses Montefiore returned from his first trip to *Eretz Yisrael*, he brought back a stone which he had used as a pillow, in order to fulfill the words of the same verse.

Therefore, when reciting this blessing for the rebuilding of Jerusalem, we must fill our hearts with intense longing for our Holy Land and sacred city. In this fashion each and every word will bring us a step closer to redemption.

◆§ Rebuilding the Ruins

וְלִירוּשָׁלַיִם עִירְךָ בְּרַחֲמִים תָּשׁוּב — *And to Jerusalem, Your city, may You return in compassion.*

Etz Yosef notes that we beseech God to *return in compassion* because when He abandoned the city before its destruction, He left in a fury. As the prophet said, *For this city has been a provocation of My anger and My fury from the day they built it until this day; so that I should wipe it away from My presence. Because of all the evil of the Children of Israel . . .* (Jeremiah 32:31,32).

The Talmud (*Shabbos* 119b) enumerates the many crimes that

caused God to abhor the city He once loved. Jerusalem was destroyed because its inhabitants:

Desecrated the holy Sabbath;

failed to recite the *Shema* twice daily;

interrupted the Torah studies of pure, innocent Jewish children;

humiliated and degraded Torah scholars;

were corrupt in their business and financial affairs;

were brazen faced, unashamed, and unrepentant of their sins;

failed to rebuke one another for their misdeeds.

Above all, the Talmud explains, the Temple was destroyed because Jews hated one another for no cause (שִׂנְאַת חִנָּם) (*Yoma* 9b), and because they were so selfish that they refused to go beyond the letter of the law to help others (*Bava Metzia* 30b and *Tosafos* ibid.).

So long as we fail to rectify this list of sins, the Temple and the Holy City will remain in ruins. The Jerusalem Talmud (*Yoma* 1:1) teaches: Any generation that does not merit to rebuilt the Temple is considered to have had the Temple destroyed in its time!

The Talmud (*Shabbos* 139a) teaches that Jerusalem will be redeemed only through righteousness, as the prophet said, צִיּוֹן בְּמִשְׁפָּט תִּפָּדֶה וְשָׁבֶיהָ בִּצְדָקָה, *Zion will be redeemed with judgment, and those who return to her, with righteousness* (*Isaiah* 1:27). Thus when we pray, *to Jerusalem Your city may You return in compassion*, we must pledge to treat our fellow Jews with sensitivity and kindness. This will surely arouse God's compassion for His people, and hasten His return to the Holy City.

⧼ *Heaven and Earth in Harmony*

וְתִשְׁכֹּן בְּתוֹכָהּ כַּאֲשֶׁר דִּבַּרְתָּ — *And may You rest within it, as You have spoken.*

This refers to the prophecy of Zechariah: *So says HASHEM, Master of Legions, "I was zealous for Zion with great passion; I was zealous for her with great fury." So says HASHEM, "I have returned to Zion, and I will dwell in the midst of Jerusalem"* (*Zechariah* 8:2,3).

The repetitive nature of Zechariah's words shows the duality of Jerusalem, a city which exists on two levels, in two worlds. The celestial source of blessing is known as יְרוּשָׁלַיִם שֶׁל מַעְלָה, *The Upper (Heavenly) Jerusalem,* because it corresponds to יְרוּשָׁלַיִם שֶׁל מַטָּה, *The Lower (earthly) Jerusalem.* Heavenly Jerusalem represents a utopian ideal, a perfect city in complete harmony with God's wishes. When David designed earthly Jerusalem, he modeled it after Heavenly Jerusalem, making every effort to establish parallel cities (see comm. to ArtScroll *Tehillim* 122:2,4).

God abandoned earthly Jerusalem in a fury when it utterly failed to conform to the righteous model of Heavenly Jerusalem. When both lower and upper cities become twins once again, God will immediately return to dwell in the midst of Jerusalem.

When we request וְתִשְׁכּוֹן בְּתוֹכָה, *and may You rest within it*, we refer to the שְׁכִינָה, *Holy Presence* of God, which dwelled in the *Beis HaMikdash*. Jerusalem is not rebuilt until God's Presence returns to the Temple which is the nucleus of the Holy City.

⊸§ Capital of the World

וּבְנֵה אוֹתָהּ בְּקָרוֹב בְּיָמֵינוּ בִּנְיַן עוֹלָם — *May You rebuild it soon in our days as an eternal structure.*

Our Rabbis tell us wondrous things about the Jerusalem of the future:

Jerusalem will never be completely rebuilt until all of the lost exiles of Israel return to her. Anyone who claims that the exiles have all returned, yet Jerusalem is not rebuilt, is lying (*Midrash Tanchuma, Parshas Noach* 11).

All the exiles of Israel will be gathered into Jerusalem, but yet Jerusalem will never be filled (*Koheles Rabbah* 1).

Jerusalem is destined to become the capital city of all the nations of the world (*Shir Hashirim Rabbah* 1).

Jerusalem will expand until its borders reach the gates of Damascus (*Shir Hashirim Rabbah* 7).

⊸§ Artificial is not Eternal

בִּנְיַן עוֹלָם — *An eternal structure.*

Visiting the modern city of Jerusalem, one beholds a beautiful urban complex replete with every type of structure and institution necessary for quality living. The rebuilt Jerusalem of our times serves all the physical and spiritual needs of her citizens. So the obvious question arises: Why do we continue to plead for the rebuilding of Jerusalem?

This question can be answered with an analogy to the patient whose heart is diseased and who receives an artificial heart. The patient is up and around and appears to be healthy, but inside he is filled with anxiety lest the artificial device be rejected or malfunction. The transplant patient is extremely vulnerable to infection, and distressingly susceptible to unexpected, lethal side effects. As advanced as technology may be, artificial is not the real thing.

Similarly, the heart of mankind in general and the Jews in particular is the *Beis HaMikdash*, the Holy Temple. In that location Adam, the father of mankind, was created and there God breathed life into his nostrils. God continued to pump vitality into mankind through the Temple until it was destroyed. Now, we are maintained artificially, but it is not the same! We are weak and fragile, susceptible to spiritual and moral contamination and disease. We are easily worn out. The whole system can collapse at any time.

All the *yeshivos, chadarim, kollelim, shuls* and other holy places we see today in Jerusalem are wonderful, but they are not the Temple. They are weak and fragile and can easily fall. There is no guarantee of their permanence. Therefore, we fervently pray for the rebuilding of Jerusalem with the Temple at its center — for that alone will be a בִּנְיַן עוֹלָם, *an eternal structure*.

⋖§ *Jerusalem: David's City*

וְכִסֵּא דָוִד מְהֵרָה לְתוֹכָהּ תָּכִין — *And may You speedily establish the throne of David within it.*

Although the next blessing of the *Amidah* is devoted entirely to the restoration of David's dynasty, he is mentioned in this blessing as well, because Jerusalem is dependent upon him and his descendants. The Talmud (*Bava Kamma* 97b) relates that a coin was issued in Jerusalem with the likeness of David and Solomon struck on one side and a relief of Jerusalem on the other side. This demonstrated how David and Jerusalem are inseparable, like two sides of one coin (*Chiddushei Griz HaLevi al HaTorah* p. 106).

King David dedicated Psalm 122 to Jerusalem and sang, *The built-up Jerusalem is like a city that is united together ... for there sat thrones of judgment, thrones for the House of David.* The plural refers to the fact that David had two thrones in Jerusalem. One was his throne of judgment in the royal palace, the other was his throne in the *Beis HaMikdash*. The Talmud (*Sotah* 40b) teaches that it is prohibited for anyone except a king from the House of David to sit down in the Temple courtyard. *Rashi* explains that God granted this extraordinary privilege to David's descendants in order to publicly demonstrate that their enduring dynasty was Divinely ordained.

✺§ Mashiach ben Yosef

The Talmud teaches that at the time of redemption there will be two Messiahs. One will be descended from Joseph, *Mashiach ben Yosef*, and the other from Judah and King David, *Mashiach ben David* (*Sukkah* 52b). *Mashiach ben Yosef* will bring about a degree of independence in a rebuilt Jerusalem, where many of the former exiles will have gathered. However, he is destined to be killed in battle (although, according to *Arizal*, the Jewish people can avert his death through prayer). After his death, tumultuous events will occur culminating with the rule of *Mashiach ben David* (see *Rav Saadiah Gaon*, *Emunos V'De'os* 8:2,5; *Ramban Comm.* to *Song of Songs* 8:13; and ArtScroll *Yechezkel* 37:8).

Arizal teaches that the phrase כִּסֵּא דָוִד, *the throne of David*, refers to *Mashiach ben Yosef*, who will be a support and harbinger for the arrival of *Mashiach ben David* (see *Ohr HaChaim Hakadosh, Numbers* 24:17 and *Darkei Chaim V'Sholom* p. 55).

✺§ Progressive Reconstruction

בָּרוּךְ אַתָּה ה' בּוֹנֵה יְרוּשָׁלָיִם — *Blessed are You, HASHEM, the Builder of Jerusalem.*

When King Solomon completed construction of the Temple, the ministering angels chanted, "Blessed are You, HASHEM, the Builder of Jerusalem" (*Shibbolei Halekket* from Midrash). This is based on *Psalms* (147:2) where it says, בּוֹנֵה יְרוּשָׁלַיִם ה' נִדְחֵי יִשְׂרָאֵל יְכַנֵּס, *The Builder of Jerusalem is HASHEM, He will gather in the outcasts of Israel.* The verse is written in the present tense to emphasize that the construction of Jerusalem is an ongoing process which is in progress at all times.

Even while Jerusalem seems toppled, God is actually laying the groundwork for its reconstruction. Moreover, even when the city was actually being destroyed and its walls broken, God was clearing out the decayed old structures to make room for new edifices that would better serve the needs of the eternal, sacred city.

Jerusalem is the heart and soul of the Jewish nation; when she was destroyed, the nation disintegrated and her citizens were cast out to the four corners of the earth, like so much refuse. When Jerusalem is finally rebuilt, the nation will naturally reassemble around its historic heart.

The Talmud (*Menachos* 87a) states that even after the destruction of Zion, God protected this sacred site by posting guardian angels around it. As the prophet says, *Upon your walls, O Jerusalem, I posted sentries all day and all night; they will never be silent; all those who remember* HASHEM *be not still!* (*Isaiah* 62:6). What do these angels say as they stand guard? Rava bar R' Shila says, "They recite the verse, *You will arise and show Zion mercy*" (*Psalms* 102:14). R' Nachman says, "They recite the verse, *The builder of Jerusalem is* HASHEM" (ibid. 147:2).

What did the angels say before the destruction? Rava bar R' Shila says, "They recited the verse, *For* HASHEM *has chosen Zion, it He desired for His dwelling place*" (ibid. 132:13). And when the Temple is rebuilt, *Rashi* comments, they will recite that verse once again.

15

מַלְכוּת בֵּית דָּוִד / Davidic Reign

אֶת צֶמַח דָּוִד עַבְדְּךָ מְהֵרָה תַצְמִיחַ, וְקַרְנוֹ תָּרוּם
בִּישׁוּעָתֶךָ, כִּי לִישׁוּעָתְךָ קִוִּינוּ כָּל הַיּוֹם.
בָּרוּךְ אַתָּה יהוה, מַצְמִיחַ קֶרֶן יְשׁוּעָה.

The offspring of Your servant David may You speedily cause to flourish, and enhance his pride through Your salvation, for we hope for Your salvation all day long. Blessed are You, HASHEM, Who causes the pride of salvation to flourish.

⇜ מָשִׁיחַ בֶּן דָּוִד — *The Messiah Descended from David*

After Jerusalem is rebuilt and the *Beis HaMikdash* is restored (*Rashi*), the kingdom of David will return (*Megillah* 17b). Thus, this blessing reflects the fulfillment of Judaism's ultimate dream — the Messianic era. Whatever his personal problems and heartaches, aspirations and goals, a Jew should always keep foremost in his mind a yearning to greet the Messiah.

Tur (*Orach Chaim* ch. 118) notes that this blessing is composed of twenty words, corresponding to the twenty words with which the prophet describes the Messianic era: *For HASHEM shall comfort Zion, He will comfort all of her desolate ruins, and He will make her wilderness like Eden, and her desert like the garden of HASHEM, joy and gladness shall be found therein, thanksgiving and the sound of melodious song* (*Isaiah* 51:3).

⇜ *The Cycle of David's Dynasty*

It is noteworthy that the first blessing of the *Amidah* (*Avos*, Patriarchs) speaks of Abraham who represents the beginning of Jewish history, and the fifteenth blessing refers to the climax of Jewish history — the ascent of David's dynasty. *Rabbeinu Bachya* (comm. to *Genesis* 38:30) explains the relationship between David and the number fifteen.

The Midrash infers from the verse הַחֹדֶשׁ הַזֶּה לָכֶם, *This month* [lit. 'this new moon'] *shall be for you* (*Exodus* 12:2), that the royalty of Israel will resemble the cycle of the moon. Initially, it will endure for only thirty generations just as the lunar month has [nearly] thirty days. The light of Jewish royalty began its ascent in the time of the Patriarch Abraham. David (whose name has the numerical value of 14) was fourteen generations from Abraham and resembled the nearly full moon. When Solomon, the fifteenth generation, became king, the royal House of David reached its zenith, like the full moon. From that point on, the House of David began to wane until it was lost from view completely with the destruction of the First Temple during the reign of King Zedekiah, thirty generations after Abraham. At that time the royalty of David disappeared into the darkness of exile, like the vanished moon. Nebuchadnezzar blinded Zedekiah (*II Kings* 25:7), symbolizing the total disappearance of the moon's light.

Every month, therefore, when we sanctify the new moon, we proclaim דָּוִד מֶלֶךְ יִשְׂרָאֵל חַי וְקַיָּם, David, king of Israel, lives on and endures! [See ArtScroll Tehillim, Overview, chapter VIII, and introduction to Psalms 120-134 for further significance of the number fifteen.]

⋖§ A Martyr's Supplication

Yaaros Dvash exhorts every Jew to shed an endless stream of bitter tears while reciting the prayers for Jerusalem and the dynasty of David, because without them the soul is estranged from God. He continues that the ministering angels weep day and night, over their absence, and that the destruction of David's throne and Jerusalem fills the Almighty with pain. On the face of this, how dare we remain calm and serene? Every Jewish heart should feel intense sorrow and misery. Yaaros Dvash goes on to say that every devout Jew should make a commitment to God that if it will help to end the exile and bring the redemption, he is ready to sanctify God's Name even to the extent of sacrificing his own life, to die a martyr's death so that the world may see that those who love God hold His Name most sacred and high!

If we genuinely yearn for redemption with such fervor, the Almighty will surely not ignore our plea.

⋖§ Redemption: Like a Flourishing Blossom

אֶת צֶמַח דָּוִד עַבְדְּךָ מְהֵרָה תַצְמִיחַ — The offspring of Your servant David may You speedily cause to flourish.

This is taken from God's solemn promise to King David that שָׁם אַצְמִיחַ קֶרֶן לְדָוִד, There [in Jerusalem] I shall cause pride to flourish for David (Psalms 132:17).

Radak explains that Israel in exile resembles a tree which has withered, leaving a small shoot sprouting from its trunk. It is dependent upon that shoot to resuscitate the rest of the tree. So too, we wait for David's dynasty to nurture and revive the entire Jewish nation. With the flourishing of the House of David we shall witness the fulfillment of Isaiah's prophecy: And there shall blossom forth a sprout from the stem of Jesse and a branch shall grow out of his roots. And the spirit of HASHEM shall rest upon him (Isaiah 11:1,2).

The prophet Zechariah (6:12) teaches that Messiah's name will be צֶמַח, Zemach — literally the growth of the plant. This indicates that the

Messianic redemption does not result from one sudden, violent act of supernatural upheaval; rather redemption is a natural, progressive process which develops gradually and is like the daily growth of a plant (*Iyun Tefillah*).

Midrash Shocher Tov (*Psalms* 18) quotes Rabbi Yudan who says, "The redemption will not come about all at once; it will appear little by little, like the dawn which slowly breaks through the darkness of night, for if the sun were to rise all at once its fiery light would blind all. Similarly, the Jewish people who have been accustomed to oppression for so long could not endure instant redemption, for the experience would shock and overwhelm them."

Despite our acceptance of a *natural* and *gradual* redemption, we nevertheless ask God to hasten this natural process and we pray מְהֵרָה תַצְמִיחַ, *may You speedily cause . . . to flourish.*

ᴈ§ *Beware: The False Messiah*

The wording of this blessing is very precise, to emphasize that the Messiah himself must grow and develop spiritually into his position before he can assume that title. *No one is born as the Messiah!* Furthermore, the Messiah will be revealed only when the actual process of redemption is about to begin. In *Milchemes Hashem* (*Battle of God*), *Ramban* writes: On the day Moses was born, he was *not* the redeemer of Israel. He became the redeemer only when he embarked upon his mission and demanded of Pharaoh, *"Let my people go"* (*Exodus* 5:1). Similarly, the Messiah will assume his role on the very day he starts his mission of redemption. Until that time, he is not the redeemer.

ᴈ§ *The Realization of Our Potential*

Each of us possesses tremendous potential. Tragically, much of our talent remains dormant and locked within us and never gains expression. Unrealized potential is life's most painful frustration. In a sense, it means that we are alienated and 'exiled' from our real selves.

The great blessing of the Messianic era is that every person will have the opportunity to completely realize his potential, to tap all of his inner resources, both intellectual and emotional. Everyone will flourish like a blossoming garden bringing forth the fruits of his labor. *Paaneach*

Razah (*Parshas Korach*) notes that the letters of the phrase מַטֵּהוּ יִפְרָח, *his staff shall blossom* (*Numbers* 17:20), have a numerical value of 358 which equals the numerical value of מָשִׁיחַ, *Messiah*.

Decades ago the holy *Chofetz Chaim* observed that the incredible scientific and technological breakthroughs of the twentieth century are a sure sign of the imminent arrival of the Messiah, because his blessing teaches us how to unleash all of our locked-up potential. Before he arrives, God gives us a glimmer of what lies ahead. Additionally, *HaRav Gifter* שליט״א explains that this is why science has only recently discovered how to split the atom to produce nuclear energy. Because this represents the ultimate technological breakthrough in understanding the universe's energy structure, it affords us an inkling of the Messiah's mission.

◄§ Hurry — The Messiah Is Coming!

Speed is a very important concept in our understanding of the pre-Messianic era. The Talmud (*Avodah Zarah* 9a) teaches that human history spans six thousand years. *Ramban* (comm. to *Genesis* 2:3) explains how each millennium represents one of the six days of creation. The last millennium — where we stand today — corresponds to the sixth day of the week, the Sabbath eve!

The *Chofetz Chaim* observed that one of the clearest indications that we are in the pre-Messianic era is that human events have speeded up to a frenetic pace. Why? Because the Messianic era is likened to the Sabbath, the seventh day, and the pre-Messianic era to *Erev Shabbos*, the sixth day. As the Sabbath draws closer, the pace of activity in the home quickens. Last-minute errands and preparations send each family member hurrying. Similarly the tempo of world events speeds up in anticipation of the Messianic Sabbath. International events race across the newspaper headlines at a blurring pace. The Messiah is coming and we are hardly prepared!

◄§ Save Us from Travail

The Sages of the Talmud describe in vivid detail the cataclysmic pre-Messianic era when the earth will be wracked by war, plague, social upheaval and utter chaos. This era is called חֶבְלֵי מָשִׁיחַ, the *birth pangs of the Messiah*, and the pain will be as intense and unbearable as that of a mother in labor. The Talmud (*Sanhedrin* 98b) quotes a number of the greatest Sages who so dreaded this period of upheaval that they exclaimed: יֵיתֵי וְלֹא אֵיחְמִינֵהּ, "Let him come — but I don't want to see him."

The Talmud (*Sanhedrin* 97a; *Sotah* 49b) also describes the earlier stages of the pre-Messianic era called עֶקְּבְתָא דִּמְשִׁיחָא, *the "footsteps" of the Messiah*. This period will also be catastrophic: Insolence (*chutzpah*) will abound and meet no protest. The young will humiliate the old, and the old will feel compelled to show honor to the young; sons will curse their fathers, daughters will attack their mothers, and wives their mothers-in-law. A man's family will turn against him and become his enemies, Torah wisdom will be despised, those who fear sin will be degraded, and the truth will be unknown.

In an effort to make these pre-Messianic periods of travail as brief as possible we fervently pray for the Messiah to arrive with the utmost *speed*.

✑ If Israel Is Deserving, the Messiah Will Hasten

The sources cited above might appear to be contradictory. Some indicate that the advent of the Messiah will be the culmination of a slow but steady series of natural events, progressively leading to his arrival. Other sources teach that the Messiah will appear after a whirlpool of swift events, leading to upheaval and chaos. Our Sages reconciled the sources, teaching that there are two possible times designated for the Messiah's advent, and the deeds of Israel will be the determining factor.

אָמַר רַבִּי אֲלֶכְּסַנְדְרִי רַבִּי יְהוֹשֻׁעַ בֶּן לֵוִי רָמֵי כְּתִיב,,בְּעִתָּהּ" וּכְתִיב,,אֲחִישֶׁנָּה"? ,,זָכוּ,,אֲחִישֶׁנָּה" לֹא זָכוּ,,בְּעִתָּהּ." *Rabbi Alexanderi said that Rabbi Yehoshua ben Levi noted a contradictory passage. Scripture says [that the redemption will occur]* בְּעִתָּהּ, *'in its appointed time.' Then it says* אֲחִישֶׁנָּה, *'I will hasten it' (Isaiah 60:22). [The explanation is] if they are deserving: I will hasten it. If they are not deserving: in its appointed time (Sanhedrin 98a).*

This seminal passage sheds light on the great body of Messianic literature. There *is* an appointed time, but there can also be ways to hasten his coming.

On that same page, the Talmud relates how R' Yehoshua ben Levi was dispatched by the prophet Elijah to inquire directly of the Messiah as to when he would arrive. The holy *Tanna* did so and the Messiah greeted him warmly. In answer to his question, the redeemer said, הַיּוֹם, *[I will come] today.* R' Yehoshua complained to Elijah that the Messiah had deceived him — that day was over, but the Exile still endured. Elijah answered that R' Yehoshua had misunderstood. The Messiah had meant to say הַיּוֹם – אִם בְּקֹלוֹ תִשְׁמָעוּ, *[I will come] today — if you but heed His voice (Psalms 95:7)* [i.e., if Israel would but obey the word of God].

It has been said on behalf of Chassidic masters that we, on earth, have the capacity to rebuild the Holy Temple through the performance of *mitzvos*. Each good deed, they say, creates a vessel in the heavenly Temple, but each sin destroys the entire structure. If only the performance of good deeds could continue uninterrupted — the heavenly Temple would be completed and it would descend to earth. Exile would end and all the glorious prophecies of fulfillment and the End of Days would be realized. Such is the power of good deeds. As the Sages have said: If only all Israel would observe two consecutive Sabbaths perfectly, *that* would bring the Messiah. But, the Chassidic masters continue, a sin destroys the entire heavenly structure, requiring Israel to begin anew.

⋞§ A Glimpse of the Future

If we are bidden to yearn for the Messiah, it would be helpful to know more about him. The following is a brief outline of what we are awaiting, based on the teachings of *Rambam*:

The Messiah will be a king who will reestablish the kingdom of David. He will rebuild the Temple (*Bais HaMikdash*) and gather together all Jews, no matter where they are scattered. All the laws of the Torah will be fulfilled as they were originally. The sacrificial system as well as the practices of the Sabbatical Year (*Shemittah*) and the Jubilee (*Yovel*) will all be restored. We will then be able once again to observe all the commandments of the Torah (*Hilchos Melachim* 11:1).

Do not think that the Messiah will have to perform miracles. Nor will he have to change the course of nature, bring the dead back to life, or anything of that sort. The main thing is that the Messiah will not change our religion in any way: The Torah that we have now, with all its laws and commandments, will remain the same forever. Nothing will be added to it nor subtracted from it (ibid. 11:3).

⋖§ The Messiah's Credentials

Rambam continues, we may assume that an individual is the Messiah if he fulfills the following conditions: He must be a ruler, from the House of David, immersed in the Torah and its commandments like David his ancestor. He must also follow both the Written and the Oral Torah, lead all Jews back to the Torah, strengthen the observance of its laws, and fight God's battles. If one fulfills these conditions, we may assume that he is the Messiah.

If he does this successfully, and then rebuilds the Temple on its original site and gathers all the dispersed Jews, then we may be certain that he is the Messiah.

He will perfect the entire world and bring all men to serve God in unity. It has thus been predicted: *I will then transform all the peoples to have a pure tongue, that they may call in the Name of God, and all serve Him in one manner* (Zephaniah 3:9).

Do not think that the ways of the world or the laws of nature will change in the Messianic Age. This is not true. The prophet's prediction — *The wolf shall live with the sheep; the leopard shall lie down with the kid* (Isaiah 11:6) — is merely an allegory, meaning that the Jewish people will live safely, even alongside the wicked nations of the world. All nations will return to true morality and will no longer steal from or oppress others. They will eat that which they have honestly acquired, in harmony with Israel. This is what *Isaiah* means when he says, *The lion shall eat hay like the ox* (ibid. 12:1).

⋖§ Fundamentals of Our Faith

Rambam also gives a detailed description of the Messianic era in his commentary to the Mishnah (*Sanhedrin* 10:1):

We believe that the Messiah will be greater than any king or ruler who has ever lived. This has been predicted by every prophet from Moses to Malachi. One who doubts or minimizes this rejects the Torah itself, for the Messiah is mentioned both in the account of Balaam and at the end of *Deuteronomy*. Included in this principle is the belief that a Jewish king can come only from the family of David through his son Solomon. One who rejects this as the family rejects God and His prophets.

The Messianic age is when all Jews will regain their independence and return to the Land of Israel. There, the Messiah will be a very great king, whose government will be in Zion. He will achieve great fame, and his reputation among the nations will be even greater than that of King Solomon. His great righteousness and the wonders that he will bring about will cause all nations to make peace with him and all people to serve him. Whoever rises up against him will be punished by God and given over into his hand.

Rich and poor, strong and weak, will exist in the Messianic Age. It will be very easy for people to earn a living, and they will be able to accomplish a lot through very little efforts. It will be an age of perfection, through which we will become worthy to enter into the World to Come.

The Messiah will then die, and his son will rule in his place, and his son after him. The prophet speaks of the Messiah's death when he says, *He shall not fail nor be crushed until he has set judgment in the world* (Isaiah 42:4).

His kingdom will last for a very long time, and every person's lifetime will be vastly extended. Worries and troubles will no longer exist, and therefore, people will live much longer. We should not be surprised that the Messiah's kingdom will last for thousands of years, as our Sages thus teach us, when this good is brought together, it will not be quickly dispersed.

We do not hope and long for the Messianic Age in order that we might increase our wealth. We do not yearn for it so that we should be able to indulge in wine and song, as those with confused ideas believe. The reason why our prophets and saints have desired the Messianic Age with such great longing is because it will be a community of the righteous, dominated by goodness and wisdom. It will be ruled by a righteous and honest king, outstanding in wisdom, and close to God. Scripture therefore says of him, *God has said to him, "You are My son, I have given birth to you today"* (Psalms 2:7).

◈§ David's Horn

וְקַרְנוֹ תָּרוּם בִּישׁוּעָתֶךָ — *And enhance his pride through Your salvation.*

The term קַרְנוֹ literally means *his horn*. Since the strength and beauty of an animal are highlighted by its horns, the word קַרְנוֹ is also used figuratively to mean "his glory." The horn has a special relationship to the glory of King David, because he was anointed with oil poured from a horn flask by Samuel the Prophet. Since a horn is very sturdy, this flask symbolized the endurance of David's dynasty which would withstand the assaults of time and treachery. King Saul, however, was anointed by Samuel with oil poured from an earthenware vessel. This was an ominous sign, foretelling that Saul's monarchy would be short lived, like pottery, which breaks easily. David had this in mind in the Song of Triumph (*Psalms* 18:3) when he refers to God as קֶרֶן יִשְׁעִי, *my Horn of salvation*.

Moreover, *Midrash Shocher Tov* (ibid.) notes that at first Samuel wished to anoint one of David's seven older brothers as king. But when Samuel attempted to pour the holy oil onto their heads it did not leave the horn. When Samuel finally came to David, however, the oil bubbled over and flowed out of the horn, miraculously pouring itself onto David's head. Thus the horn demonstrated David's glory as God's chosen monarch.

⋑ Although He Tarries, We Always Wait

כִּי לִישׁוּעָתְךָ קִוִּינוּ כָּל הַיּוֹם — *For we hope for Your salvation all day long.*
These words are reflected in the twelfth principle of faith postulated by *Rambam*: I believe with perfect faith in the coming of the Messiah and even though he may delay, nevertheless every day I anticipate that he will come.

In his commentary to Mishnah (*Sanhedrin* 10:1), *Rambam* elaborates on this: We believe and are certain that the Messiah will come. We do not consider him late, and *if he delays,* [we] *wait for him* (*Habakkuk* 2:3). We should not set a time for his coming, nor try to calculate using Scriptural passages when he will come. Our Sages thus teach us, "Those who try to calculate the time of the end, may their spirit rot!" (*Sanhedrin* 97b).

⋑ Redemption in an Instant

The *Chofetz Chaim* wrote an essay, *Tzipisa LiYeshua*, exhorting the Jewish people to yearn for the Messiah. In it (Chapter 2) he notes an apparent contradiction in the words of the prophet (*Habakkuk* 2:3). The verse begins, *If he [the Messiah] delays, wait for him*, while the verse concludes, *He [the Messiah] shall surely come without delay.* The apparent contradiction can be reconciled with a parable:

Once, a king became incensed at his son and banished him from the palace for five years. He sent him to a distant land, so far away that it would take a number of years just for his son to reach it. Eventually, the king regretted his decree, but knowing that it could not be nullified, he began to think about what he could do. He realized that even when the five years were over, it would take several more years just for his son to return. He therefore commanded that roadways be carved through the mountains and paved, and the fastest train built so that the trip home should add as little time as possible to the five-year sentence.

Similarly, God has banished us into exile and cannot redeem us until the time comes. But we should not let this delay cause us to despair, because when the right moment comes and we are ready, God has everything prepared in advance so that the Messiah can redeem us instantly.

◄§ The Messiah's Enchanted Clock

Rabbi Ber of Radaschitz lodged overnight at a roadside inn. In the morning he inquired excitedly of the innkeeper, "Where did you get that enchanted clock? Each time it chimed I felt a surge of elation, until finally I could no longer restrain myself and I got out of bed to dance with joy."

The innkeeper explained that the clock had belonged to a traveler who did not have the money to pay for his lodging, so he left the clock instead. The traveler, in fact, came from an illustrious family; he was the grandson of the holy *Rebbe of Lublin.* Understanding that the clock must have originally belonged to the *Rebbe* himself, Rabbi Ber said, "Usually a clock is a very depressing instrument because it is constantly reminding you that the precious moments of life are passing by forever. Not so the clock of the *Rebbe of Lublin.* His thoughts and aspirations were entirely focused on the imminent arrival of the Messiah. Each time his clock chimed it indicated that we are that much closer to the joyous, long-awaited redemption. So this clock's chiming continues to inspire genuine elation."

King Solomon observed: תּוֹחֶלֶת מְמֻשָּׁכָה מַחֲלָה לֵב, *Hope that is continually deferred makes the heart sick (Proverbs* 13:12). Not so the constant yearning for the Messiah; the more we wait, the more intense the yearning, the stronger and happier we grow.

Shaarei Teshuvah (comm. to *Shulchan Aruch, Orach Chaim* 118) says that when we recite the words, "for we hope for Your salvation all day long," we should have in mind to ask God to save us daily from all our personal problems and troubles. He assures us that these words are a proven method of deliverance from difficult times.

⊷§ Incessant Daily Yearning

וּמְצַפִּים לִישׁוּעָה — *And we yearn for salvation.*

These words appear in the Sephardic liturgy and reflect the Talmudic tradition (*Shabbos* 31a) that when one appears before the Heavenly Tribunal for final judgment, he will be confronted with six major questions, one of which will be צִפִּיתָ לִישׁוּעָה, *Did you yearn for the salvation* [of the Messiah]? In anticipation of this question we affirm in this world that the Messianic salvation is something we crave every day.

The Talmud (*Sanhedrin* 97a) states: "The son of David (the Messiah) won't come until the Jewish people give up all hope for redemption, and there will be no help or support for Israel." *Rav Yaakov Kamenetsky* observed that this statement apparently flies in the faces of all the Scriptural and Rabbinic sources which emphasize that Jews should never give up hope and yearning for the Messiah. He therefore interprets it as follows: Jews are misguided when they turn to the gentile nations for political and military aid or for their financial largess to assist in the redemption of the Holy Land. The Messiah will come only when we put our full faith in Hashem and trust in Him to send the true Redeemer, because we have given up all hope that the gentile nations will be our saviors.

⊷§ Salvation at the Sea of Reeds

בָּרוּךְ אַתָּה ה' מַצְמִיחַ קֶרֶן יְשׁוּעָה — *Blessed are You, HASHEM, Who causes the pride of salvation to flourish.*

When God split the Sea of Reeds for the Jewish people, they were inspired to sing the prophetic Song of the Sea, which alludes to the ultimate triumph of God's holy nation at the advent of the Messiah. Therefore, on the seventh day of Passover when we commemorate the event by reading the Torah portion of the Song of the Sea, we read the appropriate *haftarah* that compliments this theme: David's song of total victory, recorded in *II Samuel* ch. 22.

Appreciating the connection between the past miracles at the Sea of Reeds and the future wonders to be wrought for the Messiah, we understand the Midrash quoted by *Shibbolei Halekket:* When the Children of Israel miraculously crossed through the Sea of Reeds and praised God with song, the ministering angels chanted, "Blessed are You, HASHEM, Who causes the pride of salvation to flourish."

16

קַבָּלַת תְּפִלָּה /

Acceptance of Prayer

שְׁמַע קוֹלֵנוּ יהוה אֱלֹהֵינוּ, חוּס וְרַחֵם עָלֵינוּ, וְקַבֵּל
בְּרַחֲמִים וּבְרָצוֹן אֶת תְּפִלָּתֵנוּ, כִּי אֵל
שׁוֹמֵעַ תְּפִלּוֹת וְתַחֲנוּנִים אָתָּה. וּמִלְּפָנֶיךָ מַלְכֵּנוּ רֵיקָם אַל
תְּשִׁיבֵנוּ, כִּי אַתָּה שׁוֹמֵעַ תְּפִלַּת עַמְּךָ יִשְׂרָאֵל בְּרַחֲמִים. בָּרוּךְ
אַתָּה יהוה, שׁוֹמֵעַ תְּפִלָּה.

ear our voice, HASHEM our God, pity and be compassionate to us, and accept — with compassion and favor — our
prayer, for God Who hears prayers and supplications are
You. From before Yourself, our King, turn us not away empty
handed, for You hear the prayer of Your people Israel with
compassion. Blessed are You, HASHEM, Who hears prayer.

◆§ Era of Prayer

The preceding blessing expressed our yearning for David's return as Messiah of Israel. The Talmud (*Megillah* 18a) teaches that "when David returns, prayer will return with him" and in the Messianic era there will be a renaissance of prayer in the Temple, as it is written: וַהֲבִיאוֹתִים אֶל הַר קָדְשִׁי וְשִׂמַּחְתִּים בְּבֵית תְּפִלָּתִי . . . כִּי בֵיתִי בֵּית תְּפִלָּה יִקָּרֵא לְכָל הָעַמִּים — *I will bring them to My Holy Mountain and make them joyful in My House of Prayer. . .for My House shall be called a House of Prayer for all people (Isaiah 56:7).*

◆§ Born to Pray

The earliest prayer in the Torah is Abraham's unsuccessful attempt to rescue Sodom, which resulted in the salvation of his nephew Lot. David was a descendant of Lot and he keenly felt that he owed his very existence to Abraham's prayers. Describing himself, King David said: וַאֲנִי תְפִלָּה, *but I am prayer (Psalms* 109:4); to David, prayer was not just another life function — it was the essence of his being (*Pri Tzaddik Vayeira* 5).

David wanted only to be completely attached to God at all times, and no bond is stronger than prayer. The word תְּפִלָּה, *tefillah*, is cognate with תָּפֵל, which means *joined; bound firmly* (see *Tosefta, Pesachim* 5:9). The fervent supplications of this blessing echo the entreaties of King David.

◆§ Three Daily Prayers

David turned to God in prayer three times a day as he said, עֶרֶב וָבֹקֶר וְצָהֳרַיִם אָשִׂיחָה וְאֶהֱמֶה וַיִּשְׁמַע קוֹלִי, *Evening, morning, and noon I supplicate and moan — and He hears my voice (Psalms* 55:18). These three periods of prayer correspond to the three times of day when the position of the sun changes most noticeably: in the evening the sun vanishes, at dawn it appears, at noon it reaches its zenith (*Radak*).

This serves as an inspiration. First, the sight of the ever-changing sun should teach man not to remain static and stagnant but to strive for self-improvement and self-transformation. Second, the inexorable passage of time and the change of seasons should heighten man's awareness and appreciation of his Creator, who is the Prime Force behind this constant movement, although He Himself never changes.

The *Kuzari* (3:5) describes the significance of the prescribed times of prayer: The three times of daily prayer are the real produce of the day and night; they are the spiritual center of a man's time, while the other hours serve merely as the path which leads to this center. Man eagerly anticipates the approach of this time, for during prayer he resembles the spiritual, celestial beings and removes himself from mere animal existence.

Prayer sustains the soul, just as food nourishes the body. The blessed influence of one prayer endures until the time of the next, just as the strength derived from the morning meal lasts until dinner. The further the soul is removed from the time of prayer, the more it is darkened by coming into contact with the mundane world.

~§ Prayer and Psalms

David describes his psalms as prayers (see *Psalms* 72:20), but his most magnificent Psalm, 145, he entitled תְּהִלָּה, *a praise* of God, for that was the ultimate purpose of all his prayers. The Talmud (*Berachos* 4a) teaches that whoever recites Psalm 145 three times a day [corresponding to the three times of daily prayer (*Rashi*)] is worthy of the World to Come.

The Talmud cites two elements which make this Psalm so important. First, the initial letters of the verses follow the alphabet. Secondly, this Psalm supplies the physical needs of all creations, פּוֹתֵחַ אֶת יָדֶךָ וּמַשְׂבִּיעַ לְכָל חַי רָצוֹן, *You open Your hand and satisfy the desire of every living thing* (v. 16).

As explained in the Overview, the letters of the Hebrew alphabet are the basic building blocks of the entire universe and, as such, they are the keys to unlocking the bounty God stored in the universe. Thus the *Aleph-Beis* which David incorporated into this Psalm actually "opens God's hand," as it were, to make available the treasuries that supply all human needs.

When the Men of the Great Assembly composed the *Shemoneh Esrei* five centuries later, they also arranged the letters of the *Aleph-Beis* in such a way that they would activate the forces and bounties stored within creation. As explained in the commentary to the ninth blessing and to the concluding supplication, יִהְיוּ לְרָצוֹן, they often based their

The Sixteenth Blessing / 225

numbering system on the numbering of David's *Psalms*, because the *Psalms* were actually the forerunner of our formalized prayers.

⊷ Never Despair of God's Mercy

Just as David bequeathed the crown of royalty to his dynasty, so did he transmit an appreciation of the potency of prayer to his descendants. The Talmud (*Berachos* 10a) relates that when King Hezekiah lay deathly ill, Isaiah the prophet told him that God had issued a Divine decree that Hezekiah had but a short time to live. Hezekiah adamantly refused to despair, saying: "Isaiah the prophet, stop this talk! This tradition has been transmitted to me from my ancestor King David (see *Rashi*): 'Even if a razor-sharp sword is poised at a person's neck, ready to cut, he should never stop praying to God for mercy!' "

With renewed fervor, Hezekiah pleaded with God for mercy and, indeed, God listened and added fifteen years to his life.

From this we learn that sincere prayer is stronger than prophecy and can even nullify a Divine decree.

Similarly, the Divine decree mandated that the Children of Israel suffer in Egyptian exile and bondage for four hundred years, but when the oppressed slaves cried out in pain, God's compassion was aroused and the exile was ended. *Shibbolei Halekket* quotes the Midrash that when the Jews in Egypt groaned in pain, God heard their cries. At that moment the ministering angels chanted the conclusion of this blessing of *Shemoneh Esrei*, "Blessed are You, HASHEM, Who hears prayer."

⊷ A Life Not Worth Living

In Hezekiah's prayer (see above), he asked God to remember his merits, for he had performed a great service for the Jewish people by hiding the סֵפֶר רְפוּאוֹת, *the Book of Cures.* That volume (written by either Adam or King Solomon) contained a cure for every ailment. *Rashi* (ibid. and in *Pesachim* 56b) says that Hezekiah saw that people began to rely on this book instead of pleading for God's mercy. Thus the book did more harm than good, because sickness is Divinely imposed in order to compel people to plead for Divine compassion.

Harav Gifter asks: "The *halachah* is that saving a human life overrides the entire Torah. If this *Book of Cures* could save lives, how did Hezekiah dare to endanger Jewish lives by hiding it?" He answers that Hezekiah's daring action — endorsed both by God and the Sages of Israel (*Pesachim* 56b) — teaches that a life devoid of sincere, heartfelt prayer is not worth living and not worth saving! Life is meaningful and sacred when it is a vehicle to cling to the Source of life, but when man places his trust in books of wondrous cures, his life has lost its direction and purpose.

⋖§ If You Want It, Pray for It

Shulchan Aruch (*Orach Chaim* 119:1) rules that in the *Amidah's* blessings of request, a person may add his personal petition for something similar to the theme of the blessing. Thus, one may mention a sick person during the eighth blessing for healing. One may add a specific personal request for livelihood during the ninth blessing for prosperity. But this sixteenth blessing of שְׁמַע קוֹלֵנוּ, *Hear our voice*, is a general supplication petitioning God for all our needs. Therefore in this blessing one can ask for anything he desires.

Mishnah Berurah (ibid.) adds that at this time it is appropriate to confess one's sins with the standard text of *viduy*, or confession. It is also appropriate for everyone, even a rich man, to beseech God for sustenance and livelihood. And if a person has committed a specific sin, he should beg God for forgiveness, with genuine humility and in a plaintive tone of voice. But if a person fails to feel remorse over his failings, then he will be severely condemned in heaven.

Yaaros Dvash observes that now is the opportunity to ask God for anything, important or trivial. Nothing is too petty to bring to God's attention in prayer. The main thing is that one must pray sincerely from the depths of his heart.

⋖§ A Mother's Prayer

Many *siddurim* feature a variety of special prayers that are appropriate for this blessing. The following is a special prayer for success in Torah study composed by the *Chazon Ish*, to be recited by mothers immediately before the last sentence of this blessing:

יְהִי רָצוֹן מִלְפָנֶיךָ ה' אֱלֹהֵינוּ וֵאלֹהֵי אֲבוֹתֵינוּ שֶׁתְּרַחֵם עַל בְּנִי
(name of child) וְתַהֲפֹךְ אֶת לְבָבוֹ לְאַהֲבָה וּלְיִרְאָה שְׁמֶךָ וְלִשְׁקֹד בְּתוֹרָתְךָ
הַקְּדוֹשָׁה, וְתָסִיר מִלְפָנָיו כָּל הַסִבּוֹת הַמוֹנְעוֹת אוֹתוֹ מִשְּׁקִידַת תּוֹרָתֶךָ
הַקְּדוֹשָׁה, וְתָכִין אֶת כָּל הַסִבּוֹת הַמְבִיאוֹת לְתוֹרָתְךָ הַקְּדוֹשָׁה. כִּי אַתָּה ...

May it be Your will, HASHEM, our God and the God of our fore-fathers, that You have mercy on my son (insert full Hebrew name) and direct his heart to love and to fear Your Name and to be devoted to Your Holy Torah; remove from before him all circumstances that prevent diligent study of Your sacred Torah; establish all the conditions that lead him to Your Holy Torah . . .

✥ The Ladder of Prayer

שְׁמַע קוֹלֵנוּ ה׳ אֱלֹהֵינוּ — *Hear our voice, HASHEM our God.*

In Jacob's prophetic dream he beheld: . . . *A ladder set up on earth and the top of it reached to heaven and behold! The angels of God were ascending and descending upon it (Genesis 28:12). Baal HaTurim (ibid.)* notes that the numerical value of סוּלָם, *ladder,* (136) equals that of קוֹל, *voice* (136), to teach us that when a person prays with sincerity and concentration his voice becomes a ladder with which he rises to celestial heights, just as the angels were elevated by Jacob's prayers.

✥ Hear the Cry of the Soul

Iyun Tefillah explains that the term קוֹלֵנוּ, *our voice,* does not refer to the sounds of prayer, because *Shemoneh Esrei* should be whispered so quietly that it is inaudible even to the person standing at the supplicant's side. As we read: *"Now Chana prayed in her heart, only her lips moved, but her voice was not heard" (I Samuel 1:13).* Rather we refer here to the inner voice of the soul, which says, "I am distressed and confused. My thoughts are in disarray. More important than the *words* of my prayer — because I can't express myself adequately — hear the anguish and suffering in my voice. Hear the sincerity with which I pour out my heart to You, for only You, O God, are my salvation!"

As King David said: אָכֵן שָׁמַע אֱלֹהִים הִקְשִׁיב בְּקוֹל תְּפִלָּתִי, *In truth, God has heard, He has hearkened to the sound of my prayer (Psalms 66:19).* It was not the *words* of my prayer, but the *sound of my prayer,* its ring of truth and sincerity, that aroused God's compassion.

✥ The Power of Tears

Elsewhere, King David is more specific about the sound of his prayer, saying: כִּי שָׁמַע ה׳ קוֹל בִּכְיִי. שָׁמַע ה׳ תְּחִנָּתִי ה׳ תְּפִלָּתִי יִקָּח, . . . *For HASHEM has* heard the sound of my weeping. HASHEM has heard my plea, will accept my prayer (Psalms 6:9,10). Sh'lah HaKadosh derives from this that sincere tears make prayers more effective. Even if someone cannot cry, he should pray in a plaintive voice which sounds like weeping, so that at least his voice will arouse him to a mood of utter dependence on God. Ibn Ezra (comm. to Psalms 39:13) observes that: "The combination of prayers and tears is like a medicine prescribed by an expert physician."

The Talmud (Bava Metzia 59a) says: Since the day that the Temple was destroyed, all the gates of prayer are locked; however, the gates of tears are not locked as it says, To my tears, be not mute (Psalms 39:13). Indeed, one who cries as he prays arouses all the stars and constellations in heaven to cry with him so that his prayer must be heard (Shiltei Gibborim on Mordecai, Berachos ch. 4).

Hirsch calls a tear 'the sweat of the soul!' Indeed, a tear of repentance is an overflow of feeling which demonstrates that he who weeps has overcome his normal, calm nature and is exerting himself to be more receptive to change and renewal. If man opens the gates of his heart in order to welcome God, certainly God reciprocates by opening all the gates of heaven before his tears.

The question has been asked: If the gates of tears are never locked, why did God have to make them in the first place? The Gerrer Rebbe said that although sincere tears always gain admission above, the gates are sealed shut in the face of false tears. We might also add that although these gates are not locked, nevertheless they are closed and can be opened only as far as the forceful flow of tears will push them!

Yaaros Dvash (Vol. II, essay 11) observes that the numerical value of בְּכִי, weeping, equals that of לֵב, heart, because tears shed during prayer demonstrate that one prays from the heart. Additionally, the letters of דִּמְעָה, tear, can be transposed to read עֲמִדָה, amidah, signifying that tears are the essence of the Amidah prayer. The tears should not be a sign of discouragement or depression, however. Rather they should be the result of passionate emotion and ecstatic fervor in the presence of the Almighty.

◄§ Please Listen Graciously

Tehillah L'David (comm. to Psalms 27:7) notes that the initials of שְׁמַע allude to שַׁחֲרִית, מִנְחָה, עַרְבִית, the morning, afternoon and evening prayers. We beg God not to weary of our incessant pleas and to continue to listen to us graciously when we approach Him three times a day.

The Emperor Antoninus once asked Rabbi Judah the Prince, "May one pray continually?" "No," the Rabbi replied, "for one who acts in this manner will come to treat God's presence with levity." The Emperor refused to accept this answer [convinced that more frequent prayer was preferable].

The next day, the holy Rabbi arose early and stood before the monarch shouting, "Hail Caesar!" After a brief interval he approached again, proclaiming, "A salute to the Emperor!" Next he declared, "Peace to you, O King!"

The Emperor was very annoyed because these constant salutations seemed ludicrous. He said, "Rabbi, you are disgracing the royal name!"

Rabbi Judah replied, "Listen to your own words! You are merely a mortal king of flesh and blood and yet you feel that constant praise to your name is a mockery, rather than an honor. To an even greater extent would constant prayer be a ridiculous show before the Master of the universe!" (Tanchuma, Mikeitz 9).

◆§ A Son's Prayer Is Always Welcome

אָב הָרַחֲמָן שְׁמַע קוֹלֵנוּ — Merciful Father, hear our voice.

The Sephardic liturgy prefaces this prayer with the words אָב הָרַחֲמָן, Merciful Father, to further dramatize how intensely we must plead for God's mercy, for such an attitude is a fundamental of prayer.

Rabbi Shimon said: ... When you pray do not make your prayer a set routine, but rather beg for compassion and mercy before the Omnipresent ... and do not consider yourself to be a wicked person (Avos 2:18).

At first glance Rabbi Shimon's two lessons appear unrelated, but they are actually intertwined. Someone who feels wicked and unworthy cannot pray properly because he feels that God despises him and rejects his prayer. Only if someone has a healthy self-image and a sense of kinship to God can he pray meaningfully. Such a person feels that despite his shortcomings God continues to love him even as a father loves his wayward son.

⋖§ An Infant's Cry

Rabbi Levi Yitzchok of Berditchev observed a man who was reciting his prayers very rapidly, mumbling the words in an unintelligible manner.

The rabbi approached the man, and mumbled some nonsense syllables. "I'm sorry, Rabbi," the man said, "but I cannot understand what you are saying."

"Then why did you mumble your prayers unintelligibly?" the rabbi asked. "You should say your prayers distinctly so that each word can be understood."

The man responded, "When you hear an infant crying or saying nonsensical syllables, you may not understand what he wants, but his parents are sensitive to his sounds, and understand what each sound means. God is my Father. He understands my mumbling."

Rabbi Levi Yitzchok was thrilled. He had acquired a new plea to defend people's behavior.

⋖§ Without You, We Are Worthless

חוּס וְרַחֵם עָלֵינוּ — *Pity and be compassionate to us.*

The term *pity* refers to an artisan's special regard for the product of his hands, while *compassion* describes the emotion aroused by the sight of a pathetic, helpless person. Thus we pray, O God — *pity* us, for we are Your handiwork, and be *compassionate* toward us, for we are nothing without You! (*Vilna Gaon*).

Rav Yehudah ben Yakar cites the Midrash (*Vayikra Rabbah* 17:4): אֵין בַּעַל הָרַחֲמִים פּוֹגֵעַ בִּנְפָשׁוֹת תְּחִלָּה, *The Master of Compassion refrains from attacking human life first*, i.e., even though a sinner has forfeited his life, God tries to save his life by stimulating him to repent. First, God may damage the sinner's property. If that incentive fails, God inflicts relatively minor physical pain or illness. Only if this gradual approach fails may God feel compelled to threaten the sinner's life.

⋖§ A Treasure Trove of Compassion

וְקַבֵּל בְּרַחֲמִים וּבְרָצוֹן אֶת תְּפִלָּתֵנוּ — *And accept — with compassion and favor — our prayer.*

Rav Yehudah ben Yakar notes the Talmudic dictum of R' Yehudah: "A covenant has been struck that the Thirteen Attributes are never turned back unanswered, as Scripture states (*Exodus* 34:10): *Behold I [God] strike a covenant* (*Rosh Hashanah* 17b)." The one prayer that God pledges to accept favorably is the prayer that invokes His Thirteen Attributes of Mercy (*Exodus* 34:6-7).

What is the nature of this covenant?

The *Brisker Rav* explains that it was as if God assembled an infinite cache of mercy. From this treasury of kindness, He promised to withdraw whatever was needed in response to Israel's invocation of the Thirteen Attributes (*Chiddushei Griz HaLevi, Ki Sisa*). For this reason, any plea for the mercy guaranteed in the Thirteen Attributes can always be answered — because there is always ample mercy for those in need.

Chiddushei HaRim teaches that the most abundant of all God's treasuries is one called אוֹצָר מַתְּנַת חִנָּם, *the treasury of free gifts*, which has an endless supply of goodness. One can tap this resource, however, only if he feels sincerely that he has no claim on God and that God owes him nothing. When a supplicant recognizes his lack of worth and begs God for a *free gift*, he is guaranteed to be answered with unlimited bounty (*Sifsei Tzaddik, Va'es'chanan*).

◄§ Pleading for an Unearned Gift

כִּי אֵל שׁוֹמֵעַ תְּפִלּוֹת וְתַחֲנוּנִים אָתָּה — *For God Who hears prayers and supplications are You.*

Rashi (*Deut.* 3:23) explains that תַּחֲנוּן is a request for מַתְּנַת חִנָּם, *an unearned gift*. Truly righteous people use this expression because they know that no human being can claim that God "owes" him something. *Gur Aryeh* explains that the righteous use the term תַּחֲנוּן only when praying for themselves, but when praying for the community they use תְּפִלָּה, *prayer*, because Israel as a *community* deserves God's help.

Harchev Davar (*Genesis* 48:22) explains that *prayer* is the set, unchanging formula that the Sages formulated for all people. *Supplication* is the individual plea for personal needs. Such pleas may be inserted into relevant parts of the *Shemoneh Esrei*, or one may have them in mind as he recites the general prayer.

◄§ Like a Prayer Begging for Alms

וּמִלְּפָנֶיךָ מַלְכֵּנוּ רֵיקָם אַל תְּשִׁיבֵנוּ — *From before Yourself, our King, turn us not away empty-handed.*

This echoes the plea of King David: אַל יָשֹׁב דַּךְ נִכְלָם עָנִי וְאֶבְיוֹן יְהַלְלוּ

שְׁמֶךָ — *Let not the sufferer turn away in shame, let the poor and destitute praise Your Name (Psalms 74:21).* At this point some have the custom of stretching out their hands and cupping their palms like a pauper begging for alms (see *Shulchan Aruch, Orach Chaim 98:3*). While reciting these words, one should feel that he is unworthy, that all he can do is cast himself upon God's mercy. The supplicant should imagine that he is a wretched beggar pounding on a strange door, pleading desperately for help, uttering the plaintive cry, "Please, don't turn me away empty-handed! If you can't fulfill all that I request, at least give me *something* — anything! Don't ignore me and slam the door in my face" (*Abudraham*).

◄§ Undeserving and Undemanding

The Talmud (*Berachos* 32b) teaches that, "the person who prolongs his prayers will never be turned back emptyhanded." However, this apparently contradicts the dictum that whoever prolongs his prayer will eventually be heartbroken. The Talmud explains that one who prays at length with sincerity will surely be answered, but if one prolongs his prayer and "examines" it, he will be disappointed.

Tur (*Orach Chaim* 98) explains that one must take care lest his prayers fill him with pride to the point where he says, "God, examine my prayers; see how sincere they are, surely I am worthy of your positive response!" It is extremely hazardous to ask for Divine examination because once a person is subjected to God's exacting scrutiny, his shortcomings as well as his merits will come to light. Rather, says *Tur*, a person should feel unworthy of Divine reward. He should say in his heart, "Who am I, wretched pauper that I am, to make any demands of the King of kings? All I can do is cast myself upon His boundless mercy and compassion!"

◄§ The People of Israel Take Precedence

כִּי אַתָּה שׁוֹמֵעַ תְּפִלַּת עַמְּךָ יִשְׂרָאֵל בְּרַחֲמִים — *For You hear the prayer of Your people Israel with compassion.*

Rav Yehudah ben Yakar cites the Midrash that although the Creator listens to the prayers of all people, the prayers of the people of Israel receive special attention. Thus, King David said: "*I have called out to You, because You will answer me, O God; incline Your ear to me, hear my utterance"* (*Psalms* 17:6). When the Psalmist uses the phrase *God, incline Your ear to me* he refers to God's intense desire to hear the prayers of Jews who call out to Him sincerely.

∽§ Call God to Hold Your Hand

The Midrash further demonstrates the efficacy of calling upon God sincerely: David said to the Holy One, Blessed is He: "If not for Your support, I could not have stood up in this world!" To what can this be likened? — To a very tall [but shaky] ladder, which has a precious crown at its top. The king proclaimed, "Whoever can climb up to the top shall have the crown!"

One man climbed only two rungs and slipped down. A second man met the same fate — and so did a third.

Along came a wise man. When he got to the second rung, he too began to fall, but he cried out, "My king, my master, please hasten to my aid!"

The king responded, "Had I offered such help to the first men, they would not have fallen down and died!"

"The difference is this," the wise man explained. "The others did not call out to you, but I do. Please come to my aid and save me!"

The Evil Inclination is like that ladder. The Generation of the Flood came — and they were swept away; the Generation of the Dispersion came — and they were swept away. The people of Sodom came — and they too were swept away. After the incident with Bath-sheba, David's Evil Inclination sought to overwhelm him. He pleaded for God's help.

"Had I assisted the previous generations," God replied, "they, too, would not have been swept away."

Said David: "They did not call upon You for aid, but as for me, '*I have called out to You for You will answer me, O God, incline Your ear to me, hear my utterance*'" (*Psalms* 17:6). David declared, "Hashem, had You not grasped my hand, I could have not stood my ground!" (*Yalkut Machiri*, citing *Tanchuma*).

∽§ Every Prayer Is Heard

בְּרַחֲמִים ... כָּל פֶּה תְּפִלַּת שׁוֹמֵעַ אַתָּה כִּי — *For You mercifully hear the prayers of every mouth.*

This text follows the Sephardic liturgy. One of the Chassidic masters,

Reb Boruch of Mezhibozh, commented, "God hears all prayers, even if the words emanate from the mouth and not from the heart." [See above, "An Infant's Cry."]

What a strange notion! Does the prophet not castigate those who worship God only with their lips, without involvement of their hearts (*Isaiah* 29:13)? What kind of devotion is it if the prayer does not emanate from the very depths of one's being?

What the rabbi meant was if one thinks about the quality of one's prayer and realizes, "I have only spoken the words with my lips, but my heart was not in it," and recognizes that his prayer was lacking devotion, and consequently resolves to henceforth pray with more fervor, that is meritorious. The virtue of this resolution to improve the quality of one's prayer merits the prayer being answered.

On the other hand, if one thinks, "How profoundly I prayed with intense devotion today!" and prides himself in it, then his prayer diminishes in value.

Prayer should stimulate us to come closer to God. This can be accomplished only when we realize how far from Him we are, because only then will we put forth the requisite effort to draw closer (*Rabbi A.J. Twerski, Living Each Day*).

◆§ The Prayer of All Flesh

בָּרוּךְ אַתָּה ה׳ שׁוֹמֵעַ תְּפִלָּה — *Blessed are You, HASHEM, Who hears prayer.*
This is as King David said: שֹׁמֵעַ תְּפִלָּה עָדֶיךָ כָּל בָּשָׂר יָבֹאוּ, *O Heeder of prayer, unto You does all flesh come (Psalms 65:3).* No mortal can hear prayer as God does. A human king cannot even hear the words of two men who speak at the same time; certainly he cannot understand the pleas of the multitudes who cry out simultaneously. However, the Holy One, Blessed is He, hears the individual prayers of all mankind, even though they are uttered simultaneously (*Midrash Shocher Tov*).

This defies the normal laws of nature, for ordinarily the sound of a single voice can be understood by ten ears, but the sound of ten voices cannot be understood by only one ear (*Pesikta Rabbasi* 21:6).

Moreover, God is not like a human king, who discriminates between rich and poor, powerful and weak. The Holy One, Blessed is He, treats *all flesh* equally. He listens attentively to the prayers of every individual (*Shemos Rabbah* 21:4).

The Midrash (ibid.) notes that the vast variety of prayers are described by the Psalmist in the singular form, as תְּפִלָּה. An angel gathers the prayers from all of the synagogues and fashions them into one perfect entreaty, which crowns God like an עֲדִי, *jeweled tiara*. [According to *Yefeh Toar*, this word is related to עֶדְיִךְ.]

Shevet MiYisrael observes that the reference to בָּשָׂר, *flesh*, alludes to the Talmudic dictum (*Sotah* 5a), that a man's plea is not heard unless he humbles himself by making his heart become soft flesh [rather than tough, insensitive muscle].

Finally, by declaring that our Father in Heaven heeds even prayers of *the flesh* — meaning even those dedicated to mundane, material concerns of the *flesh* — the Psalmist refutes the heretics who claim that God hears only pleas for perfection of the soul and spirit, but not those which concern the body (*Mabit*).

✎§ Every Prayer Is Answered

Even when a person prays sincerely, there is no assurance that God will give him exactly what he requests — only that heartfelt prayer is never in vain.

When Rav Shneur Kotler, *Rosh Yeshivah* of Beis Midrash Govoha of Lakewood, was suffering from his terminal illness, a group of his students and admirers journeyed to Bnei Brak, Israel, to implore the holy Steipler Gaon to intensify his prayers on his behalf. They confided to the Steipler that they were discouraged because prayers were pouring out of tens of thousands of Jewish hearts, yet the *Rosh Yeshivah's* condition continued to decline.

The Steipler responded: "Do not be dismayed. There is no such thing as a sincere prayer that goes unanswered. Any heartfelt request addressed to God *must* be answered. It can't be otherwise. If it is not answered today it will be answered tomorrow. If not tomorrow it will be answered in a week. If not a week, in a month. If not answered in a month it may be answered in a year, or in ten years, or in one hundred years or more. If your prayers are not answered in your lifetime they will be answered for your children or for your children's children. We cannot say for sure *when* a prayer will be answered, but we can rest assured that every prayer *will* be answered somehow, someday."

The Last Three Blessings

The *Amidah* concludes with these final three blessings to which *Rambam* (*Hilchos Tefillah* 1:4) ascribes the collective title, הוֹדָאָה, *thanksgiving*.

✑§ *Our Deepest Gratitude*

The Talmud (*Berachos* 34a) states: Rav Yehudah said: "The supplicant should make no requests during the first three blessings or the last three blessings. All requests should be limited to the middle blessings. As Rabbi Chanina taught: During the first three blessings the supplicant resembles a servant who spells out the praises of his master before he makes his requests. In the middle blessings the supplicant is like a servant who presents his petition. In the final three blessings the supplicant resembles a servant whose wishes have been granted and is taking leave of his master."

Interestingly, *Tosafos* and *Rosh* (ibid.) observe that, in fact, we *do* make requests of God even in these last three blessings. The first of the three is a plea for the restoration of the Temple service (רְצֵה ה׳, *Be favorable, HASHEM*), and the last is a lengthy list of requests for peace, goodness, and all manners of blessing (שִׂים שָׁלוֹם, *Establish peace*). *Rosh* explains: "Since these are requests for the general welfare of the entire community, they actually serve to praise and glorify Hashem because His servants are proclaiming that the entire public depends on His beneficence. Therefore, these requests do not detract from the theme of thanksgiving which dominates the last section of the *Amidah*."

In a deeper sense this teaches us that there is a fundamental difference between thanks offered to man and thanks expressed to God. After receiving assistance from his fellow man, the best thanks the recipient can offer is to say: "Thank you! You have been so helpful and generous that I no longer need your help." With God, the opposite is true. The more one receives from God, the more one recognizes how utterly dependent he is on God, not just for the special needs he requested but even for the simplest needs that he always took for granted. In this sense, the sincerest form of gratitude and praise to God is to immediately request more of Him.

This idea is clearly stated by *Rambam* who devotes the tenth chapter of the *Laws of Blessings* to an exhaustive list of blessings and prayers of הוֹדָאָה, *thanksgiving*, for all sorts of circumstances. He concludes the list with this personal observation (10:26): "A person should cry out to God and plead for what he needs, and ask for mercy. He should then give thanks for what he has already received, and praise God to the best of his ability. The more consistently a person thanks and praises God, the more praiseworthy he is."

Therefore, only the middle blessing of this section solely expresses thanksgiving: מוֹדִים אֲנַחְנוּ לָךְ, *We gratefully thank You*. It is sandwiched by requests for Hashem's help, demonstrating that our deepest gratitude is that we can always depend upon Him.

17

עֲבוֹדָה / Temple Service

רְצֵה יהוה אֱלֹהֵינוּ בְּעַמְּךָ יִשְׂרָאֵל וּבִתְפִלָּתָם, וְהָשֵׁב אֶת הָעֲבוֹדָה לִדְבִיר בֵּיתֶךָ. וְאִשֵּׁי יִשְׂרָאֵל וּתְפִלָּתָם בְּאַהֲבָה תְקַבֵּל בְּרָצוֹן, וּתְהִי לְרָצוֹן תָּמִיד עֲבוֹדַת יִשְׂרָאֵל עַמֶּךָ. וְתֶחֱזֶינָה עֵינֵינוּ בְּשׁוּבְךָ לְצִיּוֹן בְּרַחֲמִים. בָּרוּךְ אַתָּה יהוה, הַמַּחֲזִיר שְׁכִינָתוֹ לְצִיּוֹן.

Be favorable, HASHEM, our God, toward Your people Israel and their prayer and restore the service to the Holy of Holies of Your Temple. The fire-offerings of Israel and their prayer accept with love and favor, and may the service of Your people Israel always be favorable to You. May our eyes behold Your return to Zion in compassion. Blessed are You, HASHEM, Who restores His Presence to Zion.

◄§ The True Service

The final blessing of the middle section of the *Amidah* began with the plea שְׁמַע קוֹלֵנוּ, *Hear our voice*, and went on to beseech God to accept all of our prayers. We realize, however, that no matter how sincere our words of prayer are, they are merely a substitute for the ultimate service of God — the sacrificial service of the Temple. In this blessing we ask that the *true* service be restored in the Temple (*Etz Yosef*).

◄§ Killing the Animal Instinct

Ramban (*Leviticus* 1:1) explains why the animal sacrifice is the most meaningful form of Divine service. God's greatest gift to man is the human intellect which enables man to discern between good and bad. But lurking inside every human heart is a wild beast, the Evil Impulse, waiting for man to let down his guard so it can overwhelm him with animalistic desires. When man surrenders his superb mind to the animal impulse, he rejects his Divine gift.

In truth, man should forfeit his life for this failure. But God in His mercy provides for another means of atonement. The sinner designates an animal, and brings it to the Temple where he leans on its head and declares: "My intellect failed to control my impulse and I behaved like a senseless beast, not a Godly human being. When I sinned, I resembled this animal upon which I am now leaning. I will therefore slaughter this animal to symbolizes that in the future I will overcome and slay the animal impulse which attacks me. The blood of this animal will be sprinkled on the holy altar, for blood symbolizes sensuality and fiery passion which I will henceforth channel toward enthusiastic, inspired service of God."

In this blessing we ask God to accept our passionate prayers as if they were fiery offerings on the altar of the Temple.

◄§ The Prayer of Abraham

Rav Avraham ben HaGra demonstrates how these last three blessings of the *Amidah* correspond to the first three blessings, which represented each of the three *Avos*. This blessing about sacrifices corresponds to the very first blessing which is primarily dedicated to our Patriarch

Abraham who went to the Temple Mount prepared to offer up his beloved son Isaac to God. Abraham prayed that God's Presence should always be manifest on this holy site as it says: *And Abraham named that site 'HASHEM will see', as it is said on this day, 'on the mountain HASHEM is seen'* (Genesis 22:14). In this blessing we pray for Abraham's wish to be fulfilled and for God to reveal His presence to His people on Mount Zion.

◆§ Seventeen — A Good Number

This blessing was designated as number seventeen because prayer is called טוב, *goodness*, and the numerical value of טוב is seventeen. As the Midrash (*Bamidbar Rabbah* 18:17) teaches: The prophet said to God, כָּל תִּשָּׂא עָוֹן וְקַח טוֹב וּנְשַׁלְּמָה פָרִים שְׂפָתֵינוּ, *Forgive all sins and accept our goodness, we will offer the words of our lips instead of sacrificial cows* (Hosea 14:3). With this, he echoed the words of the Jewish people who cried out to God, "When the Temple was standing we could offer sacrifices to atone for our sins, but now all we can offer is טוב, *the goodness* of our prayers."

◆§ God Desires Righteous Prayer

רְצֵה ה' אֱלֹהֵינוּ בְּעַמְּךָ יִשְׂרָאֵל וּבִתְפִלָּתָם — *Be favorable, HASHEM, our God, toward Your people Israel and their prayer.*

The Talmud (*Yevamos* 64a) teaches that הקב"ה מִתְאַוֶּה לִתְפִלָּתָם שֶׁל צַדִּיקִים, *The Holy One, Blessed is He, desires the prayers of the righteous.* Therefore, we first ask God to look favorably upon the people of Israel and to consider them righteous [by virtue of their sincere dependence on Him]. When the people are righteous in the eyes of God, He will surely look favorably upon their prayers and desire them (*Rav Avraham ben HaGra*).

Indeed, the very theme of Israel's prayers makes God desire them, as the Midrash (*Bereishis Rabbah* 13:2) says: Look at the difference between Israel and the nations. The gentile nations are exclusively absorbed in material pursuits and all they ask is, "When will the soil be fertile, when will the farms produce?" But the eyes of Israel turn to loftier concerns and their prayer is, "When will the Temple be rebuilt? Please, O Lord, rebuild Your sanctuary!" (*Rav Yehudah ben Yakar*).

◈§ A Return to Intimacy

וְהָשֵׁב אֶת הָעֲבוֹדָה לִדְבִיר בֵּיתֶךָ — *And restore the service to the Holy of Holies of Your Temple.*

The inner sanctum of the Tabernacle and the Temple, the קֹדֶשׁ קֳדָשִׁים, *the Holy of Holies,* is also called the דְּבִיר (see *I Kings* 6:20, 8:6,8 et al). *Iyun Tefillah* explains that the root of דְּבִיר is דִּבּוּר, *speech,* i.e., the Holy of Holies is the private chamber, the conference room where God talks intimately to the representatives of the Jewish people, as it says: *And I will meet with you there [in the Holy of Holies] and I will speak with you . . . of all matters which I will command you to tell the Children of Israel* (*Exodus* 25:22). We plead with God to restore His original love for Israel so that we may enjoy the most intimate relationship with Him. We ask God to communicate with us directly and guide every aspect of our lives.

◈§ Pray with Flaming Love

וְאִשֵּׁי יִשְׂרָאֵל וּתְפִלָּתָם בְּאַהֲבָה תְקַבֵּל בְּרָצוֹן — *The fire-offerings of Israel and their prayer accept with love and favor.*

This request for God to accept our fire-offerings seems odd since we cannot bring sacrifices in our times. Therefore, some commentaries understand וְאִשֵּׁי יִשְׂרָאֵל as the conclusion of the previous sentence and repunctuate this blessing to read: . . . *and restore the service . . . and the fire-offerings of Israel. Their prayer accept with love . . .* (*Vilna Gaon* quoted in *Mishnah Berurah* 120:1).

Tur (*Orach Chaim* 120) has a different explanation. Even though the Temple is not standing and we cannot bring fire-offerings today, this phrase refers to our words of prayer, which now take the place of the Temple sacrifices. We pray that God accept these words with love and favor as if they were actual sacrifices.

Tur also cites the Midrash (see *Menachos* 110a and *Tosafos* ibid.) that when Jews pray with sincere love for God their souls soar heavenward on wings of prayer. The archangel Michael takes these fiery souls and places them on the celestial altar where they are regarded as fire-offerings to God. Thus the word אִשֵּׁי combines both אֵשׁ, *fire,* and אִישׁ, *man,* referring to the impassioned supplicant who is consumed with flaming love for God and sacrifices himself to the Almighty (*Mishnah Berurah* 120:1).

✺ A Personal Sacrifice

Yaaros Dvash states that when a person recites this blessing he should fill his heart with a tremendous desire to sacrifice his life for the sanctification of God's Name. He should picture himself bound hand and foot, as Isaac was, and placed on a fiery altar to be a burnt-offering to God.

✺ The Fire-Offerings of Israel

There is a fire burning inside every Jew; it is the source of his energy and passion for serving the Almighty. If this flame is harnessed properly it is considered to be a fire-offering to Hashem.

In the Talmud, Rabbi Eliezer states: The blood that flows when a person stubs a toe can effect Divine favor equal to the sacrifice of a burnt-offering on the Temple Altar. Rava added: This rule applies only to the big toe on the right foot, if it is stubbed and cut for the second time — before the first cut has healed — and only if it occurs when running to do a *mitzvah* (*Chullin* 7b).

Rav Chaim Shmulevitz zt"l explained that usually after a person stubs his toe, he tends to walk very carefully, guarding his toe gingerly, because even the slightest tap will cause him great pain. But if this same person *ran* to do a *mitzvah*, giving no thought to his personal discomfort when the time came to serve Hashem, and in his haste stubbed his toe painfully *a second time*, the blood that flows from this new wound is considered like a burnt-offering, because it comes from serving God with selfless sacrifice and devotion.

Another fire-offering which can be offered every day: *Shulchan Aruch* (*Orach Chaim* 61:1) rules that *Shema* should be recited "with intense concentration, trepidation, trembling and sweat." The Talmud (*Berachos* 15b) teaches that whoever takes pains to carefully enunciate each word of the *Shema* will merit that the fires of Gehinnom be cooled down for him. *Beis Yosef* (*Orach Chaim* 62) explains that the person who recites *Shema* fervently will literally raise the level of his body temperature and be aflame with love and fear of God. Since God always rewards measure for measure, the more a person raises his body heat while performing *mitzvos*, the more Hashem will lower the heat of purgatory for him and he will suffer less for his sins.

⋖§ Israel's Unique Privilege

Rav Yehudah ben Yakar draws our attention to *Midrash Tanchuma* (*Parshas Tzav* 1) which relates how the wicked Balaam offered many sacrifices to sway God's favor from the Jews and toward the gentiles. God rejected his attempts outright, saying, *"Will HASHEM be pleased with thousands of rams or with ten thousands of rivers of oil? (Micah 6:7)*. Balaam, you are deluding yourself! I can accept no sacrifice from the gentile nations for I have entered into an ironclad covenant with Israel that only their sacrifices do I accept with favor!" With these words in mind we now ask God to favor the אִשֵּׁי יִשְׂרָאֵל, *the fire-offerings of Israel*, and to reject the offerings of the gentiles, who seek to harm Israel.

⋖§ Congregational Prayer

וּתְהִי לְרָצוֹן תָּמִיד עֲבוֹדַת יִשְׂרָאֵל עַמֶּךְ — *And may the service of Your people Israel always be favorable to You.*

The Talmud (*Berachos* 8a) stresses the importance of *tefillah b'tzibbur*, prayer with a quorum of ten men. If it is impossible to join the *minyan*, one should at least attempt to synchronize his schedule so that his private prayers be at the same time as the congregational service. God always accepts the prayers of a congregation of Jewish people who gather to pray, but the prayers of individuals may not be at a propitious time.

Rabbeinu Yonah (*Berachos* 13a) notes that the personal prayer of an individual requires a מַלְאָךְ מֵלִיץ, *an intermediary angel*, to assist it, but when one prays with the congregation the prayers need no assistance and arise directly before God. If circumstances prevent a person from praying with a *minyan*, then by following the exact liturgy of the *Amidah* which is universally used by all Jews, he invests his prayers with special favor (see comm. of *Maharsha* to *Yoma* 86a and *Levush* to *Orach Chaim* 101:4). Therefore, we now express our hope that the *standard, congregational* service of all Israel always be favorable to You.

◆§ Intimate Encounter

וְתֶחֱזֶינָה עֵינֵינוּ בְּשׁוּבְךָ לְצִיּוֹן בְּרַחֲמִים — *May our eyes behold Your return to Zion in compassion.*

Rabbi Yehudah ben Yakar, citing the Midrash, says that God declares, "In this world I am not visible to mankind, as it says, *For no man shall see Me and live* (*Exodus* 33:20). But in the future when I return to Zion, I will reveal My glory to Israel and they will see Me and live forever, as it says, *For they shall see eye to eye when* HASHEM *returns to Zion*" (*Isaiah* 52:8).

Elsewhere, the prophet foretells that in the future, *Your eyes shall gaze upon your teacher* (ibid. 30:20), meaning that Israel will sit before God like a student sitting at his master's feet, and freely ask God to explain part of the Torah. So exclusive is this privilege that even the ministering angels will come to ask Israel, "Tell us please, what did God teach you?" Even the angels will not be allowed to participate in this intimate encounter between God and Israel: Only **our** *eyes will behold Your return to Zion.*

◆§ The Gift of Vision

This is the time to thank God for the precious gift of clear vision, which is the key to joyous life. Indeed, the Talmud (*Nedarim* 64b) notes that blindness is akin to death. In fact, we should express our gratitude to the Creator for all of our limbs. The Mishnah (*Avos*) teaches: "Who is an עָשִׁיר, *a rich man?* He who rejoices over his lot." The word עָשִׁיר is an acronym for עֵינַיִם, *eyes;* שִׁנַּיִם, *teeth;* יָדַיִם, *hands;* רַגְלַיִם, *feet.*

Never stop thanking Hashem for the basic bodily organs and limbs we enjoy. Never take them for granted.

◆§ Only Pure Eyes Shall See

Our Rabbis warn us to guard our eyes very carefully, and to prevent them from seeing impure sights. The eye is truly a marvelous machine, yet even the tiniest speck of dust can interfere with vision and force a person to shut his eye tight. Similarly, with regard to spiritual vision, we are capable of witnessing the revelation of God's glory only if we keep our eyes pure. Exposure to forbidden sights contaminates our eyes and shuts down our vision (*Rav Leib Chasman*).

The Rabbis of the Midrash (*Vayikra Rabbah* 23:13) make this promise: "The person who guards his eyes from seeing anything unclean will surely merit that his eyes will behold God's Holy Presence. As the prophet says: וְעֹצֵם עֵינָיו מֵרְאוֹת בְּרָע. . .מֶלֶךְ בְּיָפְיוֹ תֶּחֱזֶינָה עֵינֶיךָ, *He who shuts his eyes from seeing evil. . .his eyes shall behold the King in all His beauty (Isaiah 33:15,17).*"

The eyes love to wander everywhere and they are the main agents of the Evil Impulse in bringing us to sin. They are very hard to control and we must pour out our hearts in prayer and shed many tears begging God to help us regulate our wayward eyes. *Tur* emphasizes this idea in his introduction to *Shulchan Aruch (Orach Chaim* 1). He observes that King David was so keenly aware of the importance of guarding his eyes that he composed a special supplication: הַעֲבֵר עֵינַי מֵרְאוֹת שָׁוְא בִּדְרָכֶךָ חַיֵּנִי, *Avert my eyes from seeing futility, through Your ways, preserve me (Psalms 119:37).*

For this reason we pray, *May our eyes behold Your return* — grant us the privilege of utilizing our eyes for holy matters, and spare us from profaning them, God forbid.

◆§ Let Us Witness Salvation

Abudraham says that the wording of this blessing alludes to the prophecy of Micah in which the nations of the earth hate Israel and hope to see her downfall. The prophet foretells: *Many nations will gather against you and say: "Let her be devastated,* וְתַחַז בְּצִיּוֹן עֵינֵינוּ, *let our eyes gaze upon Zion." But they know not the thoughts of HASHEM nor do they understand His strategy; for He has gathered them [around Zion] as sheaves are gathered to the threshing floor [to be beaten] (Micah 4:11,12).*

Thus we plead here to see with our own eyes the downfall of our enemies, and to personally witness the triumph of Zion, as the prophet says: *They lift up their voice, all together they shall sing, for they shall see eye to eye, HASHEM returning to Zion (Isaiah 52:8).*

Yaaros Dvash points out that when a person is unworthy of salvation but is saved because of the merits of others, he does not deserve to see the downfall of the enemies of God. For this reason, Lot's wife, who was rescued from Sodom only by virtue of Abraham's merits, had no right to look back and witness the devastation of the wicked city. On the other hand, the Jews who miraculously crossed the Sea of Reeds were delivered because of their own faith in God and, as such, were allowed to see the drowning of their Egyptian oppressors.

We express our hope, therefore, that when the time for redemption arrives, God will remember us on account of our *own* merits — not only those of our ancestors — so that we will be able to witness personally the destruction of our enemies, and *our eyes will behold Your return to Zion in compassion.*

✑ Feeling God's Presence

בָּרוּךְ אַתָּה ה' הַמַּחֲזִיר שְׁכִינָתוֹ לְצִיּוֹן — *Blessed are You, HASHEM, Who restores His Presence to Zion.*

The Midrash says that after the מִשְׁכָּן, *Tabernacle,* was constructed in the Wilderness and God's *Shechinah* [Presence] came to rest there, the ministering angels chanted, "Blessed are You, HASHEM, Who restores His Presence to Zion."

Rambam (Hilchos Beis Habechirah 6:16) rules that the sanctity of Jerusalem and the Temple Mount is absolutely inviolable and can never be nullified. Even when gentiles conquered these holy sites and every Jew was expelled, their unique sanctity remained entirely intact. The sanctity of the Temple site and Jerusalem are because of the *Shechinah,* and the *Shechinah* cannot be removed, as Scripture states, *And I shall make desolate your sanctuaries (Leviticus 26:31).* This implies that when it is rendered desolate it remains a sanctuary [*Mishnah Megillah* 3:3].

On the other hand, numerous sources indicate that the *Shechinah* did indeed depart from the Temple. The Talmud clearly states that five features of the First Temple were missing from the Second Temple, and one of them was the *Shechinah (Yoma 21b).* Furthermore, the Talmud teaches that the *Shechinah* departed from the Temple very reluctantly in the hope that the Jewish people would repent (*Rosh Hashanah 31a,* see *Rashi* ibid.). It did not disappear all at once, but withdrew in ten stages, slowly distancing itself further and further from the Temple.

The apparent contradiction between *Rambam* and the Talmudic sources is reconciled when we realize that there is a difference between the actual Presence of God and its perceptible manifestation. Indeed, once God's Presence settled upon the Temple Mount it never departed, and the sanctity of the area remains. But in the First Temple His Presence was so clear that one could actually sense God's proximity, so that all who entered the holy environs were overwhelmed with trepidation and awe. But when Israel sinned and distanced themselves from God, He concealed His Presence (see *Arachin* 6a and *Tosafos* s.v. כְּגוֹן כַּלְיָא עוֹרֵב). As we conclude this blessing, we therefore beseech God to favor us with His manifest presence, that He may show us clearly that He dwells in our midst, in Zion.

18

הוֹדָאָה / Thanksgiving

מוֹדִים אֲנַחְנוּ לָךְ, שָׁאַתָּה הוּא יהוה אֱלֹהֵינוּ וֵאלֹהֵי אֲבוֹתֵינוּ לְעוֹלָם וָעֶד. צוּר חַיֵּינוּ, מָגֵן יִשְׁעֵנוּ אַתָּה הוּא לְדוֹר וָדוֹר. נוֹדֶה לְךָ וּנְסַפֵּר תְּהִלָּתֶךָ עַל חַיֵּינוּ הַמְּסוּרִים בְּיָדֶךָ, וְעַל נִשְׁמוֹתֵינוּ הַפְּקוּדוֹת לָךְ, וְעַל נִסֶּיךָ שֶׁבְּכָל יוֹם עִמָּנוּ, וְעַל נִפְלְאוֹתֶיךָ וְטוֹבוֹתֶיךָ שֶׁבְּכָל עֵת, עֶרֶב וָבֹקֶר וְצָהֳרָיִם. הַטּוֹב כִּי לֹא כָלוּ רַחֲמֶיךָ, וְהַמְרַחֵם כִּי לֹא תַמּוּ חֲסָדֶיךָ, מֵעוֹלָם קִוִּינוּ לָךְ.

וְעַל כֻּלָּם יִתְבָּרַךְ וְיִתְרוֹמַם שִׁמְךָ מַלְכֵּנוּ תָּמִיד לְעוֹלָם וָעֶד. וְכֹל הַחַיִּים יוֹדוּךָ סֶּלָה, וִיהַלְלוּ אֶת שִׁמְךָ בֶּאֱמֶת, הָאֵל יְשׁוּעָתֵנוּ וְעֶזְרָתֵנוּ סֶלָה. בָּרוּךְ אַתָּה יהוה, הַטּוֹב שִׁמְךָ וּלְךָ נָאֶה לְהוֹדוֹת.

We gratefully thank You, for it is You Who are HASHEM, our God and the God of our forefathers for all eternity; Rock of our lives, Shield of our salvation are You from generation to generation. We shall thank You and relate Your praise — for our lives, which are committed to Your power and for our souls that are entrusted to You; for Your miracles that are with us every day; and for Your wonders and favors in every season — evening, morning, and afternoon. The Beneficent One, for Your compassions were never exhausted, and the Compassionate One, for Your kindnesses never ended — always have we put our hope in You.

For all these, may Your Name be blessed and exalted, our King, continually forever and ever. Everything alive will gratefully acknowledge You, Selah! and praise Your Name sincerely, O God of our salvation and help, Selah! Blessed are You, HASHEM, Your Name is 'The Beneficent One' and to You it is fitting to give thanks.

The Talmud (*Megillah* 18a) explains that the blessing of thanksgiving logically follows the blessing of the Temple service, because עֲבוֹדָה וְהוֹדָאָה חֲדָא מִלְתָא הִיא, *service and thanks are identical*. This implies that it is unacceptable to thank God for His graciousness without accepting the obligation to serve Him. How can one acknowledge that his very existence, both personal and national, stems from God's mercy, without simultaneously accepting an obligation to abide by His will (*R' Munk*)?

Thanksgiving is the essence of the Jew. Even the title, *Jew*, stems from the name יְהוּדָה, *Judah*, who was so called because his mother Leah expressed her profound הוֹדָאָה, *thanksgiving*, to Hashem for his birth (*Genesis* 29:35). So essential is the expression of gratitude that the Midrash (*Vayikra Rabbah* 9:7) teaches: In the world of the future all sacrifices will be unnecessary, except for the קָרְבַּן תּוֹדָה, *thanksgiving offering*, which will remain. Similarly, all prayer will be discontinued, except for the blessings of הוֹדָאָה, *thanksgiving*, which will remain.

❧ *Gratitude: The Essence of Life*

It is appropriate that this is the eighteenth blessing of the *Amidah* because חַי [*Chai*], *life*, has a numerical value of eighteen and the purpose of life is to recognize God's kindness and to thank Him for it by devoting one's life to His service, as the prophet said: חַי חַי הוּא יוֹדֶךָ, *the living — only the living — will gratefully praise You* (*Isaiah* 38:19).

The Midrash (*Bereishis Rabbah* 14:11) says that for every single breath we take, we should express our thanks to God for the gift of life. Furthermore, our Rabbis tell us that a person takes eighteen breaths per minute, for חַי, *eighteen*, symbolizes life.

❧ *An Attitude of Gratitude*

Many times we do not feel gratitude because we take what we already have for granted. We focus on what we are missing rather than enjoying what we already possess. Arrogance is a prime source of this dissatisfaction, because we always think that we deserve more. The humble person, on the other hand, realizes that nothing is owed him, so he is content with and grateful for his lot.

Rabbi Nosson Tzvi Finkel, the "Alter of Slabodka," advised his students: Make a daily practice of viewing the world as if you have just entered it. Think of the endless, glorious gifts we enjoy. The sunshine, the air, nature. Sight. Smell. Hearing. Taste. Touch. Look at everything around you with a fresh perspective each day and you will transform monotony into an exhilarating experience.

◆§ Shemoneh Esrei Is Always Eighteen

Rabbi Avrohom David Lavut (Shaar HaKollel ch. 9) notes all liturgical texts agree that this blessing is composed of exactly eighty-six words. The numerical value of אֱלֹהִים, *God,* is 86, the same as the value of הַטֶּבַע, *the nature.* Thus we bless and thank God for creating all the wonders of nature which we continually enjoy. Also, according to all texts, we begin this blessing by saying, *We shall thank You and relate Your praise —* עַל חַיֵּינוּ הַמְּסוּרִים בְּיָדֶךָ — *for our lives, which are committed to Your power.* Then we thank God for *twelve* more displays of kindness, each one prefaced by the connecting prefix ו, *vov.* The emphasis is on the number twelve, because the *Amidah* service is composed of three introductory blessings of שֶׁבַח, *praise,* and three concluding blessings of הוֹדָאָה, *thanksgiving,* to which we add these twelve expressions of thanks, for a total of eighteen. This numerology was incorporated in order to assure every *Amidah* would contain eighteen expressions of thanksgiving and blessing, even those of the Sabbath and Festivals, which lack the central core of twelve personal requests. This also explains why we refer to the *Amidah* of the Sabbath and Festivals as *Shemoneh Esrei —* which means eighteen — even though they never were composed of eighteen blessings.

◆§ Bowing in Gratitude

We bow to Hashem twice in this blessing: at the beginning when reciting the word מוֹדִים, *We thank,* and at the end, at the word בָּרוּךְ, *Blessed.* The Talmud (*Bava Kamma* 16a) states that whoever does not bow during this blessing will incur the punishment of having his spine twisted out of shape like that of a twisting, curled serpent.

Maharsha (ibid.) explains that the original serpent in the Garden of

Eden walked vertically with a perfectly straight posture resembling man. But this made the serpent arrogant and presumptuous. Instead of being filled with gratitude towards God, he was filled with envy and contempt, always wanting more. Cunningly, he spread his discontent and convinced Eve that she too had nothing to be grateful for if she couldn't eat from the Tree of Knowledge. When God punished the ungrateful serpent, He deprived him of his upright posture (*Sotah* 9b). Therefore, anyone who refuses to bow in this blessing of thanksgiving is seen as following the example of the serpent and will be punished accordingly with a crooked spine. [See Overview: *Sovereignty Through Surrender*; ch. VII, *The Posture of Prayer*.]

The Jerusalem Talmud (*Berachos* 2:4) states: Rabbi Masnay said, "I am grateful to my head, because whenever I arrive at the blessing of מוֹדִים, *thanksgiving*, it bows down by itself." The rabbi did not mean to say that his head bent over mechanically, by rote. That would contradict the spirit of meaningful, heartfelt prayer. Rather, Rabbi Masnay realized that it is extremely difficult for anyone to humbly surrender himself to God and admit that God deserves all the credit for human accomplishments. Had the rabbi's head been filled with proud thoughts all day long it would have been very hard to bow it during one brief moment of prayer. But since his head was preoccupied with thoughts of God's greatness all day long, it bowed effortlessly when reciting the blessing of thanksgiving. For this Rabbi Masnay was grateful (*Tefillas Chana*).

⊸§ The Blessing of Isaac and Abraham

Rav Avraham ben HaGra observes that this second blessing in the "Thanksgiving" section corresponds to Isaac, the second Patriarch, who showed the ultimate gratitude to God by offering himself as a sacrifice.

Shibbolei Halekket quotes the Midrash that this blessing was composed when King Solomon dedicated the First Temple. He attempted to bring the Holy Ark into the Temple, but the gates refused to open. The Talmud (*Shabbos* 30a) relates how Solomon recited twenty-four רְנָנוֹת, *cries of prayer*, but still he was not answered. The gates finally opened only when Solomon invoked the memory of his father David. Solomon was overjoyed because this publicly displayed that Hashem had forgiven David's sin with Solomon's mother Bath-sheba.

Solomon thanked and praised God profusely and the ministering angels chanted, "Blessed are You, HASHEM, Your Name is 'The Beneficent One,' and to You it is fitting to give thanks."

◆§ One Hundred Thanks

מוֹדִים אֲנַחְנוּ לָךְ — *We gratefully thank You.*

Abudraham remarks that the numerical value of the word מוֹדִים equals one hundred, alluding to the Talmudic dictum (*Menachos* 43b) that a person is obligated to make at least one hundred blessings every day. *Megalleh Amukos* (239) observes that this is why the Psalmist placed מִזְמוֹר לְתוֹדָה, *A Song of Thanksgiving,* as the one hundredth Psalm.

The Midrash (*Bamidbar Rabbah* 18:17) relates that during King David's reign a plague ravaged the country, killing one hundred people every day, until David established the practice of reciting one hundred blessings daily. In the merit of this *mitzvah* the plague stopped (see *Tur, Orach Chaim* 46).

Why did David use blessings as the antidote against the deadly plague? *Midrash Tanchuma* (end of *V'zos Habrachah*) explains that "the wicked are considered dead even while alive" because they are oblivious to all the bounties God bestows upon mankind. They see the sunrise and sunset, yet they remain silent. They eat and drink the finest delicacies without a word of thanks or benediction. Nothing stirs their souls to bless God, so that, in the sense of their awareness of God's role, they are tantamount to dead. The righteous, however, are always alive, because they bless and thank God for His every kindness. Therefore David instituted the recital of blessings of thanksgiving to counter the plague of death, fulfilling the words of this *Amidah* blessing, *"Everything alive will gratefully acknowledge You, Selah!"*

◆§ God's Loyalty to Israel

שָׁאַתָּה הוּא ה' אֱלֹהֵינוּ וֵאלֹהֵי אֲבוֹתֵינוּ לְעוֹלָם וָעֶד — *For it is You Who are HASHEM, our God and the God of our forefathers for all eternity.*

We are deeply grateful to You for designating us as Your Chosen People and allowing us to refer to You as the God of Israel. Moreover, our many sins have provided You with reason to renounce us, yet You remain faithful to Your promise that Israel will be Your people for all time (*Etz Yosef*).

צוּר חַיֵּינוּ מָגֵן יִשְׁעֵנוּ — *Rock of our lives, Shield of our salvation.*

God protects us in two ways. Sometimes He lifts us so far above danger that we are totally unaware of it, as if He were the *Rock of our lives,* who places us atop an impregnable mountain fortress, so to speak, and guards us. At other times, God exposes us to danger, to let us know we have done something wrong. Yet even then He rescues us acting as the *Shield of our salvation.*

ᴇ§ *Never Forget a Kindness*

נוֹדֶה לְךָ וּנְסַפֵּר תְּהִלָּתֶךָ — *We shall thank You and relate Your praise.*

Rabbi Alexander Ziskind (author of *Yesod V'Shoresh HaAvodah*) wrote a lengthy ethical will to his children, in which he demonstrated in great detail how he never forgot any kindness that Hashem bestowed upon him. He recorded how every line of the *Amidah* awakened memories of Divine kindness from his earliest years, and he committed himself to thanking God repeatedly for His goodness and to relating His praises to others.

In section 32 of this will, Rabbi Ziskind reminds his children to thank God for even the most mundane things. He writes, "Thank Hashem profusely every time you need the simplest utensil and you find it — a knife, a spoon, a pen. Thank God for giving you a table and chair. Thank God for a small pinch of snuff. Nothing is too insignificant to warrant thanking Him."

ᴇ§ *In God's Hands*

עַל חַיֵּינוּ הַמְּסוּרִים בְּיָדֶךָ — *For our lives, which are committed to Your power.*

Lest anyone think that he is master over his own life, we acknowledge that our every breath and heartbeat is a direct result of Your mercy (*Olas Tamid*). Furthermore, as a nation we are controlled by You alone. While celestial forces rule the lives and fates of the gentile nations, through sincere prayer Jews can release themselves from their control. As the Talmud (*Shabbos* 156a) teaches: אֵין מַזָּל לְיִשְׂרָאֵל, *no celestial forces direct Israel's destiny*, when Jews place themselves in God's hands.

◄§ A Faithful Watchman

וְעַל נִשְׁמוֹתֵינוּ הַפְּקוּדוֹת לָךְ — *And for our souls that are entrusted to You.*

The word נְשָׁמָה, *soul*, refers to a higher force that gives man his holiness, as opposed to his vital organs which merely keep him alive. During sleep, the animal soul remains in man; he remains alive and his body functions normally. But the *neshamah*, the higher spiritual soul, leaves the body and ascends to higher spiritual realms, where it can receive Divine communication, sometimes in the form of a dream. At this time, the *neshamah* is entrusted to God to be returned to man in the morning (*Derech Hashem*).

The *Zohar* teaches that if one has agreed to guard an object for its owner, he has no right to keep it even if the owner owes him money. Having accepted custody of the object on the understanding that he will return it, the guardian may not keep it to enforce a different claim. This law is derived from the behavior of God. Although He can always claim that we "owe" Him our lives because we have failed to honor our commitments to Him, He still returns our souls every morning (*K'tzos HaChoshen* ch. 4).

◄§ Nature Is a Miracle

וְעַל נִסֶּיךָ שֶׁבְּכָל יוֹם עִמָּנוּ וְעַל נִפְלְאוֹתֶיךָ וְטוֹבוֹתֶיךָ שֶׁבְּכָל עֵת — *For Your miracles that are with us every day; and for Your wonders and favors in every season.*

In this context, *miracles* are those extraordinary events that everyone recognizes as the result of God's intervention. *Wonders*, on the other hand, are the familiar things that we regard as normal, like breathing, raining, and growing. We are accustomed to them because they happen constantly, בְּכָל עֵת, *in every season*, so we call them "natural phenomena" rather than miracles. Logically, however, they are no less miraculous. There is no more reason for oil to burn than water, except that God has willed oil and water to act in different ways. In *Modim*, we thank God for both categories, because we recognize that there is no real difference between the two, except for God's will (*Etz Yosef*).

❧ Secret Wonders

We thank God also for the wonders He performs without our knowledge. King David sang, *Blessed is HASHEM, God, the God of Israel, Who alone does wonders* (Psalms 72:18). The Talmud (*Niddah* 31a) explains that God often acts *alone* — hidden — so that even the beneficiary of His miracle doesn't recognize immediately his own good fortune. The Talmud illustrates this with a parable: A merchant was on his way to board a ship, when he injured his foot, forcing him to miss the ship. Disappointed, the merchant cursed his luck. Soon however, word arrived that the ship had sunk, and everyone aboard had drowned. Now the wounded merchant understood the Divine Providence behind his accident and thanked God for His intervention.

❧ Perpetual Delight

וְטוּבוֹתֶיךָ שֶׁבְּכָל עֵת עֶרֶב וָבֹקֶר וְצָהֳרַיִם — *And for Your favors in every season — evening, morning, and afternoon.*

Every season has attractions and benefits as well as discomforts and disadvantages and we must accustom ourselves to focusing on the positive aspects of each. The same applies to the different times of the day. Some people hate getting up in the morning, while others like to get a head start on the day. Some people dread the dark of night while others burn the midnight oil. We must learn to look for the unique benefits of each time period.

Rav Avigdor Miller says: "We have the ability to delight in spring, revel in the sunny summer, love the vitality of autumn, and relish the bracing winter, and perpetually be grateful to the One Who changes the times and Who orders the sequence of the seasons" (*Awake, My Glory*, p. 369).

❧ Unlimited Resources

הַטּוֹב כִּי לֹא כָלוּ רַחֲמֶיךָ וְהַמְרַחֵם כִּי לֹא תַמּוּ חֲסָדֶיךָ — *The Beneficent One, for Your compassions were never exhausted, and the Compassionate One, for Your kindnesses never ended.*

There are wealthy men whose resources are virtually unlimited, enabling them to perform tremendous kindnesses, but their level of compassion is limited. On the other hand, there are merciful people who have boundless compassion but lack the means of actually helping those they care for. This is not the case with God — His feelings of compassion are *never* exhausted, and His ability to bestow kindness *never* ends.

◦§ We Are Confident of Your Love

מֵעוֹלָם קִוִּינוּ לָךְ — *Always have we put our hope in You.*

Even in the darkest times when You seemed unconcerned for our plight we knew that You were merely concealing Yourself temporarily, because You yearned for us to turn to You in sincere, fervent prayer.

◦§ A World of Thanks

וְעַל כֻּלָּם יִתְבָּרַךְ וְיִתְרוֹמַם שִׁמְךָ מַלְכֵּנוּ תָּמִיד לְעוֹלָם וָעֶד — *For all these, may Your Name be blessed and exalted, our King, continually forever and ever.*

Rabbi Yisrael Salanter once left his family and disciples in Eastern Europe to go to Paris and influence the assimilated Jews there to return to Torah Judaism. One day he entered an elegant restaurant to meet with some of the many Jews who frequented the establishment. Rav Yisrael was seated at his table and ordered a glass of water. When he was ready to leave, the waiter presented him with a bill for the astronomic sum of forty francs. "Why do you charge so much for a glass of water?" asked Rav Yisrael. The waiter replied, "Monsieur, you must realize that your are not merely paying for a simple glass of water. You are paying for the surroundings, the ambience. You are paying for the gorgeous furniture, tableware, carpeting and chandeliers, not to mention the view!"

The answer struck a chord in Rav Yisrael's heart. He hastened back to his lodgings and wrote a letter to his disciples: "For a long time I have been puzzled by the fact that we recite a very lofty and all-inclusive blessing for a plain glass of water, saying, *Blessed are You,* HASHEM, *our God, King of the universe,* שֶׁהַכֹּל נִהְיֶה בִּדְבָרוֹ, *through Whose word* **everything** *came to be.* But from the words of a gentile waiter in Paris I learnt that we are not merely thanking God for the glass of water; we are expressing our appreciation for the magnificent surroundings in which God serves the water to us. We are thanking God for the fresh air we breathe as we drink that water and for the sun which gives us light and for the tree which shades us. In short, whenever we thank God for *one* thing, we should use it as an opportunity to thank God for everything."

⇜ Awaken the World to Thank God

וְכֹל הַחַיִּים יוֹדוּךָ סֶּלָה — *Everything alive will gratefully acknowledge You, Selah!*

When King Hezekiah recovered from a near fatal illness he said, *The grave cannot thank You, nor can the dead praise You; those who have descended to the pit cannot hope for Your truth. The living — only the living — can gratefully thank You* (Isaiah 38:18-19). And King David said, *I will praise* HASHEM *while I live; I will sing to my God while I exist* (Psalms 146:2). Echoing these two great leaders, we proclaim that as long as we have life, we can express our thanks to God (*Etz Yosef*). Even if we do not have all the prosperity and happiness we would like, we are still *alive* and for that alone we should express our gratitude (*Siach Yitzchak*).

Chiddushei HaRim observes that the purpose of our prayers is not merely to gain personal benefit, but to awaken and revitalize the entire world, which slumbers unaware of God's Presence and Providence. The true sign of successful prayer is when the praise spoken by the individual arouses others to become conscious of God, so that *everything alive will gratefully acknowledge You, Selah!* (*Siddur Sfas Emes*).

⇜ Rehearsal for the Afterlife

Rav Yehudah ben Yakar says that the phrase וְכֹל הַחַיִּים, *everything alive*, refers to the world after the Resurrection of the Dead, when all those who are deserving will be alive to experience the ultimate life — the life of eternity!

All the praises we chant in this world are inferior to the praises that will be sung in the future. Indeed, our prayer on this world is just a short rehearsal for the "main performance" in the World to Come. *Rashi* emphasizes this point (*Berachos* 63a s.v. כבודך): "This world is merely a corridor leading into the World to Come. Accustom yourself to reciting God's blessings in this world so that you will be well prepared to recite His praises forever in the World to Come."

⋙ Four Categories of Thanksgiving

Etz Yosef draws our attention to the Talmud (*Berachos* 54b) which says that anyone who falls into one of these four categories was in such grave danger that he must show special gratitude to Hashem by bringing Him a קָרְבַּן תּוֹדָה, *a thanksgiving offering.* They are:

1) a person released from captivity or jail;
2) a person who was dangerously ill;
3) a person who journeyed over the high seas;
4) a person who traveled through the desolate desert.

The word חַיִּים, *the living,* serves as an acronym for these four circumstances:

ח = חָבוּשׁ, *imprisoned;*

י = יִסּוּרִים, *suffering and sickness;*

י = יָם, *sea;*

ם = מִדְבָּר, *desert.*

Thus all who are included in the categories of חַיִּים *will gratefully acknowledge You, Selah!*

⋙ Honest Praise

וִיהַלְלוּ אֶת שִׁמְךָ בֶּאֱמֶת — *And praise Your Name sincerely.*

Sometimes people express gratitude in the hope that their benefactor will give them even more. That is not our intention. We thank God in sincerity, and even when we request further generosity, we do so because it is His desire that we pray for our needs (*Olas Tamid*).

⋙ God's Burdens Are a Blessing

הָאֵל יְשׁוּעָתֵנוּ וְעֶזְרָתֵנוּ סֶלָה — *O God of our salvation and help, Selah!*

This phrase is based on the words of King David who said, בָּרוּךְ אֲדֹנָי יוֹם יוֹם יַעֲמָס לָנוּ הָאֵל יְשׁוּעָתֵנוּ סֶלָה, *Blessed is my Lord, day by day He burdens us, the God of our salvation, Selah* (*Psalms* 68:20). *Targum* explains that in addition to the basic precepts that are incumbent upon the Jewish people, God adds new commands, trials and challenges every day. By increasing our burden, He makes us realize how dependent we are on God and become more attached to Him (*Shemos Rabbah* 25:9).

The more attached we become to God, the more He will "burden" us with kindness and blessing (*Rashi*). Thus, to the extent that we recognize our helplessness and acknowledge God as עֶזְרָתֵנוּ, *our help*, the more He will become יְשׁוּעָתֵנוּ, *our salvation*.

◆§ Thank the Butler but Never Forget Your Host

בָּרוּךְ אַתָּה ה' הַטּוֹב שִׁמְךָ וּלְךָ נָאֶה לְהוֹדוֹת — *Blessed are You, HASHEM, Your Name is 'The Beneficent One' and to You it is fitting to give thanks.*

The Talmud (*Bava Kamma* 92a) quotes the maxim: "Although the wine belongs to the host, we give thanks to the butler who serves it," meaning that although everything in the world belongs to God we still must express gratitude to all His human emissaries who deliver His blessings to us. We must be filled with appreciation for our parents, teachers, friends, and anyone else who helps us during our lifetimes. However, we must never lose sight of the fact that Hashem is the true source of everything we enjoy, and it is entirely fitting to give thanks to Him alone.

19

שָׁלוֹם / Peace

שִׂים שָׁלוֹם, טוֹבָה וּבְרָכָה, חֵן, וָחֶסֶד וְרַחֲמִים עָלֵינוּ וְעַל
כָּל יִשְׂרָאֵל עַמֶּךָ. בָּרְכֵנוּ אָבִינוּ, כֻּלָּנוּ כְּאֶחָד בְּאוֹר
פָּנֶיךָ, כִּי בְאוֹר פָּנֶיךָ נָתַתָּ לָנוּ, יהוה אֱלֹהֵינוּ, תּוֹרַת חַיִּים
וְאַהֲבַת חֶסֶד, וּצְדָקָה, וּבְרָכָה, וְרַחֲמִים, וְחַיִּים, וְשָׁלוֹם.
וְטוֹב בְּעֵינֶיךָ לְבָרֵךְ אֶת עַמְּךָ יִשְׂרָאֵל, בְּכָל עֵת וּבְכָל שָׁעָה
בִּשְׁלוֹמֶךָ. בָּרוּךְ אַתָּה יהוה, הַמְבָרֵךְ אֶת עַמּוֹ יִשְׂרָאֵל
בַּשָּׁלוֹם.

Establish peace, goodness, blessing, graciousness, kindness, and compassion upon us and upon all of Your
people Israel. Bless us, our Father, all of us as one, with the
light of Your countenance, for with the light of Your
countenance You gave us, HASHEM, our God, the Torah of life
and a love of kindness, righteousness, blessing, compassion,
life, and peace. And may it be good in Your eyes to bless Your
people Israel, in every season and in every hour with Your
peace. Blessed are You, HASHEM, Who blesses His people
Israel with peace.

ঙ§ The Ultimate Blessing

The concluding blessing of the *Amidah* is a request for peace, for the Sages regard peace as the ultimate blessing; without it no other blessing has permanence. One may have prosperity, health, food and drink, but if he has no peace it is all worthless. Therefore all our blessings are sealed with the gift of peace (*Sifra, Bechukosei*). As the Sages taught in the very last words of the Mishnah: R' Shimon ben Chalafta said, "The Holy One, Blessed is He, could not find a container that would hold Israel's blessings as well as peace, as it says, HASHEM *will give might to His nation,* HASHEM *will bless His nation with peace"* (*Psalms* 29:11) (*Uktzin* 3:12).

The Midrash says, "Peace when you enter, peace when you leave and peaceful relations with everyone." This alludes to three levels of peace: within one's family, in the country where one lives, and throughout the world (*K'sav Sofer*).

Sforno defines peace as spiritual eternity and perfection, unblemished by punishment and failure to fulfill one's potential (see *Sforno* to *Bereishis* 49:15). Peace is not simply the absence of war. It is a harmony between conflicting forces. Within man, it is the proper balance between the needs of the body and its higher duty to the soul. In the universe it is the balance between the infinite elements as well as between the holy and the mundane. When Jews are sinful, they disrupt this balance because they are not making proper use of the human and physical resources God gives the world. This creates a barrier between God and His people, a barrier that God, with compassion, removes so that we can repent and return to the blessed condition of peaceful harmony (*Or Hachaim*; see also *Malbim*).

ঙ§ Perfection of Character

The *Vilna Gaon* (*Even Shlaimah, Megillas Esther*) comments that the blessing of שָׁלוֹם, *peace*, refers to perfection of one's character. Quality of character is truly the "container" that seals in all other blessings, because negative character traits will spoil all a person's blessings, while good character traits will enhance them.

Someone once complained to *Rav Yisrael Salanter*, saying: "Your disciple Rav Yitzchak Blazer spends too much time studying *mussar*. If he devoted his time to the study of Talmud, he would be a much greater scholar!"

Rav Yisrael replied with the law that if a person has before him a small, but uncut *challah* and a large but imperfect one, he should recite the blessing over the small, perfect *challah* (*Orach Chaim* 168:1). Similarly, שְׁלֵמוּת, *perfection*, of character and spirit, takes precedence over scholastic greatness that lacks moral perfection.

∽§ Jacob's Blessing

This third blessing of the thanksgiving section corresponds with Jacob, the third Patriarch, who asked God for peace before he left the Holy Land ("... *so that I return to my father's home in peace* [*Genesis* 28:21]). Later, Jacob's violent brother, Esau, planned to destroy him in battle, but Jacob triumphed and there was peace. It is fascinating to note that the numerical value of both עֵשָׂו and שָׁלוֹם is 376, which indicates that Jacob used peace to neutralize Esau's hostility (see *Kallah Rabbosi* ch. 3 and *Baal HaTurim* to *Genesis* 25:25).

∽§ Peace of Mind

This blessing includes a request for the most essential form of peace — the key to real fortune and success: peace of mind. The serene person is in control of his thoughts and feelings, he is not at the mercy of external events which swing unpredictably and attempt to influence human temperaments and moods. The person who is at peace with himself has developed a rich personal philosophy that helps him cope with the "slings and arrows" of life. His attitude is positive, and even life's cruelest blows cannot crush his spirits.

An essential component of genuine peace of mind is to accept what life apportions to us and not to demand that life conform to our dreams and expectations. This attitude is expressed by *Rosh* who said: "Want whatever your Creator wants for you. Enjoy whatever you have, whether it be a little or a lot" (*Orchos Chaim* 69). With this in mind, *Rabbi Mordechai of Lechovitz* would say, "If things are not as you want them to be, you should want them to be as they are." And *Mivchar Hapeninim* says, "He who calmly accepts that which is beyond his control is the truly prosperous person."

So as we pray, we make this commitment: "I am prepared for

anything life has to offer; I hope for the best, but I am ready for the worst. With the help of Hashem, I will survive and overcome life's challenges."

◄§ Inner Peace: The Purpose of Prayer

Concentrated prayer disciplines the mind and trains a person to control his inner thoughts so that they are unaffected by external distractions. Prayer is an intimate dialogue between man and His Creator. Speak to Him as you converse with your friend and listen to Him as you listen to your friend, focusing all of your attention on Him. All around you are diversions: noise, traffic, airplanes, radios. Inside is emotional turbulence: worries, stress, dilemmas, quarrels, desires, daydreams. Then suddenly, there is only quiet and calm. The inner tranquility creates an impression of serenity and silence all around. The incessant din subsides. Noise and chatter recede far into the background — I am immersed in prayer (*Rav Shlomo Wolbe*).

A traveler once arrived in Frankfurt and carelessly misplaced his moneybag. The *rav*, Reb Avraham Abish, calmly reassured the distraught visitor, "Don't worry, your money will be found. But first recite the morning prayers."

After reciting the morning blessings the visitor suddenly remembered where he had put his bag. When he happily informed the *rav* that the money was found, the *rav* replied, "Of course you found it! I told you to pray because prayer restores your composure, giving you the peace of mind necessary to remember where you put your money."

◄§ Pray for Harmony

Yaaros Dvash reminds us that in this blessing we should pray for harmony among Jews: "Dear God, please save us from envy and enmity, fighting and friction. Help us to be patient and tolerant of one another and purge our hearts of all hatred and desire for revenge. Help us to fulfill the *mitzvah* of "Love your neighbor as yourself."

Harmony is the key to successful prayer. King Solomon said, *O you who dwell in the gardens, companions are attentive to your voice* (*Song of Songs* 8:13). The Midrash (ibid.) explains that this refers to the Jews who assemble in God's garden, the synagogue, where God's "companions," the ministering angels, listen to them. When Jews enter a synagogue to pray in unison with harmonious voice, God Himself with the angels of His Heavenly Court comes and listens to their prayers. He says: Raise your voices for all to hear! Take care not to hate, nor envy, nor shame, nor quarrel with one another so that the angels will not be able to complain, "Why did You give the Torah to the Jews and not to us? We live in peace while they do not!"

◆§ The Priestly Blessing

שִׂים שָׁלוֹם — *Establish peace.*

Abudraham explains that we ask for peace at the conclusion of the *Amidah* because much of our prayer serves as a substitute for the Temple sacrifice, and at the conclusion of the sacrificial service the Priests blessed the Jewish people, ending with וְיָשֵׂם לְךָ שָׁלוֹם, *and may He grant you peace* (Numbers 6:26).

Actually, we request five other qualities besides peace in this blessing: טוֹבָה, *goodness*; בְּרָכָה, *blessing*; חֵן, *graciousness*; חֶסֶד, *kindness*; and רַחֲמִים, *compassion.* These allude to the six blessing of *Bircas Kohanim,* the Priestly Blessing. For this reason, שִׂים שָׁלוֹם is only recited at times when the Priestly Blessing is delivered by the *chazzan* in the repetition of the *Amidah* (*Orach Chaim* 127:2). At other times a condensed version, שָׁלוֹם רָב, *Abundant peace,* is recited instead (*Etz Yosef*).

◆§ Brotherhood Arouses Blessing

טוֹבָה וּבְרָכָה — *Goodness, blessing.*

Yesod V'Shoresh HaAvodah writes that in the highest celestial realms there is a holy world called *Shalom,* which is the source for all the blessings and goodness that flow down to this earth. This is what the Talmud (*Shabbos* 10b) means when it says that God's own Name is *Shalom.* God manifests His goodness on this earth through the celestial world of *Shalom.* The person who pursues peace on earth and does everything he can to prevent interpersonal strife and hatred causes the celestial world of *Shalom* to pour forth its blessings with great intensity. Even if this person is a sinner, he will be forgiven by virtue of his pursuit of brotherhood and peace.

⋖§ Stages of Development

חֵן וָחֶסֶד וְרַחֲמִים — *Graciousness, kindness and compassion.*

Man goes through stages of development in life. When he is growing and improving, he is the recipient of God's חֵן, *graciousness.* During periods when he does not improve but maintains the level of his more fruitful period, God grants him חֶסֶד, *kindness.* There are times when his performance declines and he does not deserve God's help, but even then God shows רַחֲמִים, *compassion* (*Rav Yosef Albo, Sefer HaIkkarim* 4:35).

⋖§ Children of Faith

בָּרְכֵנוּ אָבִינוּ כֻּלָּנוּ כְּאֶחָד — *Bless us, our Father, all of us as one.*

When peace and harmony unite us as one family, we are like the children of one father. Then we can merit the blessings which God promised our Patriarch Abraham who is the symbol of unity, as it is written, כִּי אֶחָד קְרָאתִיו, *for I called him 'one'* (*Isaiah* 51:2) (*Etz Yosef*). Similarly, the Priestly Blessing which opens, יְבָרֶכְךָ ה' וְיִשְׁמְרֶךָ, *May HASHEM bless you and safeguard you* (*Numbers* 6:24), is in Abraham's merit, as God promised him (*Genesis* 12:3), "*And I will bless those who bless you*" (*Iyun Tefillah*).

⋖§ Personal Enlightenment

בְּאוֹר פָּנֶיךָ — *With the light of Your countenance.*

This corresponds with the second part of the Priestly Blessing, יָאֵר ה' פָּנָיו אֵלֶיךָ וִיחֻנֶּךָ, *May HASHEM illuminate His countenance for you and be gracious to you* (*Numbers* 6:25). The Jewish people yearn for this Divine radiance as the Midrash (*Yalkut Shimoni, Tehillim* 628) says: Israel cried out to the Holy One, Blessed is He, "Master of the universe! All we ask for is that You shine Your light upon us, as it says, הָאֵר פָּנֶיךָ וְנִוָּשֵׁעָה, *set Your face aglow that we may be saved*" (*Psalms* 80:20). *Sforno* (ibid.) explains that the final salvation of the Jewish people can be meaningful and permanent only if it is accomplished through intellectual enlightenment resulting from intense Torah study, because, through Torah, God illuminates the mind and banishes all confusion and doubt. *Rav Samson Raphael Hirsch* explains that when God "shines the light of His face upon us," He endows us with the ability to understand His ways and to recognize our personal mission in attaining His goals for the world.

⋖§ A Measure of Scholarship

Tanna D'bei Eliyahu Rabbah (chapter 3) teaches that in both the future epoch of the Messiah and in the World to Come, the faces of the righteous Torah scholars will literally shine. The intensity of the light radiating from each scholar will be an indication of the level of his scholarship and piety: "Some scholars will shine like the weak sun in the early morning, some will be ablaze like the flaming sun at high noon. Some will be a mere sliver of light like the new moon, some will be silver bright like the full moon. Some will shine like large stars, some will be mere specks like the smallest stars. God's countenance will illuminate every individual according to the measure of his Torah knowledge."

⋖§ The Radiance of Torah

כִּי בְאוֹר פָּנֶיךָ נָתַתָּ לָנוּ ה׳ אֱלֹהֵינוּ תּוֹרַת חַיִּים וְאַהֲבַת חֶסֶד — *For with the light of Your countenance You gave us, HASHEM, our God, the Torah of life and a love of kindness.*

The Torah of life refers to the Written Law while *a love of kindness* refers to the Oral Law which the teacher teaches to his students out of kindness. As King Solomon said (*Proverbs* 31:26), וְתוֹרַת חֶסֶד עַל לְשׁוֹנָהּ, *and a lesson of kindness is on her tongue (Etz Chaim; see Sukkah 49b).* תּוֹרַת חַיִּים וְאַהֲבַת חֶסֶד וּצְדָקָה וּבְרָכָה וְרַחֲמִים וְחַיִּים וְשָׁלוֹם — *The Torah of life and a love of kindness, righteousness, blessing, compassion, life, and peace.*

Koheles Yitzchak (Parshas Behaaloscha) explains that these seven blessings represent the seven flames of the Menorah of the Holy Temple, which radiated Divine light to the Jewish people and the entire world.

⋖§ Eternal Peace

וְטוֹב בְּעֵינֶיךָ לְבָרֵךְ אֶת עַמְּךָ יִשְׂרָאֵל בְּכָל עֵת וּבְכָל שָׁעָה בִּשְׁלוֹמֶךָ — *And may it be good in Your eyes to bless Your people Israel, in every season and in every hour with Your peace.*

This reminds us that we need the blessing of peace at all times — not only in life, but even after death, as the prophet said: *He who walks straightforward will enter in peace to be with those who rest in the grave (Isaiah 57:2).* The Talmud (*Berachos* 8a) teaches that one should constantly pray that he be spared from dissension and strife, not only in this world, but even at his funeral — עַד זִיבּוּלָא בַּתְרָיתָא, *until the last spadeful of earth* is shoveled over his grave.

A person should pray to be spared trauma and undue suffering before he dies. He should pray that he receive a dignified burial and that his body should be prepared, protected, and purified in accordance with *halachah*. He should pray that his children will recite the *Kaddish* and commemorate his memory appropriately so that his soul will rest in peace and tranquility. And finally he should pray that the Heavenly Tribunal judge him favorably so that he may enjoy a peaceful eternal reward.

◆§ Peace in the Holy Land

בָּרוּךְ אַתָּה ה' הַמְבָרֵךְ אֶת עַמּוֹ יִשְׂרָאֵל בַּשָּׁלוֹם — *Blessed are You, HASHEM, Who blesses His people Israel with peace.*

When the Children of Israel first entered the Promised Land they enjoyed God's blessing of וְנָתַתִּי שָׁלוֹם בָּאָרֶץ, *and I will establish peace in the Land (Leviticus 26:6).* The Midrash teaches that when the Jews finally settled in the Holy Land in peace and harmony, the ministering angels chanted, "Blessed are You, Hashem, who blesses His people Israel with peace."

In our times, when we see *Eretz Yisrael* wracked by turbulence and terror, we pray with intense fervor that Hashem bring enduring peace to our beloved Land.

◆§ The Final Peace

The Midrash (*Vayikra Rabbah* 9:9) states: How great peace is! Whenever God showers His blessings, prayers, good wishes, and words of comfort on the Jewish people, He concludes with the word שָׁלוֹם, *peace.* Moreover, when the Messiah arrives to redeem the Jewish nation, he will begin with a call for peace, as it says: *How beautiful upon the mountains are the feet of him who brings good tidings, who announces peace (Isaiah 52:7).*

The word שָׁלוֹם means peace in a way that is שָׁלֵם, *complete, wholesome*. True peace is the presence of harmony, when every man fulfills his proper function and every resource is utilized properly. Therefore, *Rambam* describes the שָׁלוֹם of the Messianic era in these terms:

> The Messiah's only purpose is to bring peace to the world ... Our sages and prophets did not long for the Messianic Age in order that they might rule the world and dominate the gentiles. They only wanted one thing, and that was to be free to devote themselves to the Torah and its wisdom. They wanted nothing to disturb or distract them, in order that they should be able to strive to become worthy of life in the World to Come.
>
> In the Messianic Age, there will be neither war nor famine. Jealousy and competition will cease to exist, for all good things will be most plentiful, and all sorts of delicacies will be as common as dust.
>
> The main occupation of humanity will be to know God. The Jews will become great sages, know many hidden things, and achieve the greatest understanding of God that is possible for a mortal human being. As the prophet (*Isaiah* 11:9) predicted, *The earth shall be full of the knowledge of God, as the waters that cover the sea* (Hilchos Melachim, 12:2-5).

Conclusion – Personal Supplication

יִהְיוּ לְרָצוֹן אִמְרֵי פִי וְהֶגְיוֹן לִבִּי לְפָנֶיךָ, יהוה צוּרִי וְגֹאֲלִי.

May the expressions of my mouth and the thoughts of my heart find favor before You, HASHEM, my Rock and my Redeemer.

◈§ Epilogue

Prayer is an experience that leaves a strong impact on the soul. When one recites the *Amidah* properly, with intense feeling and devotion, he concludes this intimate encounter in a spirit of ecstasy that elevates his soul. Before the Men of the Great Assembly composed the uniform text of the *Amidah*, prayer was a spontaneous, personal outpouring of the heart. Even after they introduced a standard prayer text, their purpose was not to stifle spontaneity but to inspire it. Every blessing of the *Amidah* ignites a spark in the soul, and when all the blessings are completed, the soul is aflame with passionate love for Hashem. The tongue has been freed, the heart has been opened — now is the time for the soul to overflow with personal petitions and praises (*Tzlach, Berachos* 16b).

◈§ A Prayer Flowing from Prayer

יְהְיוּ לְרָצוֹן אִמְרֵי פִי וְהֶגְיוֹן לִבִּי לְפָנֶיךָ ה' צוּרִי וְגֹאֲלִי — *May the expressions of my mouth and the thoughts of my heart find favor before You, HASHEM, my Rock and my Redeemer (Psalms 19:15).*

The Talmud (*Berachos* 4b) designates these words of King David as the appropriate conclusion of the *Amidah*. King David realized that no matter how eloquently and exhaustively a person expresses himself, many deep feelings and wishes remain inexpressible and confined to the inner recesses of his being. Therefore, he asked God to favor not only the expressions of his mouth but the intimate thoughts of his heart as well. Furthermore, sometimes we pray only with our lips and not with our hearts. We may say words without thought. Such prayer is superficial, and is not absorbed and integrated into our being.

But if at the very last moment we realize that we did not internalize our prayer, and that we only said words which did not penetrate us, it is not too late. This moment of realization is invaluable, and we can actually salvage our entire prayer with this momentary awareness.

That is why we have a prayer after the main prayer.

✎§ *Prayer and Psalms — a Parallel*

The Talmud (*Berachos* 9b), as explained by *Maharsha*, states that there is a special connection between these words and the number of blessings in *Shemoneh Esrei*. Originally, the first two chapters of *Psalms* were a single chapter, so that the above verse was at the end of chapter 18, thus corresponding to its position at the end of *Shemoneh Esrei*, which consisted of eighteen blessings. Five centuries later, when Rabban Gamliel added the nineteenth blessing to the *Amidah*, the Sages split the first Psalm into two separate chapters so that the Psalm which ends with this verse, *may the expressions of my mouth.. find favor*, would be at the end of the nineteenth Psalm, again corresponding to its place at the conclusion of the nineteen *Amidah* benedictions.

Why did the Sages go to such great lengths to assure that the *Amidah* prayer would correspond with the numbering of the *Psalms?* Because prayer and *Psalms* play similar roles in molding the events of the entire universe. In the Overview, *Sovereignty Through Surrender*, it was demonstrated how the words of prayer activate the spiritual forces that dominate the physical universe. The words and letters of the Torah, the Five Books of Moses, are the blueprint and building blocks of the universe. Thus, prayer words activate Torah words; prayer letters activate Torah letters.

The Psalms have a similar effect [see comm. to the sixteenth blessing שְׁמַע קוֹלֵנוּ]. On the verse, *May the expressions of my mouth find favor*, *Midrash Shocher Tov* comments: When David completed the entire Book of *Psalms* he petitioned God, "Please let the study of these five books be considered like the study of Torah itself — even like its most difficult portions, which deal with ritual purity." Elsewhere, *Midrash Shocher Tov* (*Psalms* 1) states: Moses presented Israel with the Five Books of the Torah and David presented Israel with the Five Books of *Psalms*. Moses concluded the Torah with the blessing אַשְׁרֶיךָ יִשְׂרָאֵל מִי כָמוֹךָ, *How praiseworthy are you, Israel, who can compare to you* (*Deut.* 33:29). David began his *Psalms* using a similar expression, אַשְׁרֵי הָאִישׁ, 'The praises of man.'

Thus, we find a chain connecting Torah with *Psalms*, and the Sages linked prayer to both. Moses taught Israel how to rule the world through Torah. David continued this mission by showing how to rule the world through *Psalms*, which bring us closer to Torah. In the same vein, the Men of the Great Assembly demonstrated how to control the world through prayer, which brings us closer to both *Psalms* and Torah.

⊷§ *A Perfect Ending*

Shulchan Aruch (*Orach Chaim* 122:2) recommends that this verse, *May the expressions . . .*, be recited both before and after the personal supplication of אֱלֹהַי נְצוֹר, *My God, guard my tongue*. Even though *Rama* (ibid. 122:1) indicates that the prevalent Ashkenazic custom was to recite it only after אֱלֹהַי נְצוֹר, *Mishnah Berurah* recommends the original custom of reciting the verse both before and after אֱלֹהַי נְצוֹר.

Mishnah Berurah (ibid. section 8) quotes *Seder Hayom*, who stresses the significance of reciting יִהְיוּ לְרָצוֹן properly. "This verse brings good fortune. Take note of the fact that it begins with the letter *yud* (which has the numerical value of ten) and it ends with the letter *yud*. It contains ten words and in these ten words there are ten *yuds* [alluding to the Ten Spiritual Emanations of Kabbalistic literature known as *Sefiros*]. Altogether this verse is composed of forty-two letters and its mystical powers are a great secret [perhaps alluding to God's Forty-two-Letter Name]. One who recites this verse slowly and deliberately, with great feeling and concentration, is assured that his prayers will be answered favorably."

אֱלֹהַי, נְצוֹר לְשׁוֹנִי מֵרָע, וּשְׂפָתַי מִדַּבֵּר מִרְמָה, וְלִמְקַלְלַי נַפְשִׁי תִדֹּם, וְנַפְשִׁי כֶּעָפָר לַכֹּל תִּהְיֶה. פְּתַח לִבִּי בְּתוֹרָתֶךָ, וּבְמִצְוֹתֶיךָ תִּרְדּוֹף נַפְשִׁי. וְכָל הַחוֹשְׁבִים עָלַי רָעָה, מְהֵרָה הָפֵר עֲצָתָם וְקַלְקֵל מַחֲשַׁבְתָּם. עֲשֵׂה לְמַעַן שְׁמֶךָ, עֲשֵׂה לְמַעַן יְמִינֶךָ, עֲשֵׂה לְמַעַן קְדֻשָּׁתֶךָ, עֲשֵׂה לְמַעַן תּוֹרָתֶךָ. לְמַעַן יֵחָלְצוּן יְדִידֶיךָ, הוֹשִׁיעָה יְמִינְךָ וַעֲנֵנִי. יִהְיוּ לְרָצוֹן אִמְרֵי פִי וְהֶגְיוֹן לִבִּי לְפָנֶיךָ, יהוה צוּרִי וְגֹאֲלִי. עֹשֶׂה שָׁלוֹם בִּמְרוֹמָיו, הוּא יַעֲשֶׂה שָׁלוֹם עָלֵינוּ, וְעַל כָּל יִשְׂרָאֵל. וְאִמְרוּ: אָמֵן.

My God, guard my tongue from evil and my lips from speaking deceitfully. To those who curse me, let my soul be silent; and let my soul be like dust to everyone. Open my heart to Your Torah, then my soul will pursue Your commandments. As for all those who design evil against me, speedily nullify their counsel and disrupt their design. Act for Your Name's sake; act for Your right hand's sake; act for Your sanctity's sake; act for Your Torah's sake. That Your beloved ones may be given rest; let Your right hand save, and respond to me. May the expressions of my mouth and the thoughts of my heart find favor before You, HASHEM, my Rock and my Redeemer. He Who makes peace in His heights, may He make peace upon us, and upon all Israel. Now respond: Amen.

⋑ Save Us from a Double Threat

אֱלֹהַי נְצוֹר לְשׁוֹנִי מֵרָע וּשְׂפָתַי מִדַּבֵּר מִרְמָה — *My God, guard my tongue from evil and my lips from speaking deceitfully.*

Sefer Chareidim (ch. 67) teaches that this supplication is a constant prayer to be saved from our Evil Inclination which threatens us in two ways. Sometimes we are tempted by a powerful desire to do something that is clearly evil. We know it is wrong but the temptation is overwhelming. That impulse is רָע, *evil*. At other times the Evil Inclination seeks to track us into sin by distorting reality and confusing our judgment so that evil appears as a virtue and iniquity masquerades as a *mitzvah*. That strategy of the Evil Inclination is called מִרְמָה, *deceit*. We beseech God to help us overcome both threats.

◄§ Protect Our Lips

אֱלֹהַי נְצוֹר לְשׁוֹנִי מֵרָע וּשְׂפָתַי מִדַּבֵּר מִרְמָה — *My God, guard my tongue from evil and my lips from speaking deceitfully.*

These words paraphrase King David's advice, where he warns against gossip and slander: *Guard your tongue from evil, and your lips from speaking deceitfully* (Psalms 34:14). In the preceding verse David says that this is the formula for the person who חָפֵץ חַיִּים, *desires life*. In his classic *sefer* on the evils of sinful speech, the *Chofetz Chaim* shows that when a person sullies his lips with gossip, his prayers are an abomination. How dare he utter prayers to curry favor with God with the same lips that have been used as instruments of evil!

◄§ Renewing the License

As we began the *Amidah* we humbly petitioned God for the right to use the Divine gift of speech. We promised to use this gift exclusively for His service, saying, *My Lord, open my lips, that my mouth may declare Your praise* (Psalms 51:17). Similarly, as we conclude our prayers, we ask for continued permission to use our lips. Being fully aware of the dangers of an undisciplined tongue, we call upon God to help us guard our organs of speech.

The Midrash (*Vayikra Rabbah* 33:1) relates that Rabban Shimon ben Gamliel once sent his servant, Tavi, to buy him some "good food." Tavi, who was famous for his wisdom, brought back a tongue. Rabban Shimon sent him again, this time to buy some "bad food." Again, Tavi returned with a tongue. Rabban Shimon asked him to explain how the same food could be both good and bad. The wise Tavi replied, "When a tongue speaks properly, there is nothing better, but when it does not, there is nothing worse."

◦§ The Supplication of Mar brei d'Ravina

The Talmud (*Berachos* 16b-17a) lists eleven sages, each of whom composed a personal supplication for the end of the *Amidah*. Of these eleven, the prayers of Mar brei d'Ravina — אֱלֹהַי נְצוֹר — has been universally adopted as the one to be said after *Shemoneh Esrei*. It is not clear why Mar brei d'Ravina's words were preferred over the others, but a careful reading of the Talmudic text offers a clue.

In reference to each of the other sages, the Talmud says that his supplication was בָּתָר צְלוֹתֵיה, *after his prayer*, implying that their prayers were separate from the just-concluded *Amidah*. In describing that of Mar brei d'Ravina, however, the Talmud says כִּי הֲוָה מְסַיֵּים צְלוֹתֵיה, *while he was finishing his prayers*, which implies that his supplication was a continuation of the preceding verse, *May the words of my mouth find favor*. His prayer was thus an extension of *Shemoneh Esrei*, as he pleaded for purity of speech.

◦§ Perfect Serenity

וְלִמְקַלְלַי נַפְשִׁי תִדּוֹם — *To those who curse me, let my soul be silent.*
One of the great benefits of sincere prayer is that it suffuses the supplicant with a sense of complete calm and equanimity, allowing him to rise above the annoyances and aggravations that disturb his peace of mind. A serene person will not allow himself to be dragged down by feelings of anger or resentment. He strives for the state of tranquility that *Chovos Halevavos* describes as הִשְׁתַּוּוּת, *equilibrium*. It makes no difference to the humble, well-balanced person whether he is praised or insulted by others. His self-esteem comes from within himself.

◦§ Abandon Yourself

The word שִׂמְחָה, *joy*, contains the root מחה, to erase. If one truly wishes to rejoice, he must first erase his conscious desire to place his feelings above others'. In a sense, he must forget about himself.

A pious man was asked, "What was the happiest moment in your entire life?" He replied, "I was once traveling on a ship. Because of my poverty, I was assigned the worst quarters — in the hold, together with the cargo. A group of rich merchants was also on board and, as I lay in my berth, one of the merchants came down to the hold and dumped his waste on me. I was so despicable in his eyes that he pretended I wasn't there. Though I was shocked by the man's audacity, I was pleased to find I felt no anger at being offended. When I realized how indifferent I was to my own prestige, I was truly overcome with joy. I recognized I had achieved a level of genuine humility" (*Rambam*, comm. to *Mishnah Avos* 4:4).

❧ Absolute Selflessness

וְנַפְשִׁי כֶּעָפָר לַכֹּל תִּהְיֶה — *And let my soul be like dust to everyone.*

The dust of the earth is the epitome of selflessness. Everyone steps on it and crushes it underfoot, yet the dust and soil take no offense and continue to give forth a rich bounty of produce. In the first blessing of the *Amidah* we cite the example of Abraham, who was utterly selfless, and said, וְאָנֹכִי עָפָר וָאֵפֶר, *I am but dust and ashes* (*Genesis* 18:27). In this merit God promised Abraham, *And I shall make your seed like the dust of the earth* (*Genesis* 13:16). *Sfas Emes* explains that God promised Abraham that his descendants would be as selfless as dust and emulate his example of sincere humility. Thus, *Shemoneh Esrei* begins with the merit of Abraham, who surrendered to God like dust, and it concludes with the pledge that Abraham's descendants will be as numerous as dust. This fulfills the words of King Solomon who said, הַכֹּל הָיָה מִן הֶעָפָר וְהַכֹּל שָׁב אֶל הֶעָפָר, *All come from dust and all shall return to dust* (*Ecclesiastes* 3:20).

Iyun Tefillah explains this prayer for self-effacing humility. Everyone uses the dust of the earth, yet no one pays attention to it; it is taken for granted. Similarly one should not seek credit for his good deeds, and should shun attention and accolades. The less a person cares about his prestige, the less he will let selfishness interfere with his service to God and his efforts for self-improvement (see comm. of *Tosafos, Berachos* 17a).

❧ Humility and Scholarship

פְּתַח לִבִּי בְּתוֹרָתֶךָ — *Open my heart to Your Torah.*

A precondition to genuine success in Torah study is extreme unselfishness. After a person makes his *soul like dust* he can hope to be open to Torah. The Talmud (*Eruvin* 54a; *Nedarim* 55a) teaches that a person should not feel that Torah is his private possession, rather he should treat it like the open land in the wilderness that belongs equally to everyone. Moreover, the student of Torah should be humble like the wilderness. If one does not respond when others degrade him, he will be worthy of retaining his Torah knowledge.

~§ Seize the Opportunity

וּבְמִצְוֹתֶיךָ תִּרְדּוֹף נַפְשִׁי — *Then my soul will pursue Your commandments.*
This alludes to the teaching of the Mishnah (*Avos* 4:2): *Ben Azzai said: Run to perform even a 'minor' mitzvah, and flee from sin; for one mitzvah leads to another mitzvah, and one sin leads to another sin; for the consequence of a mitzvah is a mitzvah, and the consequence of a sin is a sin.*

When someone performs a *mitzvah*, he becomes conditioned to obey God's will; conversely, each wrongful act dulls the conscience. *Rav Chaim of Volozhin* (*Ruach Chaim* ibid.) explains that it is natural for man to gravitate towards sin because man is physical and temptation is physical — so if one fails to flee sin he will surely be ensnared by it. Conversely, since *mitzvos* are spiritual, they are naturally remote from physical man. Thus if man does not exert himself to pursue *mitzvos*, they will always be distant from him.

~§ Protection from Pursuers

וְכֹל הַחוֹשְׁבִים עָלַי רָעָה מְהֵרָה הָפֵר עֲצָתָם וְקַלְקֵל מַחֲשַׁבְתָּם — *As for all those who design evil against me, speedily nullify their counsel and disrupt their design.*

When a person pursues God's commandments, he is not pursued by enemies and evildoers. This idea was emphasized by King David who said: *All Your commandments are faithful, they pursue me with lies — help me! They had almost destroyed me on earth, but I did not forsake Your precepts* (*Psalms* 119:86,87).

Like David, we follow our commitment to pursue the *mitzvos* with a plea to nullify the evil counsel of all who design evil against us (*Abudraham*).

In *Psalms* (117:1,2), David said, *Praise HASHEM, all you peoples; laud Him all you nations! For His kindness to us was overwhelming . . .*

Once, a Russian prince asked *Rav Yitzchak (Reb Itzaleh) of Volozhin* to explain why *non*-Jews, instead of Jews, are expected to praise God for his kindness to Israel. *Rav Yitzchak* replied without hesitation, "You princes plan countless anti-Semitic schemes with which to destroy us, but our Merciful God always manages to foil your plots. Your secret councils are so well guarded that we Jews don't even realize all the ways in which you intended to harm us, nor how God saved us. Only you gentiles see clearly how God's *kindness to us was overwhelming*; therefore only you can praise Him adequately!" (*Chiddushei Griz HaLevi on the Torah, Yisro 18:10; Iyun Tefillah*).

◆§ Redemption Will Sanctify G-d's Name

עֲשֵׂה לְמַעַן שְׁמֶךָ, עֲשֵׂה לְמַעַן יְמִינֶךָ, עֲשֵׂה לְמַעַן קְדֻשָּׁתֶךָ, עֲשֵׂה לְמַעַן תּוֹרָתֶךְ — *Act for Your Name's sake; act for Your right hand's sake; act for Your sanctity's sake; act for Your Torah's sake.*

Shulchan Aruch (*Orach Chaim* 122:3) quotes *Tur* that whoever recites these four petitions זוֹכֶה וּמְקַבֵּל פְּנֵי שְׁכִינָה, *is worthy of personally welcoming the Divine Presence.* These requests sum up the essential purpose of all our prayers: our main concern is not for personal welfare, but to intensify God's sanctity and glory in the world.

The numerical value of לְמַעַן, *for the sake of*, is 190, which is the numerical value of קֵץ, *the final end*, a term used widely both in Scripture and the Talmud to describe the end of the exile and the advent of the Messianic epoch. Thus, at the end of the *Amidah*, we beseech God to end the exile for the sake of His Name and sanctity. Indeed, the Talmud (*Sanhedrin* 98a) says that God's proclamation לְמַעֲנִי לְמַעֲנִי אֶעֱשֶׂה. . .וּכְבוֹדִי לְאַחֵר לֹא אֶתֵּן, *For My own sake, for My own sake, I will do it. . .* (*Isaiah* 48:11), is a reference to the coming of the Messiah.

◆§ Release and Relief

לְמַעַן יֵחָלְצוּן יְדִידֶיךָ הוֹשִׁיעָה יְמִינְךָ וַעֲנֵנִי — *That Your beloved ones may be given rest; let Your right hand save, and respond to me.*

This verse appears twice in *Psalms* (60:7, 108:7). *Meiri* comments that it is a plea for mental tranquility, a release from tension and worry. The Talmud (*Yevamos* 102b) comments on the verse וְעַצְמֹתֶיךָ יַחֲלִיץ, *He shall release your bones* (*Isaiah* 58:11), that the most sublime blessing is when the body and its incessant physical demands release their grip over the soul. Then one can find genuine relief.

In the special benediction offered at the circumcision ceremony, Isaac is called יָדִיד, *beloved*, because he was the cherished son of Abraham (see *Rashi* to *Shabbos* 137b) who was beloved to God. Similarly we ask God to look upon us, the descendants of the Patriarchs, as His beloved ones.

ঙ্গ Three Steps Backward

At this point, the supplicant bows like a servant taking leave from his master (*Orach Chaim* 123:1, *Mishnah Berurah*) and, while bowing, takes three steps backward. Various reasons are given for these three steps.

— When one prays before God, the place where he stands becomes holy and the *Shechinah* [Divine Presence] rests over it. Upon concluding his prayer, he steps out of this holy area (*Shibbolei Halekket*).

— The daily prayer is like a sacrificial offering. When the priests left the altar, they had to step across three rows of stones to reach the ramp back to the courtyard (*Rav Hai Gaon*).

— The Sages teach that Nebuchadnezzar once took three steps in honor of God [see *Maharsha, Sanhedrin* 96a], and was rewarded by victory in his attempt to destroy the Temple. In response, we too take three steps to pay honor to God's Presence (*Mishnah Berurah* 123:2).

After having gone three steps backward, the supplicant bows to his left, saying, עֹשֶׂה שָׁלוֹם בִּמְרוֹמָיו, *He Who makes peace in His heights;* bows to his right, saying, הוּא יַעֲשֶׂה שָׁלוֹם עָלֵינוּ, *may He make peace upon us;* then bows straight ahead and finishes with וְעַל כָּל יִשְׂרָאֵל וְאִמְרוּ אָמֵן, *and upon all Israel. Now respond Amen.* We first bow to the left because, with God before us, our left is His right, and the right side is always honored first (*Bais Yosef* 123).

R' *Munk* comments that the bow to God's right (our left) symbolizes God's spirit of mercy, represented by the angel Michael who stands at the right of God's throne. The bow to God's left (our right) symbolizes God's spirit of exact justice, represented by the angel Gabriel, who stands to the left of the throne. Finally we bow forward, to God Himself, acknowledging that ultimately He resolves all conflicts and unifies all forces in the universe.

⋖§ Harmony in Heaven

עֹשֶׂה שָׁלוֹם בִּמְרוֹמָיו — *He Who makes peace in His heights.*

This appellation for God is found in *Job* 25:2. *Rashi* and *Ibn Ezra* explain that God's messengers often appear to contradict one another, such as angels of mercy, and angels of judgment. Nevertheless God creates harmony above so that all the various agents function harmoniously in obedience to His Will. "Peace," in this sense, is God's implementation of concord between all His forces, with the result that each functions within the bounds assigned to it, and without interference from others (*Etz Yosef*). For example, there is a delicate balance between tropical, temperate, and frigid temperatures. If the earth were too close to the sun or too far, life could not exist. There are endless instances of cosmic forces that interact so as to further God's ends. This is the peace He imposes from above.

⋖§ An End to All Strife

הוּא יַעֲשֶׂה שָׁלוֹם עָלֵינוּ וְעַל כָּל יִשְׂרָאֵל — *May He make peace upon us, and upon all Israel.*

If the heavenly forces require God to make peace among them, surely human beings who are so prone to jealousy, hatred, and fractious conduct require God's mercy to bring peaceful harmony into their midst (*Etz Yosef*).

Rashi (comm. to *Berachos* 17a) explains that every nation has an angel which represents it in heaven. When God causes strife among the angels above, war breaks out between the nations they represent on earth. Therefore we ask God not to punish us by means of a celestial conflict that will lead to hostility on earth.

יְהִי רָצוֹן מִלְּפָנֶיךָ יהוה אֱלֹהֵינוּ וֵאלֹהֵי אֲבוֹתֵינוּ, שֶׁיִּבָּנֶה בֵּית הַמִּקְדָּשׁ בִּמְהֵרָה בְיָמֵינוּ, וְתֵן חֶלְקֵנוּ בְּתוֹרָתֶךָ. וְשָׁם נַעֲבָדְךָ בְּיִרְאָה, כִּימֵי עוֹלָם וּכְשָׁנִים קַדְמוֹנִיּוֹת. וְעָרְבָה לַיהוה מִנְחַת יְהוּדָה וִירוּשָׁלָיִם, כִּימֵי עוֹלָם וּכְשָׁנִים קַדְמוֹנִיּוֹת.

May it be Your will, HASHEM, our God and the God of our forefathers, that the Holy Temple be rebuilt, speedily in our days. Grant us our share in Your Torah, and may we serve You there with reverence, as in days of old and in former years. Then the offering of Judah and Jerusalem will be pleasing to HASHEM, as in days of old and in former years.

◆§ The Temple and the Torah

יְהִי רָצוֹן מִלְּפָנֶיךָ ה׳ אֱלֹהֵינוּ וֵאלֹהֵי אֲבוֹתֵינוּ שֶׁיִּבָּנֶה בֵּית הַמִּקְדָּשׁ בִּמְהֵרָה בְיָמֵינוּ וְתֵן חֶלְקֵנוּ בְּתוֹרָתֶךָ — *May it be Your will, HASHEM, our God and the God of our forefathers, that the Holy Temple be rebuilt, speedily in our days. Grant us our share in Your Torah.*

Rabbi Moshe Isserles (Rama) writes in his gloss to *Orach Chaim* (123:1): "Today, our prayers are a substitute for the sacrificial offerings in the Holy Temple. Therefore, at the very end of the *Amidah* we make one final plea to God to rebuild the Temple, so that we may actually serve Him with real offerings and not merely verbal substitutes."

Vilna Gaon (comm. to *Shir Hashirim* 6:4) explains that we juxtapose our request for the reconstruction of the Temple with a request for our share in Torah, because as long as the Temple is in ruins and the Jews are exiled the quality and quantity of our Torah studies is drastically diminished, as we read, מַלְכָּהּ וְשָׂרֶיהָ בַגּוֹיִם אֵין תּוֹרָה, *Her king and her princes are among the nations, there is no Torah (Lamentations 2:9).* With the Temple restored, we will once again be able to study Torah to the highest degree.

◈§ Torah Insight — A Divine Gift

וְתֵן חֶלְקֵנוּ בְּתוֹרָתֶךְ — *Grant us our share in Your Torah.*

A Jew is obligated to study the entire Torah, not merely part of it, however, every person has his own insight into the wisdom of the Torah. The longer one analyzes a Torah theme, the more one exerts himself to comprehend its true meaning, the deeper one delves into the essence of a Torah concept — the closer he comes to discovering the unique interpretation that is his own exclusive share in the mass of Torah knowledge. But even after all his exertion, one should not feel that his comprehension is a result of his mental abilities, because Torah, God's infinite wisdom, is far beyond human capacity. Rather Torah insight is God's reward for the toil we have invested in its study. Here we pray that we be worthy of that gift despite our shortcomings.

◈§ The Preferred Share

Rabbi Chaim of Volozhin (*Ruach Chaim, Avos* 2:12) observes that there are two ways to acquire a share in Torah. One can either study on his own, or he can enter into an Issachar-Zevulon partnership wherein "Zevulon" the breadwinner supports "Issachar" the scholar. Although Zevulon earns an equal share in the reward for Issachar's Torah study (see *Yoreh Deah* 246:11 and comm. to the thirteenth blessing), nevertheless, there are some benefits in which Zevulon has no part. First, the Talmud (*Bava Metzia* 85a) teaches that three consecutive generations of Torah scholars earn the title of אַכְסַנְיָא שֶׁל תּוֹרָה, *a home of Torah*, and God assists future generations of this family to study Torah. This blessing is reserved for those who actually study Torah, not for those who merely "invest" in Torah with financial support.

Secondly, the Talmud (*Yevamos* 97a) teaches that when one constantly studies and speaks words of Torah in his lifetime his lips will not be stilled even in death, and they will continue to move and whisper Torah even in the grave, especially when the living repeat his teachings. This blessing is also reserved for those who actually study Torah. Therefore, in this prayer we ask God for the preferred share in Torah — the share of one who personally studies God's word.

৯৪ Reverence at All Times

וְשָׁם נַעֲבָדְךָ בְּיִרְאָה כִּימֵי עוֹלָם וּכְשָׁנִים קַדְמוֹנִיּוֹת — *And may we serve You there with reverence, as in days of old and in former years.*

As we conclude our prayers and prepare to embark upon our daily activities, we reinforce our resolve to serve God with reverence and awe.

The Torah commands: אֶת ה' אֱלֹהֶיךָ תִּירָא, *You shall fear* HASHEM *your God (Deuteronomy 10:20).* To live in awe of God is one of the six hundred and thirteen *mitzvos.* This *mitzvah* is constant, it applies in all places at all times, every moment of the day and night. This obligation is incumbent upon every member of the human race, Jew and gentile alike. It is especially important, however, to feel the awe of God in situations that try one's moral stamina. It is easier to overcome temptation when one realizes that God scrutinizes human actions, and mournfully records every transgression (*Sefer Hachinuch; Mitzvah* 432).

৯৪ The Buried Treasure

And now, Israel, what does HASHEM *your God ask of you — only that you fear* HASHEM *your God. . . (Deuteronomy 10:12).*

Mesillas Yesharim cites numerous sources that one must learn to serve God with pure intent. The most essential ingredient, he writes, is striving for a genuine fear of heaven:

King Solomon stated: *If you seek it out as you seek silver and search for it as you search for buried treasures — then will you comprehend the fear of* HASHEM *(Proverbs 2:4,5).* He does not say: "Then you will comprehend philosophy; then you will master astronomy; then you will understand medicine; then you will grasp the meaning of the fine points of law." These pursuits, while commendable, are not the ultimate purposes of life. It is only comprehension of fear of God that truly warrants constant study and research.

Mesillas Yesharim suggests that one set aside a specific period of time in his daily schedule to contemplate a personal approach toward increasing his fear of God. He also describes one way of acquiring this fear (ch. 25): One should constantly be aware that the Divine Presence is found everywhere, and the Holy One, Blessed is He, carefully watches everyone and everything, great and small. Nothing is hidden from His eyes. . . When one lives with this awareness, he is filled with awe. He is genuinely afraid to act in a manner that is not in accordance with the Almighty's wishes.

◆§ The Gift of Ecstasy

וְעָרְבָה לַה׳ מִנְחַת יְהוּדָה וִירוּשָׁלָיִם כִּימֵי עוֹלָם וּכְשָׁנִים קַדְמוֹנִיוֹת — *Then the offering of Judah and Jerusalem will be pleasing to* HASHEM, *as in days of old and in former years.*

These are the words of Malachi, last of our prophets, in the final chapter of his book (3:4), where he foretells that the Jewish people will return to God and He will return to them. Then the sacrificial service will be restored as it was when Moses built the Tabernacle and when Solomon constructed the Temple. In those early times Israel's love for God was pure and innocent, and God displayed his affection for Israel by sending down a heavenly fire that consumed their sacrifices on the Altar (*Yalkut Shimoni, Metzudas David*).

Rabbi Levi Yitzchok of Berdichev (*Kedushas Levi, Mishpatim*) writes that every Jew must strive to delight his Maker. This is the ultimate goal of service. When God "delights" in his prayer, man senses his success. He feels his heart suffused with fire and passion for all that is sacred.

Sefer Chassidim (§18) teaches that prayer and joy are natural companions: הִתְהַלְלוּ בְּשֵׁם קָדְשׁוֹ יִשְׂמַח לֵב מְבַקְשֵׁי ה׳, *Glory in His Holy Name; be glad of heart, you who seek* HASHEM (*I Chronicles* 16:10). David, King of Israel, accompanied his prayers and praise with the music of his lyre, in order to fill his heart with ecstasy and love for God, which is the goal of Divine service.

We conclude the *Shemoneh Esrei* with the wish that our prayers bring Israel closer to God's favor and the restoration of the Temple service.